The Women Who
Got America Talking

SELECTED OTHER WORKS BY KERRY SEGRAVE
AND FROM McFARLAND

The Hatpin Menace: American Women Armed and Fashionable, 1887–1920 (2016)

Police Violence in America, 1869–1920: 256 Incidents Involving Death or Injury (2016)

Chewing Gum in America, 1850–1920 (2015)

Wiretapping and Electronic Surveillance in America, 1862–1920 (2014)

*Beware the Masher: Sexual Harassment in American
Public Places, 1880–1930* (2014)

Policewomen: A History, 2d ed. (2014)

Extras of Early Hollywood: A History of the Crowd, 1913–1945 (2013)

Parking Cars in America, 1910–1945: A History (2012)

*Begging in America, 1850–1940: The Needy, the Frauds,
the Charities and the Law* (2011)

*Vision Aids in America: A Social History of Eyewear
and Sight Correction Since 1900* (2011)

Lynchings of Women in the United States: The Recorded Cases, 1851–1946 (2010)

*America Brushes Up: The Use and Marketing of Toothpaste and
Toothbrushes in the Twentieth Century* (2010)

Film Actors Organize: Union Formation Efforts in America, 1912–1937 (2009)

Parricide in the United States, 1840–1899 (2009)

*Actors Organize: A History of Union Formation
Efforts in America, 1880–1919* (2008)

Obesity in America, 1850–1939: A History of Social Attitudes and Treatment (2008)

*Women and Capital Punishment in America, 1840–1899: Death Sentences
and Executions in the United States and Canada* (2008)

Women Swindlers in America, 1860–1920 (2007)

Ticket Scalping: An American History, 1850–2005 (2007)

America on Foot: Walking and Pedestrianism in the 20th Century (2006)

Suntanning in 20th Century America (2005)

Endorsements in Advertising: A Social History (2005)

Women and Smoking in America, 1880 to 1950 (2005)

Foreign Films in America: A History (2004)

Lie Detectors: A Social History (2004)

Product Placement in Hollywood Films: A History (2004)

Piracy in the Motion Picture Industry (2003)

Jukeboxes: An American Social History (2002)

Vending Machines: An American Social History (2002)

Age Discrimination by Employers (2001)

Shoplifting: A Social History (2001)

The Women Who Got America Talking

Early Telephone Operators, 1878–1922

KERRY SEGRAVE

McFarland & Company, Inc., Publishers

Jefferson, North Carolina

LIBRARY OF CONGRESS CATALOGUING-IN-PUBLICATION DATA

Names: Segrave, Kerry, 1944– author.
Title: The women who got America talking : early telephone operators, 1878–1922 / Kerry Segrave.
Description: Jefferson, North Carolina : McFarland & Company, Inc., Publishers, 2017 | Includes bibliographical references and index.
Identifiers: LCCN 2017030422 | ISBN 9781476669045 (softcover : acid free paper) ∞
Subjects: LCSH: Telephone operators—United States—History. | Telephone companies—United States—History.
Classification: LCC HD6073.T32 U574 2017 | DDC 384.6/4—dc23
LC record available at https://lccn.loc.gov/2017030422

BRITISH LIBRARY CATALOGUING DATA ARE AVAILABLE

ISBN (print) 978-1-4766-6904-5
ISBN (ebook) 978-1-4766-2815-8

Front cover: C & P Telephone Co. Switchboards, 1905 (Harris & Ewing Collection, Library of Congress)

Printed in the United States of America

McFarland & Company, Inc., Publishers
Box 611, Jefferson, North Carolina 28640
www.mcfarlandpub.com

Table of Contents

Preface

This book looks at the telephone operator in America from 1878 to 1922. Originally males were destined to be phone operators. Men were never contemplated to fill the jobs as the telephone companies had no intention of paying enough money to attract and keep men. What was envisioned was the use of boys (never specifically defined but ranging in age from about 16 up to the very early 20s) to take those jobs. However, the boys proved to be unsuitable from the beginning as they were too prone to get into arguments with subscribers.

Thus, a bold experiment took place with women being tried out. It was successful. The vast majority of the female operators ranged in age from 16 up to perhaps 25. Even younger girls were sometimes utilized. Girls began to replace boys as operators circa 1878 or '79, and by the middle 1880s they held almost all the jobs as phone operators. A few boys held on as night shift operators beyond the mid–1880s but usually only in areas were labor laws forbade the use of "women and children" on night work. Even those boys disappeared long before 1900. The only other exception to girl operators could be found in some police departments that used male operators throughout the period covered by this book.

Between 1878 and 1922, every call a subscriber made had to be routed through an operator and involved the subscriber talking directly to the operator. That included calls in the subscriber's own city. The year 1922 marked the beginning of the end for the local operators as the system became automated to the extent that automatic exchanges began to be utilized. Frequent attempts had been made before that year but none were efficient or successful. Still, the transition period was a decade or more in many cases as every phone in every home and business had to be removed and replaced with a new one for the new direct-dial automatic system and it meant the number of operators employed went up, at least for a little while, after 1922.

The story of the telephone operator over the period covered by this book is a story of low pay, poor working conditions, arbitrary rules and discipline, vigorous surveillance by management, and many cases of labor disputes in the form of union strikes and unorganized, spontaneous walkouts.

Research for this book was done using online databases with the Library of Congress' "Chronicling America" being the most useful. Also used were newspaperarchive.com and various other newspaper databases.

Introduction

Chapter 1 of this book looks at the beginnings of the telephone industry and at the initial attempts to fill these new jobs in a new industry with boys. It proved to be so disastrous that within a year or so, the first women (and girls) were hired to replace the boys and within about five years there were very few boys left as operators, and even those had a limited time left. The experiment of employing females made the industry nervous but it proved successful beyond anyone's hopes. Most of those very young women still lived at home and proved very obedient and tractable, never answering back to the subscribers. Such docility was happily embraced by the phone companies. Such docility also made it easier for the phone companies to establish and maintain a low-wage female working ghetto with poor working conditions and a high level of surveillance.

The story of the operator until 1900 is told in Chapter 2. Within a short period of time, she was given the nickname of "hello girl" by the media. That was done for the obvious reason that the operators used to answer the subscribers' call with the word "hello." That proved less than efficient from the perspective of the phone companies who quickly substituted "Number, please." But the nickname of "hello girls" remained. During the period from 1879 to 1900, there was very little in the way of union activity, strikes or organizing drives. It would require more outside drivers such as greater acceptance from the male labor movement and greater activity, support and agitation from the feminist movement of the era.

Much of that happened in the period 1901 to 1922. The story of the operator in that period is told in Chapter 3. The industry was more mature and the operators, if still in the same age range, seemed to be more sophisticated, more prone to action. The shortage of operators, always present to some extent, grew worse with the demands of the period around World

War I, with women able to select from a greater variety of work options, almost all of them an improvement over telephone girl.

Chapter 4 looks at the various types of discipline, and surveillance, exercised over the girls. Perhaps most ludicrous of all were the dress codes that various phone companies imposed. They were ludicrous because hello girls worked away from the public. No one ever saw a telephone operator except another telephone operator.

Chapter 5 looks at the effects the work had on the health of the operators. It also looks at the effect of swearing at operators and some of the responses made to obscenities by the phone companies. Sexual harassment is also looked at in this chapter, as is "love." The media loved to present accounts of how many hello girls got married and how quickly they wed and thus fled their employer. This image was helpful to the telephone companies since they could use it to explain the perpetual shortage of operators. It wasn't the fault of the companies if service was bad; they just couldn't fill the holes in their workforces fast enough when their operators rushed off en masse to marry. It was nonsense but it helped the companies avoid dealing with the real reasons for the labor shortages: low pay and poor conditions.

Strikes and labor union activities are covered in Chapter 6. Hello girls were perhaps one of the least likely segments of society to engage in such activity; they were too young, still mostly living at home, and trained and socialized, as all females were then, to defer to men. But they did become radicalized: Strikes by operators took place all over America, especially in the years from 1901 until the end of the period covered by this book.

Finally, Chapter 7 looks at the efforts to replace the telephone operators with an automatic system. The search for a "girl-less" system began as early as 1891, almost before the women had got their seats warm. And while many such systems were announced and hyped, and even put in place, none were successful. The New York Telephone Company, which announced its automatic system in 1920, came up with that workable system. It was late in 1922 when its subscribers first began to make automatic dial-it-yourself local calls. That marked the beginning of the end for the hello girl.

1

In the Beginning, Men vs. Women

With the arrival in America of the first telephone exchanges at the end of the 1870s, a new era in communications began. A December 1877 article in an Arizona newspaper remarked about the time a few months earlier when the telephone first came before the public, singing its praises, about all the wonders that the invention could perform and would lead to. Up to that time, the only speedy communications medium was the telegraph, itself only some 30 years old at the time the telephone arrived. The change from the old to the new was dramatic for, as the news account observed, operating a telegraph "requires months of constant and arduous practice, while all who can speak, can operate the telephone."[1]

The new invention required telephone operators at the exchanges springing up all over America. Those operators were going to be males; there was no question about that. However, they were not going to be men (those beyond their mid–20s) because the telephone companies (telcos) had no intention of paying high enough wages to attract and retain men. Those operators would be in the age category of 16 through the early 20s.

In January 1881, a Washington, D.C., newspaper reporter went to the office on G Street to find out more about the telephone in his city. George C. Maynard, a company official, took the journalist from the firm's general business office to the John O. Evans building on New York Avenue between 14th and 15th Streets. At that location he was taken to a room "full" of phones. In the room, 35 or so operators were at work with a man named Warren Choate in charge. According to the reporter, "The talkers were nearly all young ladies, seated at small desks, upon each of which there was a telephone raised to a height to accommodate the conversational orifice." They were answering calls, ringing up those who were wanted and closing the verbal correspondence when they were over. The journalist then added that since talking and listening were the essential virtues of the operator, "it is but natural that there should be about an equal number of male and female operators. The males are all boys and the females budding damsels."

A full force of operators was on duty during business hours and then dwindling down to four or five at work during the small hours of the morning. There were never less than four or five operators on duty. As well, the reader was assured that the operators never listened in on conversations nor even accidentally overheard them. Most calls were directed to grocery stores, newspaper offices, department stores and doctors. That Washington telco then had 35 miles of wire and over 700 subscribers. When the company started, there were only 50 subscribers. It was also reported that operators always listened to complaints, responding to callers' impolite comments without "sassing back" or showing any surprise.[2]

An 1882 report noted that salaries for "nurse girls" were $30 to $35 a month; general housework, $37 to $55; cooks, $55 to $65; housekeepers, $65 to $80; washerwomen, $50 to $58; female farm domestics, $8 to $12 (including board, lodging and washing). Females in bookbinderies received $3 to $8 per week (nine-hour days) while boys received $3 to $10 (ten-hour days). Girls employed in shirt factories were paid $4 to $8 a week; girls in laundries, $7 to $10 a week. The principal woman in the shirt factory earned $50 a month while the male clerks in the shirt factories earned from $45 to $50 a month. Girls employed in millinery and dressmaking establishments earned from $6 to $20 per week. A first-class dressmaker could earn $100 per month; that compared favorably with skilled and unskilled labor of men in factories. In dry goods stores, female clerks received $6 to $15 a week; first-class saleswomen were paid from $65 to $85 per month. Wages of male clerks in dry goods and clothing stores ranged from $25 to $75 with an average being about $50. Female operators in the telegraph offices received pay according to "capacity," that pay ranging from $25 to $65 a month. Lastly, girls employed by the telephone company as operators received from $25 to $32 per month with the report noting, "This class of work requires very little skill."[3]

That same year it was reported from New York City that young women "are employed almost entirely in the exchanges. Men could not be induced to sit ten hours a day in a chair and respond to the call of 'hello.' When boys start in to learn to be operators they tire before they attain proficiency. Women are the only ones who will stick to the work. They are sober and trustworthy, and are contented with the pay they receive." The reporter did have some reservations in late 1882 as girls rapidly replaced the boys as operators in exchanges around the county: "Following out the popular idea which has prevailed, the conclusion would be that their natural curiosity would unfit them for the duties. There is nothing that will cure a woman of this propensity so quickly as to put her in a position where she is obliged to hear."

At that same time, the New York City telco adopted a new system to run tests in the morning to ensure that all its phones were functioning. Thus the first thing an operator did after she started her morning shift was to ring up all her subscribers and say to them, "Hello, this is your daily test." Perhaps because of being awoken too early, a common response by the subscriber was, "You are my daily pest."[4]

A reporter described the situation in Philadelphia in March 1883 when he went to the telco office in a building at Fourth and Chestnut Streets where in the exchange area, "a roomful of girls" handled the demands of the Bell Telephone Company's 2000 telephone subscribers. According to the reporter, a typical operator "must possess naturally or else carefully cultivate a store of rare and excellent graces, by comparison with which Job's possessions seem mere and trivial. They also have quicker ears, and are more obedient to rules and susceptible of discipline. But their natural restraints of temper and freedom from outbursts of bad language are considered their primary recommendation." On average, every girl while she was on duty at the Philadelphia exchange (from 7 or 8 a.m. until 7 p.m.) has the supervision of 80 phones. Under a new system then just introduced, each girl has a group of 100 wires to respond to. Each wire had at least one telephone attached to it. The reporter explained that, as the number of girl operators increased, the telco introduced a clause into their agreements with subscribers, providing that "any use of the telephone for profane, indecent or rude language, or for any purpose rather than respectful, bona fide business or social messages, shall terminate the contract, and the company insists on this to the best of its ability, although not always meeting with entire success." In describing the operators, the reporter continued:

> The young girls employed, coming from refined homes, though poor, have always shown great sensitivity against any indignity or indecorous speech reaching them through the telephones. It sometimes happens that one of them seated at her post, with the repressed air which all telephone girls get from hearing messages all day long and not being allowed to speak a syllable to each other, will burst into tears and become almost hysterical. Very often she will not tell what is said, but usually some insult has been offered, very often coming from a clerk or other person in the employ of a subscriber so that it is hard to discover the culprit.

Lately, a journalist revealed, a great deal of trouble had been experienced by the telco on account of sickness among its girls:

They nearly all become subject to long periods of nervous prostration. Several are under treatment for cerebro-spinal meningitis. The very qualities of forbearance and patient endurance which fit them for their positions cause them to break down, physically, under the continued strain. The telephones which the girls wear on their ears, strapped around their head, in the new system, are heavy and produce deafness and in place of them pretty silk caps, with light telephones attached to them, have just been introduced, and are looked upon by the operatives as a great improvement in every way.[5]

Females were first employed as operators probably around the year 1879. In November 1883, Superintendent Cochrane of the Metropolitan Telephone Company in New York City stated that some of the girl operators employed by his firm had started about four years earlier.[6]

A news account from Minnesota in May 1885 declared,

In the telephone business, ladies have also an undisputed field…. The telephone, it appears, is too monotonous to the male nerves. After a month's service as telephone operator a man is willing to saw wood [sleep]. Not so with women, provided they are young, for those who have attained a certain age do not take readily to the telephone business. Eighteen to twenty-four years are about the limits. The salaries are from $18 to $35 per month and the working day is ten hours…. The ladies are not allowed to talk back to saucy subscribers; it is supposed that they would work for half the salary if this privilege were granted. Although the employment is sedentary and keeps the eye and ear ever on the alert, it is claimed that is it healthful, and delightful, too, no doubt, as it gives the misses plenty of exercise of the faculty whose use they most enjoy.[7]

A reporter in 1892 looked back at the beginnings of the telephone industry and declared:

When the telephone was first introduced, boys between the ages of 16 and 19 were employed, but the results threatened to be destructive to the interests of the company. The boys would not obey the rules as to impertinent profanity when dealing with a "crusty" subscriber, and the consequent dismissals were so numerous that an immense relay force had to be employed. In consequence of this the experiment of employing girls was made, with most satisfactory results.[8]

In that same year, 1892, another reporter wrote that when the phone was introduced for general service 15 years earlier (1877), it was those boys of 16 to 19 who were first employed. "Incessant and emphatic stress was laid upon the necessity for absolute civility of speech on the part of the boys. [There were rules] forbidding the operator to add a syllable more than was necessary to answer the subscriber's question." As a further check, the monitor stations were added to oversee and discipline the "sayings and doings of the boys." But the average boy was no respecter of persons and when a "cranky money-bags" got verbally nasty, the boy was as likely as not to curse the subscriber in return. "Such flagrant violation of the rules resulted in immediate dismissal, but notwithstanding, similar offenses were of daily

Sketch of an operator, 1902.

occurrence and necessitated the employment of a relay [relief] force as large as the original staff of operators." The reason why men beyond their early 20s were never hired for such positions and never really considered by the telcos was summarized by this reporter: "To employ the services of men of mature judgment and business sagacity would have entailed greater expense than the corporation cared to stand…." As a last resort, the telephone girl was introduced. At first, continued the journalist, "she was an old girl, quiet, sedate and thoughtful." There was no more swearing or blowing up, no back talk, no serious complaints or threats on the part of subscribers to withdraw patronage. But the service was still only "a mediocre success." Continued the reporter; "By degrees sprightly, girlish girls were taken on the force … and they "caught on" so readily and swung into line so naturally that they all but unconsciously solved the problem of efficient telephone service. From that time the decline of telephone widows and old maids began, and a decided preference was shown for girls less than 25 and more than 16 years of age."[9]

Two years later, in 1894, a journalist reported that at first, many in the telcos opposed girls and thought terrible things would happen. Then the experiment of using girls was undertaken and several things were learned. For one thing, the female voice was soft and low "and admirably suited to be heard over the wires. It was also found that girls were nimble-fingered, and that they were conscientious, faithful and industrious in the discharge of their duties." He said there were then thousands of girl telephone operators in the U.S. ranging from small offices in country towns where one operator sufficed, all the way up to the biggest offices in cities such as New York, Chicago, Boston, etc., where from 75 to 100 or more girls were at work in exchanges.[10]

An 1898 news story contended that women were employed as telephone operators to the exclusion of men "because the women are more patient. They have not the element to fight in them which characterizes many men, and when they hear a gruff voice say 'Gimme 571 and be in a hurry about it,' they do not assume a pugilistic attitude and talk back, but respond promptly to the call, or if it is not caught say 'Number, please?' with the most interesting rising inflection that is calculated to tone down the roughest of tempers."[11]

Also in 1898, it was reported that about one out of every 1500 American women was a telephone operator. This story also reported boys were first employed at that job but young boys were not easily taught to be either civil or accurate, and telephone operating in its early days was accompanied by many unnecessary difficulties with boys looking after subscribers. So telcos turned to women, reluctantly at first because they thought that machines needed men to tend them. But girls, that is, most girls are naturally polite and soft-spoken and politeness and soft-speaking go a long way over the telephone. Also girls, in spite of the perennial jokes in the comic papers written by men, can be accurate whey they are taught to be and are made to keep it up by judicious supervision. So the girl replaced the boy, and so great was the improvement that the telephone girl promptly became an established institution.[12]

The girl telephone operator was something that swept the world. A 1900 publication reported that female operators in the Paris exchange were being displaced by men. That journal noted that women had heretofore been universally employed because their voices "are lighter and carry better and also because they have more patience and diplomacy." In spite of those qualities, the women had to go, reportedly because "[a]ll beseeching and disciplinary measures have been powerless to prevent girls from chattering among themselves instead of devoting their sole attention to subscribers." The account was accurate about women being employed as operators, giving the same reasons as were used in America for their employment. The piece also made use of the stereotype of women being uncontrollable chatterboxes. What was also nonsense about the piece was the idea that women were to be replaced by men. They were not.[13]

There was one exception to the rule that telephone operators were always female: American police departments. Many of those departments continued to employ males as their operators. In 1906 it was reported that the men who answered the phones at the Richmond, Virginia, police stations did so on an average of every three minutes, day and night. They worked 12 hours straight with no coffee breaks, meal breaks or breaks of any kind. The city police commissioner was asked to appoint another man to each station, therefore allowing the men to work eight-hour shifts instead of 12 as was then the case.[14]

Consternation reportedly broke out among the girls of the Forest Exchange of the Bell Telephone Company in Chicago in February 1908 when it became known that operator Helen Iles was in fact a boy in disguise. That secret came to light when one of the girls complained to the chief of the exchange, Miss Burns, that Helen was not what she seemed. She had applied for her position five months earlier, giving the name of Helen Iles, 22, of Chicago. At the beginning of February, a new operator named Margaret was assigned to the exchange. Helen, seemingly forgetting her disguise, told Margaret he was a man and asked her to marry him. Margaret refused and immediately told Burns, with the result that Helen was quickly discharged.[15]

In 1921 there was a worsening shortage of girl operators. It was becoming

At the New York City Police Department in 1909, male telephone operators lined up at the switchboard. Some police departments held out against the idea of women operators and used men. They were the only places that did so.

increasingly difficult for telcos to fill their switchboards. When people asked why the telcos did not hire men, an article explained that boys were used in the early days when "girls were never thought of. In the early '80s, girls were not working as much as they are today. In fact, it was 'not being done' by the 'best people' in those days." When a subscriber could not get a number, the subscriber often found that the boy operator often cursed more than the subscriber did. And when a subscriber got into an argument with a boy, the other boys stopped work to listen in and the cheer on their co-worker. Washington, D.C.'s first telephone boy was B.L. Nevius Jr., who was then (1921) manager of De-Sales Hand Laundry. The second male operator Ben Steinmetz was in 1921 an F Street merchant. Third was Everett Bossell, who also still lived in Washington. "It was soon learned that the boys were not serious-minded enough for telephone operators and that subscribers, especially if they were men, did not hesitate to cuss them out if everything did not go well," explained the reporter. In those days (around 1878), Washington telephone service was available only from 8 a.m. to 6 p.m. When the exchange moved in 1879, the switchboard was

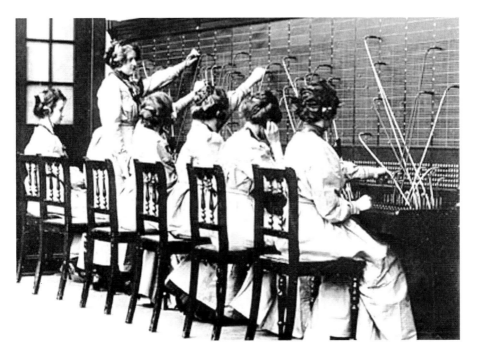

Telephone exchange in Detroit, 1880. Even at this early stage females had almost entirely taken over the job of telephone operator.

enlarged and girls were hired for the first time. The exchange then was kept open until 11 p.m., with girls and some of the boys during the day and "a man at night." That first exchange in Washington (1878) had about 20 subscribers, mostly business houses and stables. The night operator in that era was George E. Danninx. The first girls employed were the Misses Lloyd, Dant, Donaldson, French and Stone. All had left the business years earlier but some of them still lived in Washington. With the advent of the girl operator came the slogan of the telco, "Politeness and 20 seconds." Another observation from this journalist: "The boys in the old days not only cussed out subscribers, but they quarreled among themselves, carved the switchboards with their initials and played tricks with the wires and the subscribers." Girl operators were found to be more attentive to their work and their voices were more adaptable to the telephone than the voices of boys. Between 1878 and 1884, boys were employed here as operators but by about 1880 they began to be replaced by girls until by about 1885 only girls were employed during the day but the boys still held on as night operators, at least for a little while longer.[16]

In 1930, Elizabeth Good retired as a telephone operator at St. Paul,

Minnesota, after 50 years of service. She had begun her career in 1880. When she retired, she was the longest serving operator in America.[17]

In those very earliest years of 1878 and 1879, central telephone exchanges were operating in several cities. There was much noise in those early exchanges. In some cases, all the calls came to a single boy who yelled the order to the other boys. It often took from two to six boys to handle each call. However, within a few short years, technology had advanced to turn the exchanges quiet with the female operators' work barely being heard. By the early 1880s, they all sat before their switchboards with a headset attached and handled the call themselves, from subscriber to desired party, and they handled the call quickly and quietly.[18]

2

The Hello Girl to 1900

The girl telephone operators soon came to be called "hello girls," presumably because that was how they answered the phone, at least at the beginning. Telcos soon became unhappy with that as an opening word as it was too vague and open-ended and made it easier for a subscriber to go off on a tangent. Within a few years, the telcos all had their girls answer by saying, "Number, please." But the nickname "hello girls" remained firmly in place and the operators were rarely referred to in the media by any other name.

In the first few years of the industry's existence, there were no numbers at all. Subscriber Smith cranked his instrument and when the operator answered, Smith simply asked for Dr. Jones or Brown's Grocery Store. That lasted until the early to mid–1880s, when numbers were introduced. The change was introduced by the Washington, D.C., telco on May 1, 1884. When asked by the operator "Number, please," the subscriber was to give the number desired first, then their own number. For example, Smith picked up his phone and asked for 248 (Brown's Grocery Store) for 733 Smith. Throughout the period covered by this book, *all* calls had to go through a live operator. There were a few abortive attempts to introduce automatic direct dialing for local numbers during this period but none had lasting success. It was only in 1922 that automatic dialing arrived in America for all, although it took many years to implement it. Every phone had to be replaced with an instrument containing a dial. In the period covered by this book, no one owned their own phone. They were installed in the home by a fixed link and could not be moved or unplugged in any way. They were on loan by the telco and remained the company's property. When a subscriber discontinued service, he had to see that the phone was returned to the telco.[1]

One of the early changes in the lives of operators came in the mid–

1880s with the introduction of the monitor station. It began in the Washington, D.C., telco at the start of January 1885 and it was introduced in order that the company could get control of "idle chatter" by the operators and "love-making" between operators and the clerks in subscribers' businesses that were often on the other end of the line. The monitor desk was said to have been invented by E.A. Eckert, chief operator of the Metropolitan Telephone Company in Washington. Within a few days, he said, every central telephone office in the city would have its own monitor desk. All the operators were annoyed with that development. At the first monitor station installed sat Manager Thompson. He could watch every girl in the operating room. "The instant I suspect any girl is flirting with a subscriber, or carrying on a personal conversation with an operator in another exchange, all I have to do is to put a plug in the [monitor desk] switchboard in the hole corresponding with her wire, and I am instantly connected with the circuit on which she is talking," explained the manager. "She has no means of knowing that I am listening, and yet I can hear all that is said on both sides. I can listen to as much of it as I care to and then I can say 'come off,' or 'take a drop,' and both parties hear me. In this manner, no girl will dare to fritter away her time, for she does not know whether she is talking directly into my ear or not." He admitted the girls "don't like it." Eckert stated that with this method, he could catch a wayward operator every time. He had first used the monitor system on the regular telegraph wire so he could break in on telegraph operators at any time.[2]

Wages of St. Paul, Minnesota, women workers were reported in May 1885. At the time, there were said to be 1000 girls employed in the city's business district. In shoe factories they earned $3 to $10 a week with the hours of work being 7 a.m. to 6 p.m. with one hour for lunch. Forewomen in those plants received $15 a week. Dry goods stores employed 300 females aged 14 and up at pay rates of $3.50 to $10 a week with the average being $5 to $6. Dressmakers received $1 a day, worked 7 a.m. to 6 p.m. and were aged 18 to 25, with very few of the latter age. When they resided at boarding houses, they paid $3.50 to $4.50 per week for room and board. Millinery workers were paid $3 to $15 a week with skilled hands making $10 and working from 8 a.m. to 6 p.m. Salesladies earned from $6 to $12 a week. Hello girls in St. Paul were paid from $18 to $35 a month ($4.15 to $8.10 a week).[3]

An August 1886 article from an Omaha newspaper was sympathetic towards them, pointing out how hard they worked and yet were unappreciated. The Omaha central telephone exchange was located on the second floor of a building at the northwest corner of Fifteenth and Farnam. Eleven girls were employed there, including a head operator and a night operator. In addition, one young man helped during the noon hour and after supper. There were rarely more than six or seven working at the same time, the others being held in reserve for relief duty. Mr. E. B. Smith was office manager. The operators' average working day was eight hours. Sometimes a girl worked less but sometimes she was "compelled" to work longer, occasionally 10 or 12 hours a day. Once or twice a week she had a half-day off; every eighth Sunday, she was assigned to do a half-day's work, and on the Sunday following, she worked a full day. That compelled the reporter to observe that "on the whole, the length of her average working day is not excessive." He pointed out that the telephone girl had to possess intelligence, had to be rapid in thought and action, efficient, had to work error-free, be cool-headed and keep her composure. Above all, she had to avoid getting ruffled when customers got cranky, yelled or were obscene. The best-paid girl in that exchange, the head operator, was paid $50 a month. From that figure, salaries were graded down to $20 a month, where the beginner started: "The operator of fair ability and average experience receives from $30 to $40 a month." The longest serving hello girl had been on the job for about five years. The beginner started at $20 a month and was placed beside an old hand who taught and guided her. The reporter concluded; "Owing to the fact that many of the girls become thoroughly worn out by the arduous labor, or retire to seek exchange of work, new additions to the force are constantly being made."[4]

In 1888, the Minneapolis Telephone Company exchange was located at the corner of Nicollet Avenue and Second Street and contained 1500 wires that led to the businesses and homes of its subscribers. Each operator sat before a callboard that contained 75 to 100 subscribers, all of which she had to answer and then direct to the desired party. Suppose subscriber #483-2 wanted 795-4. The operator, when drop 483 fell, listened while the person ringing told her what he wanted. Then she inserted a plug in the hole numbered 483 and placed the companion plug in the hole 795 and pressed 4X on a black button. That connected the lines 483 and 795 and rang all the bells on the line numbered 795. There may have been six telephones on line 795 but the only one to answer the ring was the subscriber whose number was 795-4.

Most people at this time, and well into the future, were on what were called party lines: Several households completely independent of each other and living at different addresses had the same telephone number. When that number rang, it rang differently (for example, two longs, one short; one short, one long, one short] so that only the intended party would answer. Of course, somebody else with the 795 number could quietly pick up the receiver and listen in. Such eavesdropping was common, of course. According to this piece, it was the duty of the chief operator "to find out what operators are not attending to their duty, stop all lolly-gagging and talking between operators and outsiders over the wires and to receive all protests of poor service and all reports of wires or telephones not working." No telephone operator was allowed to receive a message for herself over the wires. Any and all such messages were sent to one of the chief operators who passed it on to the girl for whom it was intended. That exchange then had some 2300 subscribers on its 1500 wires. There were then about 900 "special wires," that is, wires on which there was only one telephone. The average number of calls answered during the day was 11,409. The busiest hour of the day was between 3 and 4 p.m. A total of 45 employees were at the exchange: 27 regular operators, two chief operators, four "trouble" men, seven linemen, one foreman and four officers.[5]

Later in 1888, reporter Eva Gay visited the St. Paul, Minnesota, exchange and wrote, "I understand that telephone girls have a perfect horror of being classed as working girls. I don't know just how they figure it, but for one of these favored mortals to walk upon the same side of the street or hold any conversation with a 'factory girl' would be forever to lose caste with her own companions." There were 25 operators. Sixteen of them had regular switchboards to attend while the other nine were relief operators who took the place of anybody who was absent or who needed to leave her post for a few minutes. The exchange manager told Gay the girls were paid $15 the first month of employment, $20 for the second month, and $25 a month for "always" after that. When Guy asked if it was not possible for a girl to earn more, the reply was, "Not unless under special circumstances." One example of that was the night operator who worked "long hours" and got $40 a month. Another example was a girl who chose to work from 10 a.m. to 10 p.m. with two one-hour meal breaks allowed; "she can earn $31 a month. Otherwise the highest wages are $25 a month." Each of those hello girls had from 50 to 75 lines under her charge and from one to six subscribers on each line. An operator told Gay that it took two weeks to learn the job "and no pay is given for that time." Regular operators worked nine and a half to ten hours a day (a one-hour meal break allowed). Some shifts ran from 7 a.m. to 5:30 p.m. Each operator had to work about three hours every third Sunday.[6]

Pittsburgh had its first phone installed in 1879, with 203 phones installed locally that year. Since that time, the average number of phones installed in the city had been 300, with a total of 3200 in place in 1889. In

Sketches of Minneapolis hello girls from 1888.

the district there were some 9000 phones that same year, about half of them business phones, half in private residences. A business paid a yearly rental of $94 for a phone while a private residence paid a yearly phone rental of $75. Out-of-town calls cost 25 cents for five minutes and about 300 of those long distance calls were placed each day. All 26 operators were young women "and they are bright and good looking," commented a reporter. The exchange manager, Mr. Gray, observed that women were more equable than men in temper and more patient and self-possessed. Their rejoinders to angry subscribers were based on the old doctrine "A soft answer turneth away wrath." The operator's headset was an eight-ounce contraption held on by a steel spring on the top of the head with the ear piece on the left ear. In an operator's first year on the job, she received what was called an "average" salary. At the end of two years, a raise of $5 a month was "always" made and the same again after four years of service. Hours of work were from 7 a.m. to 6 p.m. with time for lunch. Relief operators were always on hand to fill in as the need arose. An average day's work for an operator ranged from 450 to 1150 calls (those were the lowest and highest days on record). Six boys were employed to operate the exchange from 6 p.m. to midnight. Those six were relieved at midnight by two other boys who ran the switchboards until 7 a.m. Busiest times for phoning were from 9 a.m. until noon. According to the account; "The aforementioned boys are chiefly remarkable for impudence."[7]

Thirty-one operators were employed at the Omaha central exchange in the summer of 1890. They were girls of all descriptions, shapes, sizes, ages and so on, observed a journalist, "but they are all telephone girls, which, in itself, means the personification of patience, usefulness and general assistance to the world at large." Of those operators, 21 were on day duty, two were employed at night and eight were relief operators. The latter were on duty at noon, and in the morning and evening when the regular operators were on meal breaks or when one of the regulars was off work sick. Each operator had charge of 100 subscribers while 32 linemen looked after 1200 miles of wire.[8]

In 1892, a reporter in Arizona described the hello girls by saying the phrase "frisky telephone girl" was a great misnomer "as this young woman is almost a part of her instrument having just enough individuality to give to subscribers a line of communication. The girls themselves are absolutely forbidden to talk over the lines." Each girl had 50 subscribers to look after and, no matter how often a subscriber called, she made the connection he required. They women worked from 7 a.m. to 7 p.m. with three separate shifts, each of which worked nine hours with half an hour for a meal break and 15-minute "recesses" (coffee breaks) in the morning and afternoon. Salaries in this location ranged from $30 to $50 per month "according to aptitude and experience." Monitors receive $12 ($51 per month) each week.[9]

When a national magazine summarized the occupation in 1892, it was said that the telephone girl may not be educated but she had to be nice and must be possessed of a medium grade of intelligence:

> She must be able to write a letter, make a clear statement in good English, hold her tongue, keep her temper under every provocation and give her undivided attention to the business of the office. Any defect in speech or hearing would necessarily disqualify her for the work.... Tact and judgment are indispensible, and lacking one or the other, she will break down in a very short time, for nothing so quickly develops a pugnacious tendency as service at a public telephone.

In an office where 120 girls were required, eight boys were also employed. Their work consisted of the mechanical operation of making connections between the trunk wires running to different exchanges. Those boys received their orders by telephone from the operators and had no communication with the subscribers. No girls were employed on the night shift because, said the account, "The exposure to such uncanny hours is considered undesirable by the company and wisely so, although many girls apply for night work." That force of 120 hello girls worked 7 a.m. to 7 p.m., divided into three shifts: 7 a.m. to 5 p.m., 8 a.m. to 6 p.m., and 9 a.m. to 7 p.m. Every second Saturday was a "half-holiday" and, said the reporter;

"the girls are in every respect as well treated as college students." Reportedly, no fines were imposed on the operators for infractions and the company provided a suite of five rooms for the girls' use. One was a toilet room, with an adjacent dressing room that included lockers. Another was a dining room with a cook who made coffee. Also provided was a reading room stocked with magazines and newspapers and a "sick ward." The matron in charge of those rooms was a retired operator. Salaries ranged from $30 to $50 a month "beginning the very day the girl is engaged, although she may not be useful as an operator for a month or more." The girls who were able to "take charge without assistance" and attend to 50 wires received $35. Monitors received $12 a week while operators in the relief force were paid $1 a day. That relief force was always on hand "to facilitate matters when disasters, public excitement or unusual events increase the business of the office to an extent that overtaxes the capacity of the regular force." Examples of such events were a run on a bank, a big fire, a train accident or news of a shipwreck.[10]

On October 18, 1892, an exchange of telephone messages took place between a telephone operator in the American Exchange in New York City and another in the office of the same company on Quincy Street in Chicago. Reportedly this exchange of messages "was over the longest telephone lines ever successfully used."[11]

San Francisco reporter Marie Evelyn visited the central telephone exchange building in that city in November 1892. The telco employed seven operators on long distance work and 40 hello girls as regular operators. They were paid $30 to $40 a month and the company provided a lunch room where a matron made tea for the girls. Evelyn found that some of those operators were very young, little more than 18; "Not a few of these hello girls, still in their teens, are the mainstay of some invalid mother or younger sister. When a telephone girl is suspended, it often means privation and want for a whole family."[12]

A piece published in the summer of 1893 dealt with the stereotype of females being unable to keep secrets. The reporter mentioned the possible problem of secrets betrayed because the operator heard all kinds of things:

> The Central girl must have a hard time to keep all the secrets she hears, and she would be more than mortal if she did not occasionally divulge. Then sometimes a secret gets out, and central is occasionally blamed for an offense of which she is not guilty.... The reporter sometimes blames the telephone girl for tipping off "scoops" to the other papers. The central girl is often accused of impertinence or lack of attention, and a thousand and one faults are laid at her door, while she is doing better than could be expected when her manifold calls for service are considered.

Every city, he added, "has its many instances of choleric persons going to the local manager and demanding the discharge of an operator. In very few cases is the demand complied with, as it generally turns out that the operator is not blameworthy."[13]

In the summer of 1894, the central telephone exchange in Salt Lake City was located on the top floor of the Deseret National Bank Building. When a reporter stopped in for a visit, the temperature was 95 degrees. Eight operators (out of a total force of 14) were on duty; they worked from nine to five while two operators were in the relief group and one was in the toll (long distance) room. From 5 p.m. until 8 a.m. the next morning, two operators alternated, one sleeping on site while the other manned the switchboard. Also, one operator worked daily from 5 p.m. to 8 p.m. According to the account, the proportion of telephone messages sent outside of business hours (8 a.m. to 5 p.m.) "is, of course, comparatively small, the bulk being by the newspaper and railroad offices." Chief operator Jennie Smith was a veteran of six years on the job. She provided general supervision and taught the novices, although the exchange had what was described as a stable workforce and had no turnover in the operator ranks for over one year. "An applicant for a position in the central office is expected to be quick-witted, deft and polite. It is not required that she be pretty, but she usually is. She is sweet-tempered, too," declared the reporter. Also, "she has the tact of the society woman and the discretion of the businessman."[14]

Some idea of the class divisions in play could be seen in a brief account that appeared in April 1895 in a Stockton, California, newspaper:

> The four hundred of Santa Rosa [the elite] must feel slighted because a telephone girl was elected the queen of the rose festival. The election is not complimentary to Santa Rosa society, but is highly creditable to Santa Rosa in general…. The people have shown themselves to be pretty good Americans by bestowing the distinction on a self-supporting girl, whose beauty must be unusual to have overcome the power of wealth in such a contest.[15]

When the Missouri and Kansas Telephone Company moved to a new office at Sixth and Delaware Street in Kansas City, Missouri, on May 1, 1895, it had a total of 2700 subscribers. Telephone service had cost $60 a year before the move but was reduced to $48 a year with the move. Hello girls employed there were paid $1 a day and that was, said a reporter, about twice as much as salesladies received. Some operators had worked for the telco for 10 or 12 years. According to the account, the telephone company was always "on the lookout for the welfare of the girls." The exchange received 40,000 calls per day with each subscriber using his phone some 15 times per day.[16]

Sketch of Kansas City Missouri's new exchange, in 1895 just after moving into the location.

A story that appeared at the start of 1896 proclaimed that hello girls had to learn telegraphy. Within a few months, the entire staff of the Pacific Telephone Company would be carrying telegraph messages ticked by the girls who heretofore had only been required to say, "Number, please." Those telephone lines were to be used for both telephone and telegraph messages.

A Montreal telephone exchange in 1895.

This San Francisco–based telco saw big profits as it would have no expense for linemen (already employed for the phone lines) and would need no extra operators. President and general manager of Pacific Telephone Company, John L. Sabin, declared; "There is one thing you can be sure of, that is that it will not be long before candidates for positions to take charge of telephones will be required to be expert telegraph operators." It never happened. Early telcos were often both telephone and telegraph companies at the same time but none ever integrated their staffs; phone operators remained hello girls while telegraph operators remained telegraph operators.[17]

When reporter Mamie Loretta Nallin visited the Scranton, Pennsylvania, central telephone exchange in May 1896, she found that it employed 18 young women and two men (the chief operator and the electrician). The switchboard operated by the women was in 12 different sections, including two sections for the long distance messages. On average, each operator answered 700 calls a day. Each girl had a section with 50 wires and with an average of five subscribers on every wire. The operator was required to know every subscriber's number and when a call came in—say the number was 4762—the operator connected the number of the wire (the call was on wire number 476) and then rang two bells; the last figure in the call number was the number of bells to ring for the specific subscriber, who shared number 476 with four other households.[18]

When the Southern States Telephone Company completed the work of putting in a new switchboard in Norfolk, Virginia, in December 1896, it had a capacity of over 900 telephones; 500 subscribers on the old board were transferred over. On December 17, six "pretty" Norfolk girls went to work on the new board, having been trained by Mr. J.D. Hobbs, the telephone exchange manager. It worked as follows: The subscriber went to his phone, rang his bell and listened. Soon that subscriber heard an operator at central say, "Number, please," which meant the subscriber had to give the number of the phone with which he wanted a connection. When that subscriber first rang his bell, his number on the indicator board at central fell and the operator moved a little lever in front of her and placed a jack in the hole corresponding to the subscriber's number. When she received the desired number she put a jack in the hole corresponding to that number and a connection was made. After the subscriber finished his conversation, both parties to the chat were expected to ring their respective bells and let the operator know the conversation was over. At that point, the operator unplugged both jacks. Each operator had 100 numbers in front of her. When the number desired was not one of those 100, she, by an "electrical contrivance," connected the caller to wherever the number was in the central station or on the exchange.[19]

A lengthy article describing the New York Telephone Company in New York City appeared in February 1897. At that time, there were 12 central exchanges with more than 17,000 subscribers connected to those 12 exchanges, besides many private lines. The reporter noted that when a man made a call and was told the desired number was "busy," he "doesn't for an instant believe the girl has told him the truth [and] begins to scold the girl roundly over the wire, threatening to have her discharged. He does this because he believes that it is one of the privileges of every subscriber and, furthermore, he believes that the managers of the telephone system employ girls to work the switchboards because men would do it better." Many separate exchanges instead of one large exchange in big cities existed because it would have been impossible to run all the cables into one building. A building of the necessary size would have had to occupy more than an entire street. One of this telco's exchanges, the Cortlandt Street exchange, had more than 250 feet of switchboard. The front of that board was divided up into 43 sections with one girl in change of each. When Mr. Bethel, the manager of that exchange, was asked what qualifications were needed to be a hello girl, he replied, "A girl must be well-natured" and "She must bring references as to her general character and the references we set the most store by is one from one of our own girls." Bethel said most of his girls had been with him for five to seven years: "This work is not like the holiday work in our great shops. It goes on night and day … and often life, death, success and failure depend upon the promptness of the girls at the switchboard. We give each applicant a general examination to determine her fitness for the work, and very many are turned away as unfit." If she got through the system that far, she was taken on by the telco on probation for six months. During that time, she was paid $3 a week during which time she could be discharged for any reason (that is, no cause was necessary). Once she had passed her probation period, she could only be discharged for cause. When a reporter asked Bethel what were causes for dismissal, he stated, "The main one is flirting over the wire, or perhaps I should say talking, and making engagements. Another is being pert to subscribers. It is next to impossible for the girls to do either, for they are listened to from outside and inside, and are watched by the lynx-eyed young women walking and sitting behind them."

Behind each group of 12 girls, a young woman walked up and down on a raised platform. She was called a supervisor and her eyes were ever on the alert for "anything that needs correction." She was also there to help girls when they had more calls than they could handle. Each girl had charge of 40 to 75 subscribers and sometimes that number went up to 100. Seated at desks back of the supervisors were a number of girls called monitors. At any time, they could break in on a girl and hear what was going on. If a monitor spotted a girl laughing and talking, she broke in. Another function of monitors was to take subscriber complaints. When a subscriber scolded a girl for telling him a desired number was busy, and would not stop complaining, the operator could route him to a monitor.[20]

Bethel admitted that "very occasionally" they had to fire a girl for being rude or for making an engagement. On the occasion of the first such offense, a warning was issued; discharge was the result for a second offense. The manager told the reporter they had tried men on the job at night but they were not "nearly so satisfactory" as the girls and to his surprise they found plenty of girls willing to work nights. "Girls are more attentive and deft with their hands and their soft voices smooth out many a rough place in the business world that would only be made rougher by man's gruff voice in the Central exchanges," Bethel explained. Busiest times in his office were from 10 a.m. to noon and from 2 p.m. to 3 p.m. In those times, the New

York Telephone Company received an average of 19,000 calls an hour. Hours of work for the day shift were those found in other telcos: 7 a.m. to 5 p.m., 8 a.m. to 6 p.m. and so on. When there was a lull in business, said the reporter, "the girls can speak to each other, though regular chats are forbidden." In the company lunchroom, the girls brought their own food but the firm supplied hot tea, coffee, chocolate and milk. There was a reading room with periodicals and newspapers. In that room sat a young woman at a desk who carried the title of assistant manager but the girls called her "our mother," according to Bethel. They went to her with all their troubles and if necessary she took them to the superintendent. However, no trouble was taken to the higher level of manager unless it involved a subscriber's contract. Subscribers were, reportedly, cut off and refused service if they talked "outrageously" to an operator over the line. The operator was allowed to report such behavior to a "sympathetic woman" instead of to a man. After an operator served out her six months of probation, her salary moved to $10 a week, which was as high as it went for a regular operator. A great many big businesses and public offices had started their own private exchanges, which were, of course, connected with a central exchange. In all those cases, those private exchanges were staffed by young women as operators.[21]

The hello girl had become such a widely known personality and a large enough part of American culture that she made it to the stage. Described as a "frothy comedy" with musical pieces, *The Telephone Girl* opened on stage for the first time on November 29, 1897, at the Columbia Theater in Washington, D.C. It starred Louis Mann and Clara Lipman.[22] One month later it was presented at the Casino Theater in New York City. It was said to have been an adaptation from the French of Anthony Mar and Maurice Desvallieres. This company also starred Mann and Lipman. Mann had the comic part of inspector of wires and Lipman was the telephone girl. This operator, employed in a central office, heard a message sent by another young woman to her (the operator's) lover. She became jealous and went so far as to disregard the confidential nature of her position to the extent that she acted on her fears. She got a place as a maid in the household of her supposed rival in order to watch her. And it went on, getting sillier and sillier.[23]

A year later, *The Telephone Girl* was still making the rounds. When it appeared in Norfolk, Virginia, in December 1898, a reviewer observed; "The first act shows the interior of a telephone exchange. Prettily uniformed girls sit around the sides and back working at the phones, when they are not singing, talking or dancing." The cast featured 40 "bewitching" tele-

An 1898 newspaper ad for the long-running play *The Telephone Girl*. It was very popular and also very unrealistic.

phone girls. Later that same month, the play was performed in Washington, D.C. Reportedly it was a very successful play that ran in a lot of cities, played for a long time and generally got very good reviews. By then, a number of different casts were on the road with the play.[24]

That play was still on the go at the end of 1902 and then playing in Spokane, Washington. When asked about it, and whether her hello girls were going to see it, the Spokane telco office's chief operator declared, "No, we don't intend to go. None of the girls are going as far as I know, and under no circumstances are we going in a party." According to the reporter, "The Spokane hello girls draw the line on the play. They claim it is a burlesque on their profession and, in short, they think the play is under the wrong *nom de plume*."[25]

When journalist Eva Mitchell Cook visited the central exchange in Los Angeles in the first month of 1898, she learned that there were some 4000 telephones scattered around the city and only 56 girls to handle the boards at the main office. In that main office were 60 boards, each of which connected with trunk lines, party lines, the chief operator and so on. Each board had 200 holes for jacks. All the holes were numbered and divided into A and B boards. On the former, the calls were received from subscribers while on the latter the ringing was done. Sitting facing the boards were the girls, in long lines. Against the ear of each, usually the left, was a black rubber receiver that was bound to her head by means of a curved double steel band. Suspended from the board in front of each operator's mouth was the transmitter for that specific board. During working hours, the operator's conversational powers were limited "by strict rule" to "Number?" "The line is busy" and "Party called for does not reply." Any complaints were routed to a supervisor. Cook wrote,

> The girls are all chosen with discrimination and care. Some of them are related to the best people in the city, and even as the company exacts scrupulous obedience to its rules, so does it protect and shield its employees from unjust criticism or harsh treatment from the outside.... If a subscriber swears at an operator, the manager immediately warns him that a second offense will deprive him of his telephone—and when the second offense comes his telephone is taken out forthwith.

Walking behind the girls were the chief operator and the manager. Girls never knew when one was directly behind them.[26]

In June 1898, it was reported that Chicago had nearly 500 telephone operators in the city and of those, over 200 were located in the central exchange. Every one was a woman. Women were preferred, declared the article, because the feminine voice "suits best the delicate instrument" and they were more patient. Telco general manager Angus Hibbard explained that all applicants were tested for acuteness of hearing and as to mental alertness. They did not want girls who had to say "I beg your pardon" and so forth. "Boys and men are less patient. They have always the element of fight in them. When spoken to roughly and rudely, they are not going to give the soft answer. Not ever. And every man is a crank when he is on a phone." According to the reporter, "Mr. Hibbard is a strict disciplinarian but he is perfectly just." At the Chicago telco, obscenity was not tolerated. One warning to a cursing subscriber was all that was delivered; upon a following offense the service was cut off. "We must and shall protect our operators," explained Hibbard. The journalist added that Hibbard "is a courteous gentleman, and through him the ways of the Chicago telephone girls are ways of pleasantness, and all their business paths are peace." The journalist went on to summarize Florence Kelly's report to the state labor committee in which she declared that the Chicago telephone girls received a higher average compensation and were better taken care of than those in any other place which she had visited in that state; that theirs, of all avocations reported on, was the most desirable. That report also declared, "[F]or pure air, perfect cleanliness and opportunities for rest, the telephone exchange could scarcely be excelled." One of Hibbard's rules was that each of his operators had to wear a black skirt that cleared the floor by an inch or two. That was to keep down dust, one of the major enemies of all the electrical equipment in the room. The air was kept clean and air-conditioned but that was done for the sake of the equipment and machinery which was prone to malfunction in the face of dust and temperature and humidity variation. None of those steps were taken with a primary view of operator comfort. When the reporter was touring the central exchange, an operator turned to look at the passing journalist. The guide pegged her as a novice because she "had no occasion to do that. An experienced operator never notices anything or anybody apart from her work."

People frequently asked Hibbard if the work of an operator affected the hearing. He replied, "It certainly does. It makes it more exquisitely keen." He added that virtually all of his operators were unmarried. In Chicago, the daily number of calls was then about 300,000, with about 16,000 subscribers. Business hours were the busiest times of the day for the telco. The most frequently asked question directed to the operators was "What time is it?" They were asked that some 25,000 times a day. A big fire, a new war bulletin, an "exciting" accident and other such incidents caused the number of calls received to spike up. The company kept its operators informed of such incidents and even sent out a man of its own to find out the details. In this era, the telephone company in each city functioned very much as an information source and gave out a variety of information that was wholly extraneous to its core business. In many ways it was very much an audio community service and information center, at least for the first couple of decades. All that sort of extraneous information-dispensing was then stamped out by the telcos. The biggest surge in calls to the Chicago Telephone Company took place in March 1897 on the occasion of the James Corbett vs. Bob Fitzsimmons boxing match that took place in Nevada. Some 10,000 men in Chicago frantically sought out the

NO WORKING WOMAN IS HAPPIER THAN A TELEPHONE GIRL.

Her Hours Are Short.
Her Surroundings
Comfortable, and
There Is a Never
Failing Interest
In Her Work.

Life of the Bright
Sweet-tempered Girl
Who Plays an Im-
portant Part
in the Business
World.

An 1898 article from Chicago that read like a cheerleading section for the telephone companies. Nobody had it better than a hello girl, reportedly.

results. Finally, the hello girls were told the news and gave out the answer to all who asked that Fitzsimmons was the victor. Another point that Hibbard emphasized to the reporter: flirting was taboo. The tone of the article was accurately captured in the title of the piece: "No working woman is happier than a telephone girl."[27]

Within the New York Telephone Company, the traffic department was the branch responsible for the operation of the subscribers' lines. It was to the superintendent of this department that the would-be operator had to go to apply for work. Almost no applicant had prior experience. Qualifications included good eyesight, good hearing, distinct enunciation, fair penmanship and general neatness. At least medium height was required, preferably a bit more. Recruits, noted an account, "should be at the teachable age, say, between 17 and 21, good elementary education and good character references." The first step was for the applicant to go on the waiting list, after she was first checked out for the above qualities. When there were vacancies or additions to staff, letters were sent to those on the list requesting them to report for duty. The beginner usually was put on the night shift, because the work was light. She went on salary from the start, although "not a very large pay at first." A raise was given according to individual abilities but took at least three months. During most of that time, no real work was done by the beginner. Mostly she watched, listened and learned for the first month and then proceeded to light work on the night shift. As vacancies occurred in the day workforce, the best night operators were transferred. From the ranks of regular operators, promotions were made through the grade of senior operator to supervisor. The bulk of the day shift worked from 8 a.m. to 6 p.m. with one half-hour meal break and two 20-minute breaks during the day, one in the morning and one in the afternoon. The night shift hours were 7 p.m. to 7 a.m. with three hours of relief time scattered over the shift. Amenities included a cloakroom, dining room and a reading room supplied with newspapers and magazines. A matron was in charge of the dining room with tea, coffee and so on provided by the telco.[28]

A lengthy article appeared in a San Francisco newspaper, *The Call*, on January 1, 1899, about a telco that violated the privacy rights of their subscribers. It used transcriptions (automatic recordings were not possible during this time) of conversations over its wires to blackmail people, or held back the transcriptions for potential use for blackmail in the future. The reporter observed that the tapping of telegraph wires was banned by law and that the privacy of the mail service was "inviolable." He declared there was a need for the law to stand guard over the telephone, to safeguard privacy. Also noted was that the use of the telephone had mushroomed, and that its usage was then (1899) universal. According to the story, *The Call* had shown "that the administration of the telephone company in San Francisco is corrupt to the core and its service a gigantic spy system and organized betrayal of its customers for the benefit of their social, political, amatory, official or business enemies or rivals, who are willing to pay the price of the treachery and violation of privacy." As proof, he revealed that a *Call* reporter had sent in exclusive information on an attempted murder and immediately the telephone operator reported it to a correspondent for the *Examiner*, a rival newspaper. On investigation, the operator admitted the offense and was discharged. That caused the *Call* to conduct an investigation of the Pacific Telephone and Telegraph Company and its subordinate company, the Sunset Telephone and Telegraph Company. The former handled local San Francisco phone calls and the latter conducted all of the long distance business. There was found to be a great deal of leakage in the *Examiner* office, where an individual gave money to use and to secure control of the operators and convert the switchboard into an

Telephone Company Has a Gigantic System of Espionage.

Every Conversation at the Disposal of the Talker's Business or Social Rivals.

Organized Betrayal of Its Customers Carried on for Pay.

The Most Confidential Messages Leaked Directly Into the Office of the Examiner.

IN THE MAIN TELEPHONE OFFICE

HELLO: "I WON'T BE HOME TO DINNER DEAR."

"ALL RIGHT GEORGE, BUT COME HOME EARLY."

THE EXAMINER REPORTER.

This series of sketches accompanied an article that purportedly exposed corruption in the San Francisco telco. That firm was accused of transcribing phone conversations for blackmail purposes and of feeding information from one city newspaper to a rival.

adjunct of the *Examiner* office. He sat in his office and listened to conversations leaked to his wire, and all sorts of private information was ascertained. The account gave a few more examples of the *Call* having information no one else should have but the *Examiner*. Concluded the piece, "It was found that the instructions given to the operators who handle the out-of-town business over the Sunset wires is to take down verbatim every conversation held over those wires, and that every conversation is transcribed, indexed and preserved in the telephone office."[29]

Reporter Cromwell Childe's lengthy study of the New York City telephone girl was published in the spring of 1899. He found her to be "as a rule, a slip of a girl, barely 20 oftentimes." His story was a supposed behind-the-scenes look at operators: "[T]he telephone girls of New York are attractive, but not markedly so when taken as a lump. They do not lend themselves particularly to romance." He did say that they were skillful. Behind every ten or so girls was a supervisor, one appointed from the ranks of the operators. She could see and hear everything each operator did. Next step in the supervisory line was the position of monitor with the largest switchboard in New York City then having four monitors. Each monitor sat at a switchboard and had queries and complaints referred to them from the operators. However, their main function was that "they listen in secretly upon the various girls in the room, a girl never knowing when the thin little wire is spying upon her." Altogether, said Childe, the operator "is a healthy, hearty, happy young woman whose privileges are many, and whose labors are not so severe, though incessant and taxing." She could get relief whenever she asked for it, he observed, always providing she was not trying to "soldier," to get out of working. She had as a right 20 minutes rest in the morning and 20 minutes in the afternoon. One conclusion he drew: "In comparison with that of the other working girls of the city, the lot is not a hard one." There were then an estimated 1200 telephone operators in New York City with the number increasing each week. About 50 men were in the telephone service, most of them being managers and their assistants; the remainder worked as operators on the night shift. Said Childe, "They are not the girls of the factory, nor yet of the shop. That a better class than this can claim them, certainly a good proportion, is evident." Those hello girls sat so close together at their work stations that "their dresses touch yet not a word of gossip is heard." Childe explained, "If it were permitted to chat with subscribers, to gossip with each other, the telephone girls would have no time. It is nothing unusual for an expert operator to answer 125 calls an hour." According to him stories about telephone flirtations "are in the main fairy stories." Each day each operator received an average of 500 or 600 calls.

It was the early morning duty of every operator to ring up all her subscribers and find out if the wires were in good working order. Within the New York Telephone Company, an operator started off as a "student" and was paid $3 a week. At first she simply listened in and observed the veteran she had been paired with and then worked her way in as an operator in the slack hours. Her pay was raised gradually according to her capacity until in two or three years, "if she is bright and quick," she reached the top of the operator pay scale, that being $9 a week. An expert chief operator could rise to about $18 a week. Childe noted, "No girl has yet risen from student to the heights of ordinary operatorhood in less than a year and a half."[30]

In July 1899, telephone girl Anita Byrne committed suicide in San Francisco by taking carbolic acid. Dr. Caglieri, acting autopsy surgeon, found that she was a "pure girl." One reporter wrote, "There were evidences that her nervous system had been undermined by overwork and constant worry—a condition that seems to be the lot of the telephone operators of this city." This was reportedly the third case within a few months of a telephone girl committing suicide "because of temporary mental derangement brought on by nervous tension and overlong hours." According to the article, an inquiry was to be held with respect to conditions at her workplace; "It is said that the treatment of the girls in the service of the monopoly is as bad as though the knout [whip] were applied to their bare backs." Coroner Hill was said to be the source of the statement that Byrne "had a horror of being discharged, and that the telephone girls are under a system of espionage so strict that they are kept in constant terror." Hill said:

> I understand that 69 detectives are employed by the telephone company to watch the girls. For the least infraction of the very rigorous rules, they are called into the office and discharged without a moment's notice. The constant tension to which they are subjected leads to all kinds of nervous diseases, and I do not wonder at the numerous suicides in their ranks.

One day earlier, the same newspaper implied that Byrne killed herself over a love affair that went bad.[31]

At the inquest into Byrne's death, telco Superintendent Lehigh swore that the girls were required to work only eight hours a day. But that idea was contested by the writer of an anonymous letter dated July 14, 1899, received by Coroner Hill and signed "A telephone girl." Hill told reporters he had received a separate letter giving the name and address of the anonymous letter writer but was then keeping it sealed. The anonymous letter read in part,

> We are worked to death. We are supposed to work nine hours every day, but more often it is lengthened to ten or twelve hours. Every other Sunday we work ten hours with a rest of 20 minutes to snatch a bite to eat. No holidays from January 1 to December 31. If a girl has a free Sunday she is often called to work some part of the day or night…. When the office is very busy, the manager is supposed to call upon the main office for assistance, but Manager Adams of the east office, instead of doing that, works the girls nearly to death and gives them ten cents an hour for their overtime. If

they are worn out and refuse to work, they are threatened with dismissal…. Don't expect truthful statements from employees of the company. They would be dismissed if they spoke the truth…. I cannot sign my name, because I work for the company, but if you will be instrumental in benefitting our case we will all say, "God bless Coroner Hill."[32]

The story of the death of Byrne created enough interest that *San Francisco Call* reporter Marian West went underground and got a job as a hello girl in that city to report on workplace conditions. West started off by commenting that the place did not look like a sweat shop "[but there] are mental sweat shops where mind is tortured at expense of body. Under this class comes the telephone office." She spent a week there and for four days and three nights she lived the life of a telephone girl. Admitting the office had large rooms that were well-lit and well-ventilated, she added, "But the hours and the wages are those of the sweat shop." Potential subscribers to the service were often given tours of the office, to see the operators at work. When such a guest asked the guide what hours the operators worked and what pay they received, he always received a vague reply; no actual figures were ever mentioned. Said West; "The telephone company criminally overworks the girls and shamelessly underpays them. I say this in the fullness of a seven-days' working knowledge among them. I went into the telephone company unbiased and without malice aforethought." Reportedly, a wave of sympathy for telephone girls had erupted in the wake of the suicides. Those hello girls had to wear either black or blue dresses. If they wore shirtwaists, they had to be white; "Color is tabooed. The telephone girls cannot speak to each other while working. They cannot say one word more than is absolutely necessary to the subscriber. They are under the constant surveillance of the chief operators. The spy system makes their lives miserable." West argued that those were the main points champions of the telephone girls made but that those were necessary and proper rules. Those champions were raising the wrong issues. She wrote:

There is one unnecessary reason for this state of affairs. It's because Central is worked far beyond the endurance of the average girl. Body and brain cannot stand it. It's fag-physical and mental fag that drives the telephone girl to the brink of death and sometimes over it. It's that which drives them to the shame and despair of worse than death…. It is impossible to get into the telephone office without more or less influence. Someone has to pull a wire for you or it is out of the question.

For West, a man, part of the financial and the political world, signed her letter of introduction to the office of Mr. Glass, who employed all the operators. Glass told West they turned away hundreds of girls and had a long waiting list but he made an exception for her and gave her immediate employment. Looking at the name on her letter of introduction, he told her, "You need no further recommendation." Three days later she received a note telling her to report for duty. She had a salary of nil for two weeks and then $20 a month thereafter. That first day she reported for work at 8 a.m., sat beside an experienced operator and listened all morning. At noon they had a 30-minute lunch break. The staff lounge area had six bathtubs; they were for the use of the girls who had no tubs at home. At 3 p.m. the operators had a ten-minute "recess," and they left work at 5 p.m. The next day, West reported at 9:30 p.m. and finished at 7:30 a.m. the following morning.[33]

There was a related incident in the Bay Area less than a month later. On September 13, 1899, it was reported from Oakland that 15-year-old Nettie Friebel was "a victim to the remarkable effect exercised on her brain and mind by five months' work at a telephone switchboard. For several days before her death she was engaged in fierce combat with a phantom receiver that would convey imaginary messages to her wrecked mind." According to Nettie's mother, five months earlier Nettie begged to be allowed to get work to help out at home, saying she could get a telephone company position. She received no wages at first and only small wages thereafter. Mrs. Friebel said her daughter was tall, strong and healthy before joining the telco, but the work made her sick. Nettie went to work at 7:30 a.m. and came home at 2 p.m. Then she went back to work at 5 p.m. and was home at 10 p.m., but sometimes it was later and she didn't get home until 11 p.m. or even later. She got little sleep, developed poor eating habits and heard a roaring in her ears. A delirium began two weeks before her death, leaving her raving and hearing voices and shouting in her ear. A physician diagnosed the problem as brain fever. Later, other medical people were called in. One declared the ravages of typhoid were added to those of the mental malady. Reportedly, Nettie's friend and fellow operator, Miss Campbell of East Oakland, had been recently taken to an insane asylum with her "mania" being the perpetual ringing of the telephone in her ears and the never-ceasing answering of calls. The most Nettie ever received was $17.75 for a month. "They docked her little salary of $20 per month on every possible excuse," stated Mrs. Friebel. Also, Nettie told her mother that Campbell had once received just $3 for a month's work.[34]

In light of Nettie's death, Robert Flemming, manager of the Oakland telco office, was asked if sickness was prevalent among the 100 girls employed at the Twelfth Street exchange. "There is really very little," he said. He didn't even recall Friebel's name. "I am inclined to think that her mother has attributed rather too much to action of the telephone on her

HAUNTED TO DEATH BY PHANTOM "HELLO" BELLS

Nettie Friebel, a Telephone Girl, Succumbs to Brain Fever.

Raving of Imaginary Messages, She Dies Under the Eyes of Her Distracted Mother—Switchboard's Work.

NETTIE FRIEBEL, A VICTIM OF THE TELEPHONE SERVICE.

With its sensational headlines, this 1899 article creates the impression that Nettie Friebel died as a result of her work as a hello girl. Most likely she died of typhoid.

girl's brain," he added. "We have an elegant retiring room with a matron to attend to girls that feel sick and wish to leave the tables for a few hours and we never question their sincerity in such matters." The journalist said that Mr. Ellis, who had charge of the girls, told him that Nellie did not work more than one month for the company. Ellis also said she worked as a substitute and "her hours were not so confining as those of the regular girls."[35]

In Kansas City, Missouri, an applicant had to be at least 5'6" in height because "short girls have short arms and cannot do the work satisfactorily."[36]

A reporter went to his local telco in St. Louis and spoke to manager Durant of the Bell exchange. Durant explained that when a businessman called for a number, he wanted it in a hurry and he wanted to receive due respect. "If the operator should speak to him in a harsh tone, he would resent it," explained the executive. "By careful observation for many years, we have tried to eliminate all the harsh ones from the vocabulary of the girls. We noticed that a rising inflection is more pleasant than any other, and you will observe that all the girls now use it. They are taught just how to say 'number,' 'hello' and all the other words constantly employed by them, and they are watched closely to see that they carry out instructions." According to this article, not more than four or five out of every 100 St. Louis applicants would come up to the requirements in every way. They had to have perfect sight and hearing and a good "reach." They were no short-armed telephone girls. Such a girl "couldn't reach the top of the board without rising to her feet, and she hasn't time for that." An applicant had to have a "quiet disposition and not be given to nerves." Each girl had from 65 to 100 lines to look after. It was a slow day when she made less than 1000 connections. In her busiest hours she made as many as 180 to 200 connections. The busiest hours were 9 a.m. to 10 a.m. and 3 p.m. to 4 p.m.[37]

For some time there had been complaints about the telephone service in Jeffersonville, Kentucky. The management employed a spy to watch the telephone girls and, said a reporter, "it seems he has reported that the girls neglected their duties, and now the girls are indignant…. It is charged, however, that the trouble is not due to the carelessness or negligence of the girls, but to the old-fashioned instruments and inefficient system of the Jeffersonville company, and the scheme to make a scapegoat of the girls will not remedy matters."[38]

An Omaha newspaper reporter commented in June 1900, "Telephone girls are exceedingly well cared for by the great telephone companies in the east. They are well fed within the exchange and provision is made to insure their getting the maximum amount of rest that their free time will allow."[39]

A brief story that appeared in a Texas paper in July 1900 stated that more than half of the telephone girls employed in the big city offices were Scottish or Irish. A manager explained to the reporter that those girls "controlled their tempers better, had clearer voices and that their politeness was more reliable than that of any other nationality."[40]

In the large exchange building in Omaha were employed eight young women, as of August 1900. "Their work requires intelligence and education and the girls are above average in dress and bearing," declared the account. Each operator had charge of 100 subscribers. One of those operators was Mrs. J.J. Ford, who had been in the phone service for ten years. She had no official title but, said the reporter, she "is to all purposes an assistant to the manager." She worked from 8 a.m. to 6 p.m. The operator lounge in this exchange also contained bathing facilities for the girls. The work day ranged from eight to nine hours in length. Election nights were very busy for operators as they fielded questions about who won. Many people called up to ask the time and to ask for weather reports, as in "Is it going to rain?" Whenever whistles went off in the city or there was loud bangs or mysterious plumes of smoke, everybody in town called the operator to find out what happened.[41]

3

The Operator, 1901–1922

The nickname "hello girls" never really left the women in that profession. However, in the late 1910s and into the early 1920s, it became somewhat more likely that the women employed by the telcos would be referred to simply as "operators."

In Honolulu, Hawaii, in February 1901 it was reported that after an "early hour of the evening," the hello girls were replaced by the hello boys. Calls were not frequent at night, especially over the period from 1 a.m. to 4 a.m. when there was an average of perhaps one call every 15 minutes. It was said that Honolulu was not a night city, that people went to bed early. According to telco superintendent Corcoran, an average day's business would be 5000 calls with 90 percent of those made between 8 a.m. and 6 p.m. Calls were steady from 6 p.m. until 10 p.m., and then "it practically ceases until the sun is up." The first group of 26 operators came on duty at 7 a.m. and remained until 11 a.m. Then relief operators took over with the first group going for lunch. Some of the first group returned to work in the afternoon. At 8 p.m., all of the regular day force went home and hello boys went on duty—three of them. They remained on duty until 7 a.m. Said Corcoran,

> The girls are mostly young and live with their parents. They are good girls, for this company could not use other. They are pleasant and bright and in spite of statements to the contrary, seem to be perfectly satisfied with their positions. There are any number of applicants for positions on file with me, which would seem to indicate that the job of hello girls is not all thorns and without any sunshine.[1]

In February 1901, one reporter remarked that with every large telephone exchange there was then a regular school for employees. Such schoolrooms were fitted with dummy switchboards and the installation apparatus corresponded to everything else found in a regular exchange. In many of those schools, if a trainee did not learn readily under one teacher, she was transferred to another teacher and was never dismissed as unfit for the work until she was given "a very fair trial." After her period of probation in the schoolroom, the newcomer was detailed to sit all day beside an expert operator to watch and learn and have a veteran explain things to her. It was said to be weeks before she was set to work alone and usually then on duty only during the slack hours.[2]

In East Liverpool, Ohio, there were about 15 telephone girls in March 1901, with seven of them employed at the Bell Telephone Company and eight at the Columbiana County Telephone Company. According to the reporter, there were always more applicants than jobs; the reporter added, "Telephone companies usually make life as pleasant as possible for the girls, and, if orders are strictly obeyed, all is well." The work day lasted from eight to ten hours. A few of the Columbiana girls had a broken day working split shifts, four hours in the morning and four hours much later in the day. The journalist noted, "These 'swings' are often objected to." Then there were the rules for the hello girls: no talking over the line, no talking back to patrons no matter what they said, no talking to "that nice young man" (meaning no flirting), no listening in on conversations. For eight to ten hours a day, the operator sat in her chair except for 30 minutes or 60 minutes for lunch. Each operator looked after 100 numbers. It was also noted that some physicians said the receiver attached to each operator's head sometimes caused "telephone ear." For her work, the telephone girl was paid what the journalist described as "fair wages." The standard scale in East Liverpool was $20 a month but it took two to three months of experience, as a rule, to secure that amount. Beginners were paid $15 a month. The reporter added; "It is said that three of five girls make a success as hello girls. It talks from two to five months to become proficient. The time depends upon the girl herself and the patience of the instructor. If, at the end of five months, she cannot care for her board, it is likely she is dismissed." The piece concluded by remarking that after the telephone girl became proficient in the regular exchange, "her ambition is then to secure a position in a private branch [switchboard of a private company]. Here the life is somewhat easier."[3]

An April 1901 article that originated in New York City told about the increasing number of rest rooms provided by employers for working women, especially in the previous three years. Several department stores and factories then had them, as did every one of New York City's 13 telephone exchanges. It went on:

> The telephone girl leads a nerve-racking sort of existence. Every one of her faculties are in commission from the moment she fastens on her nickel-plated headgear in the

morning until she takes it off at night. She sits in a room with a hundred or more girls, also on the extreme alert. The air is charged with a nervous intensity. No human being could stand it more than two hours at a stretch. The telephone girls are not required to work steadily through a morning or afternoon.

The day shift at the New York City telco worked from 8 a.m. to 6 p.m. with every girl getting a 30-minute break in the morning, 30 minutes in the afternoon and one hour for lunch. The rest room was furnished with rocking chairs, couches, a desk, writing material and a long table piled with magazines and newspapers. A matron was in charge. The firm supplied tea and coffee for the operators in the lunch room.[4]

As of June 1901, a new rule was established at the Brooklyn telco that did away with the practice of the hello girls ringing up every subscriber every morning just to see if the line was working. There were, reportedly, two reasons for that change. One reason was that subscribers objected to being disturbed every morning for the sole reason of testing the line. The other reason was that a new system had been implemented that enabled the operator to test the line without phoning subscribers. Under the old system, there had been a lot of cranky subscribers due to the test call.[5]

In June 1901, 300 hello girls worked in Chicago in the main office of the Chicago Telephone Company, located at 203 Washington Street. When they arrived for work one morning, company president Sabin showed them the new café for the employees: Half of the seventh floor was set aside for the use and comfort of the operators. Most of the area was occupied by restaurant tables that could hold half of the workforce at once. A chef and three waitresses were in attendance and meals were served any time, day or night. Until that time, the operators had to bring their own lunches or go out at noon. Sabin had come to Chicago from the San Francisco telco where the firm had fed its employees at its own expense for years. But as a reporter observed, that move was perhaps not as altruistic as it appeared. The operators worked on the ninth floor of the building and while they were allowed to take the elevator up, they were ordered to walk down the nine flights "in the rush hours of the day." Company General Superintendent S.J. Larned stated, "We have a superior class of girls, and we do all we can to make their work easy for them. At San Francisco there was an elevator accident not long ago in the telephone building there, and President Sabin was naturally nervous about the overcrowding here at noon and 6 o'clock. So he wants the girls to walk down."[6]

The local management of the Central Union Telephone Company in Columbus, Ohio, announced in July 1901 that they were voluntarily increasing the salary of all their operators about 20 percent and reducing the work day to nine hours. Almost 100 girls were affected. No other details were reported. According to the story, the same wage increase would be granted in a number of other cities where the company was located.[7]

In August 1901, describing the main telephone exchange of a big city, a reporter commented that during the day perhaps 200 girls toiled away while at night there was only one-fifth of that number on the job. On Sundays there was perhaps half the usual workforce. Often the exchange was a big room on the top floor of an office building. The operators wore black aprons to protect their clothes; false cuffs on the wrists served the same purpose. In a separate room, or patrolling the operating room, was the chief operator who supervised the business of the floor. With the exception of two or three assistants, that chief operator was the only male official in the room. At a big desk, advantageously located, the monitor kept a record of the work of each girl, as well as filling in for vacancies in case of sickness. "This responsible position may pay the incumbent $12 a week, and is one of the almost unattainable goals toward which the ambitious telephone operator strives," he wrote. Also, certain sections of the switchboard were the responsibility of a supervisor who kept an eye on the girls and occasionally lent a hand when an operator was suddenly rushed. There were six or seven such people in those large exchanges. Despite 200 girls being on duty during the day shift, the operating room was described as being very quiet, with "no conversation." An observer could hear only a murmuring voice saying "Number, please?" or "Busy." Another observation from the reporter: "It is said that girls brought up in the city are more satisfactory than country girls in telephone exchanges." Said a supervisor; "The city girls are of more even temperament and slower to resent the occasional harsh language that is used by subscribers." It was said herein that usually a year's apprenticeship was required before a girl was regarded as first class. A beginner was paid about $4 a week while a first-class operator received $9 and a supervisor got $10. Those figures varied somewhat according to circumstances but they were said to be the prevailing figures in the large cities.[8]

An August 1901 article played up the image of telephone operators as eavesdroppers who loved nothing better than to listen in on conversations. Said the reporter, "Well, there are plenty of Pandoras nowadays, but they are not called by that name. [Pandora was from Greek mythology and her fatal curiosity led to all sorts of evils being turned loose on the world.] They are known as Maude and Minnie and Susie and their sweet tones gently coo 'What number, please?'" As far as this journalist was concerned, the telephone girls were the modern Pandoras, who furnish daily evidence that fair femininity has not yet outgrown the deadly vice of curiosity. Formerly I used the phone for confidential communications, chats with friends and members of any family, in which I said things I would not want shouted from the housetop. Now I don't…. I have awakened to the fact that there is a third listener to the conversation in about nine times out of ten. There used to be an old joke about girls wanting to get jobs in the post office where they could read the postal cards. Those same girls are now obtaining positions in "Central" where there is just about ten times the fun, and there is less strain on the eyes deciphering careless calligraphy. Any girl can listen, and it is a safe gamble that she will whenever she gets a chance.

The reporter noted that in Nebraska there was a fine of $100 or six months imprisonment for any telco employee who divulged the contents of any message with which he or she may have become acquainted. The journalist remarked that she would work up a public agitation over the eavesdropping but for one thing: that law. "Now suppose that law is enforced. What would be the result? It would completely paralyze the telephone service until the companies could get more employees." Within the story, no piece of evidence was cited to confirm the reporter's allegation, save for one brief anecdotal account about a friend of the reporter. Even if the operators were as inclined to listen in as suggested, it would have been impossible since the work was incessant with barely any pauses. And, most importantly, those operators were subjected to probably the most vigorous surveillance system then in play in capitalist America. No other workforce was monitored and eavesdropped on as were the hello girls. This particular article was total nonsense.[9]

A new Indianapolis telephone company announced at the end of 1901 that it had decided to open a school of elocution "for the benefit of the hello girls on one hand and the benefit of the public on the other." The theory behind that decision was that many of the mistakes that occurred at a telephone exchange were "the direct result of the want of clear enunciation on the part of the operators." To that end, one of the elocutionists in the city had been employed and "there will be regular lessons in voice culture, free of charge, under his direction." Each operator "will be required to devote a certain number of hours each day to improvement of her voice." It was also stated that the company would hereafter make it a condition of employment that the applicant undergo certain voice training before being placed in charge of an exchange switchboard. Operators handling long distance calls were said to be most in need of this training. Many farmers were receiving market quotations over the line (involving many numbers being read out) and more were doing so as time passed.[10]

According to a January 1902 report in a New York City newspaper, the trouble for the rejected applicants lay in the physical tests: "Some education is required, as a matter of course, but the greater attention is paid to hearing and speaking." Above all, said the account, "she must not only be able to talk, but know how to talk. Defect of speech is fatal. Articulation, pitch of voice and general self-possession are most carefully considered, and examination in these requisites is of necessity conducted viva voce." In that voice testing, "Any indication of nervousness, hysteria or want of self-possession will cause rejection of the candidate." The greatest stumbling block with respect to the voice was the fact that "the majority of girls are not clear in their enunciation, and very many have a strongly marked twang that is certain to cause their rejection."[11]

New York Telephone Company had its training school for potential operators up and running no later than January 1902. Kate Smith was the principal. Students learned the switchboard, how to talk, how to be pleasant to subscribers, and so forth. Reportedly, some 50 girls a day applied for admission to the school. The course lasted four to six weeks. Just 25 percent of applicants proved eligible.[12]

On April 3, 1902, the Twin City Telephone Company moved its general offices from the Phoenix Building to Eighth and Cedar Streets in Minneapolis. It was reported that at the new location, attempts were made to maintain an even temperature and to "wash" the air coming into the building. Fresh air run into the new building first went through a spray bath that took out the dust. Then it passed over heated coils or iced coils, depending on the season. The air in the operating room was completely changed every ten minutes. That new switchboard could accommodate up to 150 operators at a time and, if necessary, the arc that they sat around could be completed to form an oval "when the force of operators can be increased to a much larger number." The new location had the usual amenities including a lunch room, a reading room and a locker for each operator.[13]

A letter to the editor published in a Washington, D.C., newspaper in September 1902 told about the hours of work imposed upon the hello girls at the Chesapeake and Potomac Telephone Company's central office, located at 14th and G Streets Northwest. Girls who had been worked daily from 4 p.m. to 10 p.m. and every third Sunday from 8 a.m. to 5 p.m. for the sum of $3 a week would, on and after Monday, September 29, be compelled to work from noon to 10 p.m. daily for the same salary and in addition they were to work every Sunday from 8 a.m. to 6 p.m.[14]

As of 1900, 18.8 percent of all females over the age of ten were engaged in gainful employment in the U.S. In 1890, the corresponding number was 17 percent and in 1880 it was 14.7 percent. In 1900, women employed in domestic service made up 29.4 percent of that female workforce while 24.7 percent were to be found in manufacturing. With respect to the occupational category of stenographers and typewriters (the word "typewriter" then referred both to the machine and to the person who operated it; the word "typist" came later), women made up most of that occupational group having 86,158 out of the total of 112,464 positions (about 80 percent). There were 75,274 female stenographers and 23,563 males while there were 10,884 female typewriters and 7753 males. There were a total of 15,349 hello girls.[15]

To assure the safety of more than 100 young female operators and other occupants of the Bell Telephone Company's building at Tenth and Olive Street in St. Louis, a new spiral fire escape was put in place on the northwest corner of the building in November 1903. About 60 young women at a time were on duty at the switchboard on the sixth (top) floor of the building. The structure was something like a spiral ladder.[16]

The United States Civil Service Commission announced that on January 20, 1903, an examination would be held in San Francisco for the position of telephone switchboard operator in the U.S. Mint located in that city. The age range specified was 20 years and over and the salary offered was $40 a month. That high pay rate explained why most hello girls, after achieving proficiency, tried to get work in the public service or on a company's private switchboard. Invariably the salary was higher and the hours were better.[17]

According to an account about the lives of hello girls, published at the end of 1902,

> Quieting sensitive and high-strung young women, who cannot imagine why a subscriber should talk to them so gruffly, is one of the principal sources of worry. Although not all or a majority of the subscribers use abusive language over the wire, the number is large enough…. Sometimes a subscriber will cause one of the supersensitive young operators to leave her board in tears, and then comes the demand for the services of the chief operator, who must put her arms around the girl and comfort her, or talk to her severely or sensibly as the case may demand…. The girl must be induced to go back to her board as quickly as possible and sometimes coaxing does better than reprimanding. If she loses very much time, another subscriber might ring up and lose his temper and cause a fresh stream of briny tears.[18]

In March 1903, Some 3000 hello girls employed in the central offices of the New York Telephone Company in Manhattan and the Bronx were made happy when the firm announced that beginning on the next Saturday, their wages would be raised to $10 a week and $20 a week for the chief operators. Most of those girls had been receiving from $7 to $9 a week. According to the account, "The company advanced the salaries voluntarily because it wished to forestall the girls from forming a labor union and going on strike."[19]

In May 1903, St. Louis girls who applied for telephone work were being trained in an "institution of learning" established by the Bell Telephone Company at its Beaumont office, located at Beaumont and Locust Streets. A class of 25 "competent" operators was graduated from that facility every month. For a long time the company had conducted a class for beginners but now the school was described as being "permanent." J.J. Crawshaw, superintendent of exchanges, was the principal of the school and he had two assistants. One was Prof. Brown, who demonstrated the electric part of the work. Nettie Foster, the other assistant, instructed in the operation of the switchboard. During that period of learning, the rookie was paid $20 a month, which was increased when she had shown herself to be proficient and able to keep up her section of the switchboard. The entrance exam given to all applicants was "a process of weeding out objectionable persons," declared the account. For example, one question asked of applicants was, "Do you chew gum?" Under the rules of the company, an operator could not run her switchboard and chew gum. The potential hello girl had to have a "soft, modulated voice." The applicant was also queried about her knowledge of the location of business firms in the city. Often someone would ring central and ask for the number of a drug store at such and such a corner but had forgotten the name of the store. According to the account, "Much depends upon the young lady's moral and social environments. Girls who live at home and are the support of a mother or little brothers and sisters receive preference because they are less likely to slight their work." In all respects, the telephone girl "must be level-headed, sweet-voiced and patient." Crawshaw usually gave the first lecture to new recruits accepted into the training school. It dealt largely with the necessity for promptness and attention: "He reads over the rules which prohibit chewing gum, sewing, eating, candy or any other feminine pastime while on duty." Then Prof. Brown took the class and explained the technical details using a dummy board. Foster had charge of the school's practice board. After graduation, Crawshaw assigned the beginners to one of the smaller exchanges where the work was light, before she was required to perform the full duties of an experienced operator.[20]

In August 1903, a New York City newspaper published a somewhat folksy and humorous piece on the hello girl. It began:

> The generally accepted belief in regard to the telephone girl is that she is the suffering victim of circumstance—circumstance being represented by hard taskmasters, long hours and low wages. There is another belief running counter to this, a creed gained

from vaudeville and popular song, that she spends her spare time doing cake walk dances, that she usually dresses in gowns that would put a concert hall singer to shame and that her salary must be commensurate with her needs.

According to the reporter, there was very little noise at all in those operating rooms. In Manhattan proper, there were 16 branches of the New York Telephone Company with an average of 120 girls at each one. Every branch had about 3000 lines under supervision. The lobby of any of those branches always had its complement of applicants, most of them sisters or friends of the girls already employed, or those who had left places vacant by res-

Above, and next two pages: **Sketches from 1903 depicting various aspects of the New York Telephone company, including a rest room, training school and a boss asking an operator about complaints.**

ignation. Those girls were usually public school graduates. An expert operator was paid $11 a week while a beginner received $3. The journalist admitted that the beginner rate was not a huge income "but when one considers that many professions offer no wages to the learner, the smallness of the sum assumes a different aspect." It was said that few girls resign and there

was always a long waiting list. At that time it was estimated that some 2000 girls were kept busy in the phone industry each day in Manhattan. When a new group started in the training school, there were usually 17 or 18 girls there and "few are out of their teens." One hundred fifty girls were on the day force and 20 on the night shift; "There is no second of the day when Miss Hello is not actively employed except at her recreation hours and this applies in the school, as well as in the regular working rooms." When the reporter asked his guide at the telco if girls could speak to each other at work, the reply was: "Not a word while they are at work. If you notice, the girls sitting right next to each other rarely turn their heads. In fact, they have no time." Then the reporter asked if the girls could talk to subscribers. The reply: "As soon as it is discovered that a girl is having any personal conversation over the line, she is reprimanded. If it occurs a second time, she is notified that her place will be filled. However, they are taught that in school, and a second lesson is seldom necessary." Finally, the reporter asked if the girls' hearing was affected by the work. The response: "It renders it more acute, if anything. It certainly does not injure it in the least."[21]

When a reporter for a Washington, D.C., newspaper looked at what type of woman was needed at the telephone companies, he declared, "No nervous girl need apply at a telephone exchange. The strain and stress of the eight hours' intense, concentrated attention to the demands of the switchboard call for coolness and poise." At first, the girl seeking employment as an operator saw the general manager and was put through "a searching test for general fitness—sight and hearing, wide-awakeness, deportment." If she passed that phase, she was turned over for training to the operating instructor. During the first week of training, she did nothing but attach her headphones to an experienced operator's position and listen. For the following two weeks she put her observations into practice, with an experienced operator always by her side. According to this article, the lot of the telephone girl is "by no means an unenviable one." Her work demanded unflagging attention, "but custom eases the strain." Reportedly, the great telephone companies were in the forefront of the modern movement for improved working conditions. Every girl in the employ of the Washington telco was given a half-hour "intermission" morning and afternoon to lounge in the rest room and read or gossip, as she saw fit. For the rare case of nervous collapse, a hospital room and a matron's care was provided.[22]

Recognizing the dangers to which lone young women of limited income were subjected to in Paris, France, the minister of commerce went among his rich friends in 1903 and got them to loosen their purse strings for the purpose of collecting enough money to erect a modern hotel for hello girls. It was said that 200 girls of "good habits" would be comfortably and cheaply housed that winter under one roof and under the care of a matron who would look after their well-being, "without spying into their business." It was reported that if that new women's hotel was a success, others would be built to accommodate women working for the government and private concerns.[23]

According to a December 1903 news story, the New York Telephone Company was sometimes so short of switchboard operators that the management was obliged to advertise and to enlist the assistance of their women employees to find girls for vacant places. The age range solicited was usually 16 to 20. That firm's training school for operators, then 18 months old, was said to have produced a better quality of operator than the old individual training methods. From that school, an average of 50 girls graduated every month. About 25 applicants to the school were examined every morning but a high proportion were rejected. Candidates were required to have a bright and alert disposition, good enunciation and a "fairly pleasing" voice. The educational test was simple. The candidate was given part of an article to read aloud; "Unless she is able to do this in an intelligent manner, with clear understanding of its meaning, she is considered below the standard of intelligence. Her ability to think and act connectedly is tested also in the reading of ordinary English prose." An application form filled out in her own handwriting showed her ability to write and spell. The story continued:

> As a rule, no girl over 20 is received. The theory of the work could be much more easily imparted to a mature woman, but the actual manipulation of the switchboard seems to be impossible to the majority of women past the formative period of life…. This calls for a certain dexterity, an accuracy of touch that becomes perfectly mechanical. It seems to be an accepted fact that it is possible to acquire these in early life, but very rarely afterwards.

Each central office had a chief operator and a number of supervisors (one for every nine operators). The student operator was paid $3 a week while in the school, and from $7 to $10 a week afterwards. The supervisors and chief operators received as high as $25 a week. New York Telephone Company had 15 central offices and each had 10 to 20 supervisors. With respect to the average salaries paid to telephone girls, the reporter noted they were "deemed rather small [but] the fact should be considered that operators are under less expense than many other working women." They were said to be not under the necessity of wearing "expensive or elaborate uniforms, as are the high-salaried clerks in department stores…. The switchboard is more or less trying to the nerves of the operator, but this if offset by the consideration with which they are treated by the company."[24]

The Chesapeake and Potomac Telephone Company in Washington, D.C., put into use at the end of 1903 a new North exchange. It employed 38 regular operators, chief operating supervisors and one monitor. The day shift was divided into three section: 7 a.m. to 4 p.m., 8 a.m. to 5 p.m. and 9 a.m. to 6 p.m.; the afternoon shift worked from noon to 9 p.m. and the

Photos of the Chesapeake and Potomac Telephone Company's new exchange in 1903.

night shift was on duty from 9 p.m. to 7 a.m. On the day force were 26 operators, one chief operator, two supervisors and one monitor; on the afternoon force were one chief operator, one supervisor and eight operators while the night force consisted of one chief operator and four operators. Girls were on duty for nine hours but had 30 minutes for lunch and two 30-minute breaks during the shift; thus they were at their boards working for seven and a half hours per shift.[25]

On April 5, 1904, Mary Schultz, formerly an operator with the Chicago Telephone Company, was awarded by a jury in Judge Haney's court $15,000 against the company to compensate her for the loss of hearing in the left ear. The accident that resulted in her deafness occurred about five years earlier: Schultz, then 17, had the receiving apparatus attached to her head and was answering calls when a bolt of electricity was transmitted through the wires with such force that she was thrown to the floor. She was rendered unconscious for an hour and was ill for several weeks. She was not aware of the permanent injury to her ear until she again reported for work. She then discovered that she had lost the hearing in her left ear. In June 1901, Schultz began her suit against the company, asking for $30,000 damages. Chicago Telephone strongly contested the case, attempting to prove Schultz was subjected to epileptic fits and had received her injury in that manner. Her attorneys refuted that claim and alleged that negligence by the company linemen was responsible for the accident. A verdict for Schultz was returned after the jury had deliberated for just one hour.[26]

There were approximately 15,000 public and private telephones in

Salt Lake early in 1905, and of that number more than 80 percent were owned by the Rocky Mountain Bell Telephone Company. A reporter visiting that firm's operating room found 33 young women seated side by side before the switchboard: "There was no laughing, no chatting, and no gossip." Three supervisors moved silently and slowly behind the operators, keeping a careful eye on the girls to see they were attentive to their duties. At two central desks were the chief operator and assistants. At another desk sat a young woman with headset in position and a stopwatch in her hand. From time to time she made entries in a notebook. Those notes were in shorthand and were later to be transcribed into typewritten notes for the benefit of the general manager, the city manager and the operating room manager. She was listening to connections over the wires and her duty was to take notes of any coarse language from subscribers or "pert remarks" by the operators to "irascible persons on the lines." Added the reporter, "It speaks well for the discipline of the operating room that she had spent the day thus far without having had occasion to report any of the young women for infractions of the rules." That journalist could not, of course, talk to the hello girls at work but he found that even after work they were reluctant to talk to him. A few finally agreed to do so but only under anonymity. On average, one of those operators had 1500 calls to answer in an eight-hour shift.[27]

S.P. Kelley of the engineering department of the Nebraska Telephone Company, speaking to the Electrical Club at the Omaha YMCA in March 1905, said the problem of securing and retaining the right kind of female labor in telephone exchanges grew more difficult year by year as the service increased and the demands became more exacting:

> It will be a matter of time only until Omaha will be forced to have a training school for operators the same as has been established in New York and other cities. This has been found to be economical and much more satisfactory than the old way of teaching a new girl the business. But getting the girls who can do their work well, not offend the public and stay with their jobs is what perplexes the exchange manager.
>
> In Chicago the decision has been reached that the Irish-American girls are the best [operators] because they are quick-witted, can handle the public easily and hold their tempers. They also remain longer than do girls of other nationalities. But St. Louis declares that German-American girls are the best there. In Omaha I do not think the classification has been made in this way.

Another problem, he said, was how to keep the girls interested in their work and the standard of efficiency maintained. In Chicago there were 16 large exchanges. They competed every month for the honor of best handled exchange, explained Kelley, and a prize was awarded in the form of books, to go into the reading room of the exchange, for the benefit of all operators

An operator working at a board in 1905, place unknown.

"and which has proved to be a refining influence with the operators. In Omaha the merit system, or graduated pay on the basis of efficiency, was tried to keep up the grade of work."[28]

Until 1905 or thereabouts, it had been telephone companies' custom to permit its subscribers to use the central station girls for early morning alarm clocks. The operators would take down the number on a slip of paper indicating the time the sleeper wanted to be called and the girl would jingle his bell at the appropriate hour. But in a short time, the phone companies found that this was a large part of its business and decided that it would have to be stopped.[29]

Another account, in the summer of 1905, observed that the efforts of the eastern telephone companies to shut down the use of their operators as early-morning alarm clocks would not be followed in Omaha, according to Vance Lane, general manager of the Nebraska Telephone Company. In New York City, the alarm clock business got so big it swamped the night shift so an order was issued forbidding it. Reading between the lines of the banning order, however, the girls were given to understand that some room existed for them to use their discretion. "We are not to a point here where we have to stop extending every convenience and courtesy to our patrons that is possible, even though such matters are not nominated in the bond," said Lane. "The extraneous work has been expanding along with the growth of the business but, as most of it is at night we can still take care of it. We probably do as much for our patrons besides making connections as anyone can ask."[30]

A journalist for a Washington, D.C., newspaper, describing the life of the hello girl in October 1905, began by writing that their lot in Washington "is about as comfortable as that of the woman anywhere who works for wages and earns her own living." Washington then had over 10,000 phones—9000 more than in 1903. Seventy-six operators handled the ever-increasing traffic. There were then 243 employees in the operating department of the local telco, including linemen who worked away from the switchboard. The aspiring telephone girl in the nation's capital had a training school where she started out at $3 a week while she was learning and would get as much as $20 a week when she got up to the position of chief operator. Girls started in the business when they were 16 to 18 years of age and their life in the service was usually about eight years. At the end of that time, it was said, they were usually promoted or got married. Those hello girls were on duty in the exchange for nine hours each day and worked for eight of those hours. Training school in this city lasted for two to three weeks. Then the novice was put to work in the hours when traffic was light. Busiest hour for telephone use in the downtown business district of Washington was 10 to 11 a.m. and for the residential districts it was one hour later. During an average day, a total of about 58,000 calls were handled. Between 4 and 5 a.m., there was an average of just 18 calls an hour. Things were slightly different in the long distance department where toll sheets were kept and the length of the conversation recorded. The phone was then used regularly for distances of up to 1600 miles. There was one Boston firm that called up its Omaha office regularly every morning for a conversation that cost $7.25 for the first three minutes and then $2.25 for each additional three minutes. The only reason that long distance was not then used over longer distances such as from New York City to San Francisco was that the traffic would not pay for the installation of the line. The difficulty was reportedly commercial and not mechanical.[31]

Two want ads appeared side by side in a New York City newspaper in November 1905. One told of a job for a telephone girl at $4 per week and it brought 100 applicants. The other ad offered $7 a week for girls to work in a factory and, reportedly, no one applied. A newspaper editor attributed that response to snobbery and argued that people invited the girls from the department stores to spend the evening and those same people passed the ones from the factory by. Said the editor; "The world is full of snobs and some of them live in palaces and more in cottages…. They are un–American, unwise, unkind and they are making life hard for those noble women whom we call 'working girls.'"[32]

In May 1906, a special report on telephones and telegraphs for the year 1902 was issued by the U.S. Census Office. For commercial phone systems, the number of telephones stood at 2,225,981; for the national system, 89,316; and for the independent lines, 55,547. As of January 1, 1901, the number of telephones in America stood at 3.3 million while in Europe the number was 485,784.[33]

A description of the life of the telephone girl, running in a Los Angeles newspaper in September 1906, was likely nothing more than a public relations plant from a telco, although it looked exactly like any other news story in the paper. The title of the article was the first clue: "Hello girls vocation both pleasant and remunerative." According to the piece, there were probably 50,000 operators in the U.S. and the great majority of them were employees of the Bell Telephone system. There were also thousands estimated to be operators in private exchanges such as hotels, department stores, big offices, government service and so on. Hello girls were thought to stand second within female professions, behind stenographers, at 100,000. Less than 2000 females were then practicing law while some 15,000 to 20,000 were engaged in the medical profession. It continued:

> The working girl is very often better off than the woman engaged in a profession, and this is particularly true of the telephone girl. Telephone companies demand reliable, intelligent and courteous service, and in return they extend to their employees, and particularly to the soft-spoken women at central, the most liberal and considerate treatment. The Bell companies, early in the history of the art, began to introduce arrangements for the comfort of the women who operate the switchboard.
> … The telephone operator is entitled to especial consideration on account of the responsible nature of her employment. Much is expected of her, consequently much is given her. [Qualified girls] will find the position of operator lucrative and promising.
> … As a rule. telephone operators are better paid than clerks in stores; they are better paid than a good many stenographers, Besides the good pay, there is always an assurance of steady employment. The telephone operator—at least in a Bell exchange—is never discharged for incapacity or intractability…. The telephone girl is one of the busiest, most up-to-date and most contented women in the world, and she has every reason to be, for she is well paid, for every want during working hours is attended to and she performs her daily tasks with the prospect that sooner or later her fidelity and industry will be substantially rewarded.

The only clues that this was simply a public relations piece planted by Bell (perhaps for consideration) was that no specific examples were cited and no names were used. While the "good" pay of the hello girl was mentioned, there were no examples or comparisons of any kind with the other mentioned professions, that is, no figures or numbers of any kind were used.[34]

Later that same month, it was reported that the number of telephones in the Bell system had reached 2.8 million in America and was growing at the rate of 25 percent a year. According to a reporter, "Telephone managers do not use stopwatches in timing operators but the tests made at regular intervals in every Bell office show that on average a subscriber's signal is answered within five seconds after it is given and communication is established over the line wanted within ten seconds after that." Over the course of the year 1905, more than 13 billion conversations passed through the offices of the Bell system and, it was noted; "After a girl takes her permanent place at the switchboard, everything she does is painstakingly supervised."[35]

Some two months later it was reported that Washington, D.C.'s hello girls were to be put through a course of vocal training to teach them the proper voice modulation, according to a report going around at one of the downtown telephone exchanges. Reportedly the scheme was not new in at least two of the big Eastern cities, Philadelphia and New York. One Washington telephone manager had recently gone to a New York City training school where he saw a vocal coach putting a number of operators through a "course of sprouts" and returned to Washington full of enthusiasm. The object of the proposed training was to teach the phone operators to concentrate the sound of their voices upon the mouthpiece of the instrument, thus enabling them to sink the voice into the pitch of a soothing whisper. To perfect the scheme would mean that any operator would be able to talk freely into the instrument without being heard more than a foot or two away. Said the manager, "It's an easy thing to learn and I think the girls will take kindly to it. In a way, they will soon get wise to a few tricks of ventriloquism."[36]

One of the communities served by the Sunset Telephone Company was Grants Pass, Oregon. December 10, 1906, was "count day" there and in Grants Pass that day the data showed 3740 local calls were made for the day. All that local business was handled by just two girls in the office. Those calls involved answering all the extraneous questions from subscribers, dealing with irate customers and so on. Six girls worked in the Grants Pass office; two were local operators, two were long distance operators and two were bookkeepers.[37]

In Oakland, California, on February 25, 1907, Dwight E. Potter, pastor of the Union Street Presbyterian Church in that city, appealed to the city's telephone operators to provide him with information and insight on the character of their work, with suggestions as to how the public could make it less arduous. Armed with such information, the clergyman planned to read to his congregation the comments and suggestions received from the hello girls. He wanted the operators to answer questions such as "What kind of people make your work hard? How?" "What suggestions would you offer to subscribers desiring to make your work easier and more pleasant?" "Name some of the peculiar faults, trials and temptation of telephone employees." "What percent of the employees are professing Christians? Why not more?" "Name some of the things that people using the telephone ought to remember." "What can the church do to help you?"[38]

On March 3 of that year, Potter preached on "Telephone Religions." He read out comments he had received from the hello girls such as "Avoid hurling sarcastic and cutting remarks at the operator"; "Men seem at times to take a delight in abusing an operator, especially when such calls originate from cafés, saloons or restaurants"; and "One of the temptations that is hard to fight against is to avoid sharp answers when spoken to in an insulting or sarcastic manner by a subscriber."[39]

An article in a March 1907 Washington, D.C., newspaper looked at the information operator as separate from the regular operator. Those girls in Washington received questions such as "Where does the president go to church?" "What is the distance from Washington to Philadelphia?" "Which is the best baggage express?" "Was the Potomac River frozen in '72?" and "Is there one 'L' or two in travel?" At that exchange, the operators no longer performed the function of alarm clocks, nor did they provide any extraneous information. Such queries went to the separate information operators. In Washington at that time, about 250,000 telephone connections were established daily by the 230 regular operators.[40]

A reporter for a Spokane, Washington, newspaper examined the conditions of the telephone girls in 1907 and stated, "About the poorest paid and most abused class of labor in the city, not excepting laundry workers, is employed by the Pacific States Telephone Co." He said the girls received wages ranging from $25 to $37.50 per month. A girl started at $25 and the company agreed to give her an advance of $2.50 in six months; "At the end of that time she is, as a rule, told she has not come up to requirements and her raise is refused. At the end of nine months or a year she realizes that there is little or no chance to secure a raise and usually quits." According to the journalist, that was what the company wanted; wages were kept

THE 'INFORMATION' OPERATORS AT THE MAIN OFFICE

The information operators at the Washington, D.C., central office in 1907.

down and dividends kept up. About 300 girls were employed in Spokane with each having to take care of 250 to 280 phones, or twice as many as they looked after before a strike that had taken place about four years earlier. "The company employs inspectors who call up the girls and time them in getting answers. This is called giving them tests. It is needless to say that a girl having the number of phones to take care of as the local girls do rarely pass a test, therefore wages remain at $25 per month," the reporter explained. Pacific States also ran the Butte, Montana, exchange and girls there received about $50 a month. Of the 300 hello girls at Spokane, it was reported that not more than 50 had been with the company for over a year. The Spokane exchange had secured ten girls from San Francisco some time earlier, to fill some vacancies. But the girls found they could not subsist on the low wages paid them and all but three of them returned to San Francisco.[41]

In the Home Telephone Company in Los Angeles, it was one of the rules in the local office that each girl was entitled to one night a week off. She could pick the night herself as long as it was not Sunday night. Once every three months, each girl was allowed a Sunday night off but many tried to get an extra one by pleading sickness. That was the only excuse the telco would accept. In that office, 25 girls were supposed to be on duty Sunday night. On a Sunday night in July 1907 there were only ten on duty. The remaining 15 were home suffering from headache, toothache, lung trouble and so on. In the rival Sunset Telephone Company office, things were just as bad that Sunday night as more than half the girls scheduled to be on duty had excused themselves on account of "sickness." According to the reporter, both of those telcos had been shorthanded for some time. "For some reason, young women seem to object to working in telephone offices, and despite the fact that fair salaries are paid and short shifts allowed they seem to prefer working in the department stores of offices," stated the reporter. "One of the reasons given for this is that the girls employed by the telephone companies are compelled to attend strictly to business during the working hours and that little time is allowed for visiting."[42]

Covering the operators' training schools in a 1907 article, a reporter wrote that in the early days, beginners learned by observing the work of experienced girls who, in addition, gave such snatches of instruction as there was time for. There was, however, one "great objection" to that method in that "it was likely to perpetuate the technical faults of the old operators, while it did not necessarily inculcate their virtues; neither did it make for uniformity. And when traffic increased so that regular operators could give no attention to training novices, special instructors were appointed." For a time, the instructors taught their pupils at spare positions at the switchboard. The lines, though, could not be connected to anything and instructional scope was limited to showing how a board was handled. Growth began to crowd the switchboards and the next step was to utilize discarded apparatus for practice purposes. But technology quickly rendered old equipment useless for training. So a school for telephone operators, equipped and conducted solely for teaching candidates for switchboard work, was established in New York City. At the time of this article, it was said the Bell companies had similar schools in all the larger cities and instruction classes in many of the smaller telephone centers, while traveling instructors took care of the needs of the little offices that required only occasional attention of that sort. In the Bell operating schools, young women were first given a working knowledge of the details of the apparatus. Then the methods of actual operation were taken up and taught by lectures, charts and experience at practice switchboards. Also taught was the phraseology to be used in all the different situations that arose and the reason why each phrase was employed rather than any other; the methods of "trunking" from exchange to exchange; handling toll and long distance calls and operating coin-in-the-slot pay station service; the treatment of requests for information, emergency calls and so on. Practice was more important than precept and teachers took the role of the public in giving would-be operators "vivid experience."[43]

In the fall of 1907 it was reported that rest rooms and libraries were being installed in the Sunset Telephone Exchange building in Los Angeles

Operators in 1907 receiving instruction in the formal training classes set up by all telephone companies.

for the benefit of the operators. Donations from subscribers and contributions from employees and officials of the firm had made possible the improvements. In the main exchange on Hill Street, there were 500 books. The libraries adjoined the dining rooms of the buildings; the operators there were provided with two meals a day. Subscription to the library was by a nominal fee of five cents per month. Newspapers and magazine were also supplied. Sunset Telephone president Scott had donated complete editions of Shakespeare and George Eliot to the library. William Dean Wilde, traffic manager of the company, contributed 50 volumes of "light fiction and poetry."[44]

At the Washington, D.C., telco, the nine operators were under the control of a supervisor. Calls were completed in two or three seconds and so it proved impossible for operators to answer "information"-type questions. So, said a journalist, "it was found expedient and for the good of the patrons of the telephone company to establish an 'information desk.' There all things not pertaining to direct communications of subscribers are referred. And among these questions are found many which are pertinent and foreign as well, to the telephone company's business." Such queries included transit travel questions, was there skating at the parks?, what was the Baltimore postmaster's name?, weather forecasts for tomorrow, give me the number of the man who runs a coal yard in the middle of the block in

16th Street, when are visitors allowed in the city jail? and can you recommend a good carpenter? That information desk kept an alphabetic list, a street address record and a numerical record of listed subscribers since the issue of the current paper directory. A monitor listened in on conversations without the operator knowing; "A continuous supervision is maintained over the operators by a series of such monitor desks. And the operators at these separate desks are also women." When the relief group of hello girls came on duty at, say, noon or 4 p.m., the change was made in military fashion. On the ringing of one bell, the assembled relief crew marched to the backs of the operators they were relieving, with their headgear already on. At the ringing of the second bell the original group unplugged their headsets while the relief group plugged in and sat down. Reportedly, all of that was done in "the bat of an eye." The reporter also stated, "The care and supervision of the telephone company over its operators do not stop with training them for their profession and attention to their physical needs. The man who offends one of the operators offends the company, provided always that she is blameless." To enter the Washington training school, a girl had to be 17, in good health, have perfect hearing, good eyesight and be free from color blindness, have a good voice and have enunciation that was clear and distinct. She also had to be even-tempered, patient, polite and courteous; "She must at all times deport herself with dignity and never forget that she is a lady no matter where she may be, whether it be on the street, in office, in parlor or hall…. The character and home life of a student are looked into and every effort is made to keep the force at a high standard." After graduating from Washington's training school, the new operator started at $4 a week and could move to positions that paid as much as $20 a week. During the year 1906 at Washington, 761 applications were made for entrance into the Chesapeake and Potomac Telephone Company's school for operators. Of that number, 368 qualified, 321 were taken into the school and 241 graduated. In most cases they were employed in the firm's exchanges.[45]

A law passed in Kentucky in 1907 took aim at privacy and targeted, among others, the hello girl:

> Whoever being an operator, clerk, messenger or employee of any telephone company discloses the content of any dispatch or message sent or received from any such office of such company, except to a court of Justice or to a person authorized to know the same, shall on conviction, be fined not less than $100 or more than $500.

As technology had passed privacy laws that existed, such as holding the mail inviolable, authorities had to scramble to keep up with new electronic communications such as telegraph and telephone. The above law was

"MANAGER'S OFFICE."
MANAGER AND CHIEF
OPERATOR.

"LONG DISTANCE."
SIX GIRLS TALKING TO
SIX DIFFERENT CITIES—
EAST AND WEST

Above and following page: Several photos showing the Washington, D.C., telephone office and its operators, in 1907.

"DROP A NICKEL,
PLEASE."

similar to ones passed during this period to bring electronic communications under the sway of privacy laws, at least in theory.[46]

According to a brief profile of the telephone girl in a Tacoma, Washington, newspaper in February 1909, "The exchange girl's voice still has its power to charm…. Telephone girls, although they work under nervous strain, are well paid and agreeably circumstanced in their work." The average wage was said to be $10 a week but that the positions coveted by telephone girls were the ones at private exchanges such as department stores and hotels; weekly wages there were in the $12 to $15 range. The highest paid telephone girls were reported to be those who worked for private exchanges in the financial districts in the service of bankers and brokers. The average working life of the hello girl was put herein at about three years with matrimony being the leading reason for resignation.[47]

According to an April 1909 report, New York City then had 310,000 phone subscribers and telephone calls in that city averaged 1.25 million per day, going through 53 exchanges and being handled by 12,000 employees. In 1900 there were 56,000 subscribers in New York City with a population

AMERICAN WOMEN WHO WORK
NO. 12—THE TELEPHONE GIRL

A romanticized sketch of the hello girl in 1909.

of 3.2 million. In 1905, subscribers there reached 190,000. The population of New York in 1908 was 4.6 million. In Chicago, the number of telephone subscribers stood at 156,000; Philadelphia had 101,500 while Boston had 101,000. These numbers came from Mr. Farranda, a director of the telephone company of Rome, Italy. Farranda came over from Europe to study the American phone system. At that time, Rome had just 8000 subscribers. The Italian thought there were many reasons to explain the much higher number of subscribers in the U.S.:

> The number of employees is not the sole cause for the regularity of service. It is to discipline that the good results must be attributed, and which makes the system so perfect. Fines are imposed on those employees who break the rules the first time, and they are dismissed from the service for the second offense. Notwithstanding the discipline, telephone girls seem well satisfied with their positions and telephone companies have less trouble with them than they do in Rome.

Chicago and New York City were separated by about 1000 miles and a three-minute call between the two cities cost $4.[48]

A journalist observed in November 1909 that Spokane, Washington, telephone girls were paid $1 a day to start and received a raise of $2.50 every three or four months. They could only afford buy things if they lived at home. Explained Spokane's chief operator, "We always try to employ girls who live at home. For although it only takes three weeks to learn the work, it requires at least six months to make a successful operator. Then, too, the girls who live at home are more steady—not so apt to be changing all the time."[49]

Late in 1909, complaints about poor telephone service were voiced frequently at Anadarko, Oklahoma. Several citizens of the city set out to find out what was wrong. To their surprise, they found that one girl operator was supposed to handle 330 drops (subscribers) besides eight rural lines, averaging 12 to a line, "which is next to an impossibility for any girl to do successfully," noted the story. It also commented that the board was too busy at times for one girl to handle the equivalent of 426 drops; "The rural subscribers find it at times impossible to get central, consequently the girl is unjustly censured and frequently it is thought she is not very courteous." It was the belief of the reporter that something should be done "to relieve the burdens of these girls by inducing the telephone company to give better service." In several towns, the citizens demanded better service and compelled the company to pay the girls better wages or furnish more help.[50]

An order went out to the Richmond, Virginia, operators that they must always answer a call with "Number, please" instead of just saying "Number." Then, in late 1909, an effort was made to enunciate the "three" by trilling the "r." Thus whenever a three came up, the operator was to trill it so that it became "th-r-ree." That was, reportedly, not done as an affectation but as a way to differentiate it from other numbers. Telephone managers were then said to be at work on a method to differentiate "five" and "nine" as those numbers were often confused.[51]

As 1910 began, the Sunset Telephone Company hello girls in Seattle were attending a school for courtesy. P.J. Lynch, commercial manager at Sunset, declared, "It doesn't take any more time to be polite, and it makes everybody a whole lot better." So he established a "School for Courtesy." This all took place on company time. Primarily it seemed to have been set up to ensure that the operators took subscriber abuse quietly and did not talk back.[52]

Labor Commissioner Charles Neill of the U.S. Department of Commerce and Labor reported on the hello girls in 1910, on the instruction of the Senate. His 200-page report discussed the conditions of the more than 20,000 telephone girls at work in America. Reportedly complaints from hello girls that they had to walk up too many flights of stairs to get to their work stations were the chief reason for Neill's investigation. With respect to that point, he stated; "Of the 73 exchanges reported by the agents of the bureau, it was found that 33, which were located above the first floor, requiring the climbing of one flight of stairs, ten on the third floor requiring the climbing of two flights of stairs, and six on the fourth floor required the climbing of three flights of stairs." Maximum number of operators required to climb one flight of stairs was 60, required to climb two flights was 108, while 75 found it necessary to climb three flights of stairs. Neill figured the average working life for a switchboard girl was three years. He had good things to say about their lunch rooms and the "great precautions taken to insure the health of the employees." He regarded 225 calls an hour as the breaking point of efficiency for an operator, although he admitted an operator sometimes handled as many as 600 calls in an hour. The journalist who wrote the piece concluded by remarking, "Some of the hello girls may be surprised to know that the 'spasms of rush' that last only a few minutes are regarded as 'fun' by them. 'They really enjoy the excitement and exhilaration,' says the commissioner."[53]

Commissioner Neill also found there was no use in short girls trying to become telephone operators. "None of the companies employ short girls; they want girls that can reach," he explained. He also found very few telephone companies took girls without first subjecting them to a physical examination. In some cities, the girls objected, but they would have been surprised to learn that they were examined without knowing it. Neill

This 1910 photo shows Colorado Telephone Company operators doing calisthenics as required by their employer. Note they are wearing what amounted to uniforms despite the fact the customers of the company, and the general public, never saw these women at work. Just another form of company control.

explained, with respect to one of those cities that appeared not to give an exam, "It is ascertained that the applicants are interviewed by a woman whose exact height is known, and in talking to the applicant can by comparing the level of the eyes with her own tell within a fraction of an inch the height of the girl with whom she is talking. Experts in other lines interviewed the applicant and ascertained their exact physical condition." Some companies required their candidates to have good eyesight and hearing plus "a good appetite and a rosy complexion" and demanded that they have "a steady hand and a firm set jaw; also that they should not be easily excitable." Of 6152 applicants whose data was reviewed, the commissioner found that 2229 were unable to quality, 544 being too small, 53 too old, 436 too young, 11 refusing to work on Jewish holidays, six declining to be vaccinated and 189 "lacking in personal appearance."

Neill also found that many of the companies, especially the New York Telephone Company, to be "engaged in a system of welfare work among its employees." They had libraries and "parlors" where girls could lounge during rest breaks and also boat ride excursions, theater parties and art museum parties. Declared Neill, "The loyalty and *esprit de corps* among telephone girls is greater than in any other industry in the country." When Neill observed that the hello girl had to watch 100 telephone signals, the reporter remarked,

With all this confusion in front of her, the hello girl has to contend too with a supervisor, who stands behind her and calls out the numbers to other operators when she falls behind in her work. She is in fear also of the monitor cutting in at any minute and reprimanding her.… Under the rules of the companies she is allowed to say only "Number, please" no matter how much she is abused. When the peevish party begins to scold and asks why in thunderation he hasn't got his number, he is delaying her with the other calls that are coming in, and is not only lessening his own chance of getting quick service, but is delaying other people and making it hard for the switchboard girl.

Neill learned that 92.7 percent of the hello girls were either unmarried or "conjugal condition unknown" while four percent were married and 2.7 percent were widows.[54]

Short girls in Neill's report seemed to be those under five feet in height. They had to be taller than that in order to reach the top of the switchboards and to reach a "reasonable" distance sideways. Neill's report data was furnished by 27 telephone companies in 26 states with a total of 17,210 operators. Agents of the Labor Department visited 73 separate phone exchanges and found the operators therein to be well-housed. According to the report, wages for telephone girls varied from the highest monthly average of $36.96 in New York City to the lowest monthly average of $22.40 in Nashville. In some of the smaller cities, the average went even lower, particularly in the South. The Bell Telephone Company system employed 16,266 women operators at an average monthly pay of $30.91.[55]

Generally, the educational requirement to be a hello girl was usually that the applicants must had passed the sixth or seventh grade, according to the Neill report. Boston preferred girls who had a high school education but it was not always successful in obtaining them. Said the writer of this article, "The [Labor] bureau has reached the conclusion that the operator who has not enough to do to keep her constantly busy does not properly attend to what she has to do—'is inclined to loaf.'"[56]

From the data collected by Neill, it was found that 71 percent of the telephone companies' hello girls were between 16 and 24, 22 percent were from 25 to 35, and seven percent were over 35. During the investigation, the agents received a total of 76 complaints; of which 51 concerned the lack of elevators or their hours of operation. Companies investigated by Neill's agents were employed by the three main phone systems in America at the time: Bell, the Independent and the American Telephone and Telegraph company. Those firms had 23,298 salaried employees; they also had 2766 male and 76,638 female wage-earners. The average wage of the female worker was $301.31 a year. The other complaints received from operators concerned the abusive and foul language used by subscribers.[57]

A May 1910 article that was likely a public relations plant was done by a journalist called Laura Smith. Once again the title of the piece was a giveaway: "Great care is exerted for telephone girls' comfort." She observed,

> The nervous strain of the city operators makes the work a great bugbear to girls seeking employment. Consequently, while managers are studying constantly how to improve the equipment and to introduce inventions, they are also studying how to make the work attractive to girl operators…. All companies were doing their best to alleviate nervous strain…. Recently I went through a telephone building, just completed, where every modern device was invoked for the health and comfort of the girls employed. [It had a roof garden, a sickroom and a lunch room wherein tea and coffee were furnished.] I have gone through big manufacturing plants also, where this same care is taken by girl employees, and feel it is a fine tribute to American men who thus smooth the pathway of the little working girl…. Do not feel that any kind of girl can become a hello girl. The standard is very high, both as to morals and attainments [and] the wages of telephone operators compare favorably with those of girls in stores or offices.

Other giveaways that this piece was a p.r. plant can be found in the fact that no specifics were mentioned: Where was the great new building?, what city?, what company? If wages were so much better than in other occupations, where were the figures? If Smith knew hello girls' wages were so much better, then she must have known the figures.[58]

In June 1910 it was reported that a Los Angeles telephone company had ordered its exchange girls to speak "gently and sweetly" to its customers. To make that rule effective, it had provided courses in "vocal culture" for its girls. They were "compelled to learn how to talk sweetly" and once having learned the method they were expected to use it. A Cleveland, Ohio, newspaper editorial about this development said, "[I]t is well to cultivate a pleasing and soothing voice, for general purposes or, if necessary, to turn away wrath. The Los Angeles company has taken an important step in the right direction."[59]

According to a July 1910 report, one-twentieth of the ten million telephones in existence in the world were in New York City and the city's phone system "is so much more efficient in the speed and smoothness of its workings" that delegates from France, Japan and the U.K. had come to the U.S. within the past six months to study it. A little more than 30 years earlier, circa 1880, a list of about 250 telephone subscribers was printed—that was the first telephone directory in New York City. By 1910, that directory was a bulky quarterly published to the tune of two million copies a year (500,000 copies per quarter). New York Telephone Company kept 25 people busy every day of the year in the work of revising the directory and reprinting it. In the course of a day, there were 1,250,000 calls made. Reportedly, in 1875, the general public was indifferent to the new invention and labeled the phone a rich man's toy. Efficiency had reached such a point by 1910 that the average time required for an operator to receive calls and repeat them to the calling subscribers was 7.5 seconds. The average time used in making connections and starting the required telephone ringing was 13.5 seconds. Subscribers answered calls, on average, in 10.5 seconds and the time required to disconnect the line after the conversation was 3.8 seconds. Said the reporter,

> At work in large, airy buildings, almost as secluded from the outside world as the average nunnery, with ample opportunities to rest from the strain of their work, with well-stocked reading rooms, with tea and coffee served to them free of charge by their employers at all hours, with reasonably good pay, and with experienced kindly women to superintend their work while they are novices, the telephone girls lead a life that is not without its points of charm…. No masculine intruder mars the peace of those retreats and the life there moves with a quiet rhythm that makes it a thing to be sought by any girl who must earn a living. The employment is particularly suited to girls who have a home but are constrained to add somewhat to the family income…. The central idea of training is to teach the operator that she must never allow herself to become annoyed or confused and, above all, that she must do all things after a certain set form, by prescribed, habitual motions, in a certain natural order.[60]

A Part of the Gramercy Exchange

Above and following page: Photos and sketches for the New York Telephone Company in 1910. Note the disappearance of phone wires in less than 20 years, moved from above ground to below ground.

1,250,000 Conversations a Day Is the Record of the Work Done by the System, Which Embraces One-Twentieth of All the Ten Million Telephones in the World

Broadway and John Street 1890

Broadway and John Street 1908

Typical Lineman

In September 1910, Joseph Myers, Texas State Commissioner of Labor, finished an investigation of the conditions surrounding the employment and work of women telephone operators in Texas. He said their duties were arduous and their salaries exceedingly small, the average wage of a Texas hello girl being $22.80 a month. Myers stated,

> If the telephone user would investigate the nerve-racking duties of the operators they would be more patient. Considering the strain and stress of their task they do remarkably well and should not be upbraided in the manner so commonly resorted to…. They sit at the switchboard an average of nine hours a day, serving perhaps 185 subscribers. The number of calls per hour that an operator efficiently may handle varies from 230 to 275, and they have been known to handle as many as 450 calls in an hour…. The rooms in which operators have to work are in many cases poorly ventilated, and the little breeze they get comes from electric fans. In some operating rooms artificial lights are necessary. Exceptions are in the exchanges in Dallas, Fort Worth, and a few other places.

Based on records from 105 telephone exchanges located in 82 different counties, the average annual earnings for 1909 of 1475 operators were $273.65 each, or an average of $22.80 per month. Myers said the requirements were good eyesight, good hearing, alertness, good memory, clear enunciation, "patience, tractability, and a good disposition." At the larger exchanges, Myers found that the highest age at which an operator could enter the service was 25 and the youngest was 16. One large company reported having 2235 applications received during the year with only 1400 being accepted. So many were rejected because they did not come up to the requirements. Myers concluded, "Many of these girls have no homes, and the meager wages they receive compel them to live in little rooms and do their own cooking and washing after their hard day's work at the switchboard. They have little time to enjoy life and little opportunity to improve their social, moral and educational conditions."[61]

Late in 1910, it was reported that young women admitted to the school of instruction of the New York Telephone Company got $5 a week while learning the business. Formerly they received $3. The increase was instituted because the company wanted to attract a class of young women from the country who were "well equipped" for the business in all respects and who could manage to live on $5 a week in New York City while learning. (Eking out an existence on $3 a week was impossible for some of them.) At that time, more than 4500 women were employed at the city's 55 central exchanges. Lately only five percent of the school's applicants had been accepted and some of *them* were discharged after a week of instruction, "not having come up to the standard in alertness or general intelligence or dignity of deportment." Management was said to be very particular: "The manifestly frivolous young person has no chance at all of being kept very long at the telephone school." Said a company official,

> There was a time when telephone girls, whether they merited it or not, were not classed with the serious hard workers of the community. Rather they were a synonym for trifling, un-businesslike behavior. That day is past…. Today recruits to the service

must have not only a fair education, considerable intelligence and a wide-awake alert manner, but they must show a first-class aptitude for attending strictly to business in business hours…. The country girl is bound to make good as a general thing. She is already in earnest, her manners are good and what she may lack in alertness at first is more than offset by her dogged perseverance.

About 20 percent of the operators employed at his central exchanges dropped out each year: Some got married, some moved to other cities, some filled better positions with other business concerns. Supervisors were paid $15 a week; $10 a week "with few exceptions" was the maximum paid to women operators. Those who wanted more had to look to work at private switchboards. New York City girls who wanted to be operators reportedly made a splendid first impression with their intelligence and alertness but did not have perseverance enough to go through the school, nor patience enough to master the complexities of the work.[62]

A Tacoma telephone girl received a wage of $25 a month at the beginning of 1911. Her costs included room rent at $1.25 a week, or $5 a month; lunches at 15 cents a day for 26 days, $3.90 a month; laundry at $1 a week, $4 per month; and housekeeping expenses of $2.50 a week, $10 a month. That total came to $22.90 a month, leaving the hello girl a balance of $2.10 a month. However, an editor pointed out that each month contained nearly half of a week more than the above figures indicated; each month had 4.33 weeks, not 4.0. Thus the prorated extra expense claimed another $2.80 per month and thus there was no balance left. That theoretical balance of $2.10 was meant to be used for items such as clothing, entertainment, vacations, illnesses and so on. The editor pointed out that the telephone girl's work paid for her subsistence, and hardly *that*. "Now what we want to say to you comfortable folk, who sometimes complain of agitation, labor unions and unrest by the masses, is this. Every dollar taken in dividends on watered stocks and bonds of telephone companies is a dollar coined out of the blood, health and comfort of this girl and thousands like her. As such, it is a crime against humanity."[63]

In April 1911, David Belasco presented on stage in Washington, D.C., a three-act play called *The Women,* written by William C. deMille. It revolved around the telephone and the heroine was a hello girl. It showed the important role the telephone played in modern life and how it could shape and control the fates and destinies of modern men and women. In the play, the central girl Wanda Kelly (played by Helen Ward) entered a phone conversation and interfered "to save a woman's honor and avenge her father's memory."[64]

When the play was staged a year later in Salt Lake City, a reviewer commented of its hello girl heroine, "She is the central pivot of a plot that shows up all the romance and mystery of the switchboard and the part it plays in the hurry-scurry life of a big city. Politics, intrigue, love, finance and business are mixed in the plot of *The Women*."[65] In October 1912, when *The Women* was running in San Francisco, the *San Francisco Call* took 62 hello girls from the local exchanges to see the play as its guests at an afternoon matinee.[66]

Mary Marshall had a book published in 1911 that was a sort of career guidance volume for young women. Part of it excerpted in a New York City newspaper late in the year. Marshall said there were then over 100,000 telephone girls in the U.S.: "To serve in this army is an education in itself. It does for a young woman what a training in the National Guard does for a man. It sets her up, quickens her senses of sight and hearing and, above all else, it steadies her nerves." Out of every eight or so applicants for admission to the position of telephone girl, only one was found to be acceptable, at least for the large cities. Said Marshall, "For the girl with no previous training, save a grammar school education, who wants to be self-supporting for a few years or for many—who wants to work up to a steady position of from $15 to $25 a week in the course of four or five years—there is no more healthful, womanly work than that of a telephone operator." (The wage figures were outrageous exaggerations.)

According to this guidance counselor, only three things were needed to gain admission to telephone training school: good health, being at least five feet tall, and to have passed through grammar school. If she had those three attributes, it got her admission to an interview where a female advisor sized her up. Girls of 18 to 25 years were preferred and "if she has not earned money before it is in her favor, for if she had worked in a factory or a store—so the telephone authorities are inclined to think—she may have acquired careless habits which unfit her for the exacting work of the switchboard." At that point, the applicant was put through a series of sight and hearing tests. She had to read a paragraph aloud to see if she could speak distinctly and she had to write a sentence or two to show that her handwriting was legible. During the course of the interview, the questioner studied "the girl's general manner and appearance. If her coat lacked a button or her shoelace was untied, showing carelessness, if she came out with a quick, snappy answer, revealing a tendency to impatience or rudeness, or if in any of her actions she seems listless or indifferent—a fatal defect in the telephone business—the examiner was likely to turn her application down."[67]

Marshall continued by remarking that if the girl was accepted, she went into training school at a pay rate of $4 or $5 a week, depending on the size of the city. Once the operator was through the school and had started regular employment, she usually got $5 a week, "and if she shows any sort of ability she is advanced within a few months to $7 and from there to $8 or $9." The next line of advancement was to one of three positions (supervisors, information or long distance operator) where she was paid from $10 to $12 or occasionally as much as $15 in the big cities. A supervisor had charge of about nine operators. To work on the information desk, an operator had to have all the aforementioned qualities and in addition had to possess much general information. It was from the ranks of supervisors that the assistant chief operators were drawn, with a salary of $15 a week. From assistant chief operators were drawn the people who filled the positions of chief operators, at a salary of $25 a week. Marshall added,

> visit to one of the telephone exchanges would convince anyone that the telephone girl is about as well provided for as any working girl, whether in the store, office, factory or schoolroom. The exchange quarters are almost always in new, airy, fireproof, spick and span buildings, and as you watch the young women at their work you will see that the various motions they go through—chest expanded, head held erect, and arms in motion—look like a physical culture drill…. Each exchange has its rest room, provided with magazines and newspapers. There is usually a matron on duty who in case any of the operators are taken ill knows just what to do. But telephone girls don't often fall ill, for, from carefully kept figures, it had been proved that telephone girls on the average enjoy better health than their sisters who work in stores or offices or schoolrooms.

Perhaps the telephone business' greatest attraction for a young woman, Marshall speculated, "lies in the work itself, which is far from monotonous…. [S]he knows that all the great leaders in the world's affairs, men of wealth and men of might, social queens and the nation's rulers talk over her wires and she knows, too, that no big transaction can be put through without the aid of her deft fingers and ready wits."[68]

On March 4, 1912, it was announced that Estelle Cahoun had been appointed welfare matron for the Spokane central telephone exchange and its branches operated by the Pacific Telephone and Telegraph Company. Her duty was to look after the health and general welfare of more than 100 young women and girls in the offices and at their homes. A room had been set aside in each office as an emergency hospital. The purpose, Cahoun explained, "is to secure the services of the best class of girls and make their surroundings such that they will be glad to remain in the company's employ."[69]

Reporting from Missouri in March 1912, a journalist said that a typical insult delivered to a hello girl was, "Say, Central, would you just as soon

A New York City telephone exchange in 1910.

put down that Duchess novel, shift your gum to the other side and answer this phone?" Set phrases used by operators were very limited and consisted of "Number, please," "The line is busy" and "They don't answer." The reporter said that the hello girl "may speak only in set phrases over the wire, regardless of sarcasm or foolishness or rage from the telephone user. Only when the wrathful one becomes too unbearable does she transfer him to the chief operators, who is privileged to cut him off without further ado."

Columbia, Missouri, then had 1,837 telephones where five years earlier the number had been 950. The eight switchboard girls answered on average 16,000 calls a day. One problem faced by the telephone company: "It can't keep its girls. The entire personnel of the force has changed in the last two years. Why? They got married."[70]

Dispatches from Flushing, Long Island, telling of how the exchange's telephone girls there had been forbidden to powder their noses brought the following remarks from an unnamed telephone official at the exchange in Washington, D.C.:

Our girls evidently know how to do both the powdering and the operation of the switchboards well. To this time we have received no complaint to the effect that the powdering of noses had interfered with girls doing their duty on the wire. Hence we have issued no orders against our girls applying perfumed dust to eliminate the shine.

The Roseburg Telephone Company Exchange in Oregon, circa 1910.

Until something showing inefficiency develops with the powdering as the cause, we will take no steps against the practice.[71]

In the fall of 1912, complaints about the poor service of the El Paso telephone company were brought to the notice of the directors of the Chamber of Commerce by director Crawford Harvie. A committee was appointed by that organization to visit manager C.E. Stratton of the Tri-State Telephone Company. He showed the committee members around the plant and told them of the firm's problems. The Chamber of Commerce then issued a report that declared Stratton had been doing his best to bring the El Paso telephone service up to a proper standard. Stratton agreed that the service had been unsatisfactory for some time and said there were three main causes. The first was the inability of the management to employ and retain the necessary number of telephone girls to handle its business; the second was the inability to promptly secure additional equipment (switchboards), and the third was the large increase in business due to the sudden closing of the plant of the Automatic Telephone Company (a rival phone service in the city). The Chamber of Commerce committee added that Stratton showed them that the salaries paid to the telephone girls at his exchange were higher than the average throughout the area and that the best in amenities were provided for them, including rest rooms, a heated and air-conditioned plant, and the best of current literature. There was even a player piano. Stratton said he had advertised extensively, applied to the YWCA for names of potential operators and written letters to every minister in town asking their assistance in finding girls to operate the boards. He added that not only was it necessary to have a sufficient number of girls but that it was necessary for *them* to remain in the service "for a considerable length of time." Records from Stratton's office showed that on September 1, 1912, out of 44 girls employed, 12 of them had been with the company less than one month, 24 less than six months. Only ten had been with the company for two years or more. When the Automatic Telephone Company shut down, the number of daily calls received by Tri-State in El Paso increased from 33,000 to 53,000.[72]

The shortage of hello girls existed everywhere in America at this time. One response that soon became popular could be seen in New York City in October 1912 when the New York Telephone Company announced a plan for making additional payments to operators who remained in the service two years or more. All classes of operators (day, night, chief operators, assistant chief operators and supervisors) were included. A sum of $25 was to be paid to those women at the end of two years of continuous service; $50 at the end of each year from the third to the ninth years of continuous service; and $100 at the end of the tenth year of continuous service and at the end of each year thereafter. Beginners were to have their pay increased by $1 a week. In December 1910, the New York Telephone Company reduced the working hours for day and night operators from nine to eight and for evening hours from eight to seven. At the same time, the wage scale was increased. According to a reporter, "Eight hundred new operators were required at that time by the decrease in working hours" with an increase in the salary bill of around $425,000. The firm was hoping, by those changes, to attract "new operators of the right type so that the present efficiency may be maintained."

The turnover rate among hello girls was notorious with the phone companies usually claiming it was all due to the high marriage rate among their very young women (17 to 25 for the majority). Some of that was true. That was an age range that saw a lot of women get married and leave paid employment. Yet it was a problem that did not bedevil factories and department stores (with female employees of the same ages) to anywhere near the same extent. The reality was that the pay for the hello girls was poor and the working conditions were terrible. No other workforce was con-

The resting room of the York Telephone Exchange in Denver, around 1910.

trolled and supervised to the extent and with the vigor displayed by the telcos. Those firms hoped that the automatic phone would arrive (at least for local calls) and that the hello girls would disappear almost overnight. But in 1912, that did not appear to be just around the corner.[73]

Early in 1913, it was announced that telephone operators who had been in the employ of the Bell Telephone Company in Pennsylvania for two or more years of continuous service were to receive an annual bonus on the same basis as in the above account: $25, $50 and $100. Those sums were to be paid on the anniversary of the beginning of service. The rule went into effect on January 1, 1913.[74]

Later in 1913, the Chesapeake and Potomac Telephone Company in Washington, D.C., announced the same bonus system. In addition, the wages for regular operators were increased by $1 a week. Reportedly the bonus system had already been called a success in Philadelphia. The Chesapeake and Potomac said it would extend the system to Baltimore. Other concessions were reported to be additional pay for overtime, Sunday and holiday work, although no details were provided.[75]

In 1913, the Minnesota Legislature amended the hours of labor law

The Asheville, North Carolina, Telephone Exchange, in the 1920s.

for women to include operators in telephone exchanges in cities of the first and second class. Under the new law, hello girls could be employed for a maximum of 58 hours in any one week. For girls who worked seven days a week, that would give them an average of an eight-hour day. It was reported that many operators had been compelled to work from 63 to 70 hours in a week. With respect to that new law, a reporter commented, "It will be rigidly enforced by the State Bureau of Labor."[76]

Telephone girls employed in Bell's Cleveland exchanges were surprised in the spring of 1913 when the company announced a wage increase. Some 150 girls were affected with the increase amounting to $1 or $1.50 a week. The minimum wage paid to girls in the company's training school was raised from $20 a month to $24 a month.[77]

At the end of 1912, there were reportedly 12,318,000 telephones in the world. The U.S. had 8,357,625 and Europe had 3,153,000. New York City had 441,128 and Chicago had 279,833. Los Angeles and San Francisco tied for the percentage record with each of those cities having one telephone for about every four inhabitants.[78]

Working women who submitted estimates of their costs of living in early 1914 to the Washington State Industrial Welfare Commission gave $12.11 as the necessary weekly wage for living expenses and a reasonable allowance for possible illness, vacations, insurance and so forth. Estimates by their employers, previously provided, gave an average of $10.29 for the same list of items. When those figures were broken down by occupational group, it was found that the estimates of laundry girls averaged $10.44 a week while the estimates from telephone girls gave the highest occupational estimate at $13.65. Factory girls gave an estimate that averaged $12.01; employees of mercantile establishments, $12.08; office workers, $12.27; and waitresses, $13.07. Various items of dress, which the working women estimated much higher than did their employers, were chiefly responsible for the difference between the estimates from the two groups.[79]

Representatives of the employers, employees and the public met in conference in Olympia, Washington, in June 1914 and then recommended to the state Industrial Welfare Commission that the minimum wage of girls employed in telephone offices be set at $9 a week. The vote was nine to three in favor of that figure with all three employers involved, noted a journalist, "voting against such a high figure." Nonetheless, it was believed the Commission would accept the recommendation.[80]

And on July 10, 1914, the Washington Industrial Welfare Commission established a minimum wage of $9 a week for telephone girls over the age of 18 and $6 a week for those under 18. Every female employed in connection with telephone and telegraph lines came under the provisions of the order. The $6-a-week minimum also applied to messenger boys under 18 years of age. Minors (under 18) could only be employed between the hours of 6 a.m. and 9 p.m.[81]

In January 1915, a new three-reel musical comedy film, *A Woman's Way*, opened. In it was Irene Hough of Omaha, winner of a newspaper contest: She was chosen as the most beautiful telephone girl in America. Hough was selected by a committee from hundreds of candidates. She received $100 as a fee for playing a part in the film and her expenses and those of her parents were paid to Chicago where the film was shot by Essanay."[82]

Frank P. Walsh, chairman of the Commission on Industrial Relations, speaking before an audience of the Woman's Trade Union League in Chicago on February 14, 1915, declared that when his commission found capitalists and corporations using autocratic powers over the working class, the commission would not hide that condition but was going "to tear it

A Salt Lake City Utah exchange, circa 1914. Note again the *de facto* uniforms. Several women are seen standing behind the operators. Most likely they are getting ready to relieve operators who are going on a break. Companies had what amounted to a precision drill to minimize the amount of time "wasted" when one operator replaced another.

open." He said that if American Telegraph and Telephone Company was working thousands of hello girls at "less than a living wage," the commission would say so. "It's the business of the public which controls the wire corporations by regulative laws to see that the hello girls get the decent pay of decent women," stated Walsh. His commission was made up of nine members; three each from labor, capital and the general public. Walsh added,

> What reason is there for a telephone girl getting less than a living wage? The American Telephone and Telegraph Co. owns or controls all phone companies of the United States. Their rates are fixed by governmental bodies. Labor is the greatest factor in their operation. This implies inherently the right to fix wages…. Those girls are working for the telephone company at a wage lower than it costs them to live decently. That is a condition all of us are responsible for. This is your own crime and not the crime of the corporation. You, the public, have the power to fix the wages higher.

The Most Beautiful Telephone Girl in the United States

"A WOMAN'S WAY," the Essanay moving picture play in which Irene Hough of Omaha was chosen as the most beautiful telephone girl in America to play one of the roles, is to be shown at the Alhambra for four days beginning today. Miss Hough was selected by a committee from hundreds of candidates entered through the Seattle Star and its sister papers over the United States. She was paid $100 for her part, and her expenses and those of her parent paid to Chicago, where the play was filmed, and, while there, was elaborately entertained by the Essanay people.

IRENE HOUGH in "A WOMAN'S WAY"

This Picture Is Complete. It Is Not a Serial

IN ADDITION WE OFFER

A 3-Reel Feature

A RIP SNORTING COMEDY

ALL-STAR TRIO IN NEW SONGS

Thursday Friday Saturday Sunday

10c The Entire Lower Floor 5c Balcony Children

THE ALHAMBRA

WESTLAKE PINE AND FIFTH

Selected as the most beautiful telephone girl in America, Irene Hough of Seattle received as a prize, a role in a 1915 film (which had nothing to do with telephone girls).

Directors and stockholders in corporations, Walsh declared, "must be held responsible for the labor conditions in the enterprise out of which they derive their profits."[83]

An investigation of wages and general conditions of telephone operators in Chicago, Kansas City, Madison, Salt Lake City, San Francisco and Los Angeles was completed on July 21, 1915, for the Commission on Industrial Relations. The investigation, done by Nellie Curry, took six months. According to that report,

> The wages paid are too low to enable a girl dependent on her own energies to maintain a proper standard of life; that the wage scale remains too low for the following reasons: (a) Because of the employment of a large number of young girls; (b) On account of the competition of girls living at home and partly supported out of the earnings by parents or others employed in various occupations; (c) On account of the lack of organization; (d) The telephone girls, because of their youth and inexperience, are peculiarly unqualified to insist on fair conditions for themselves. As a substitute for organization, the report recommends Government supervision and publicity.[84]

The report also recommended a six-hour day and a minimum wage for telephone operators. The nervous strain attending telephone operating, the report stated, "is exceptionally severe and is responsible for physical and nervous breakdowns of a large number of girls."[85]

Government statistics that became available in April 1916 showed there were more than eight million women workers in America. Numbers for various job categories were as follows: 263,315 stenographers and typewriters; 14,061 linotype operators; 2,530,846 domestics; 1,820,980 factory and mill girls; 76,508 trained nurses; 111,117 midwives; 2,000,000 women farm laborers; 100,000 women bakers; 8,219 telegraph operators; and 88,262 hello girls.[86]

Nell Taylor had spent 24 years in continuous service as a telephone operator in Columbus, Ohio, as of September 1916. She said she had answered 2.4 million calls over that period. The first eight years she spent at the switchboard handling calls at the rate of 1000 a day. She spent another eight years as a supervisor answering what she described as "foolish" questions such as "Will you marry me?" which she said was "the silliest and most frequent question asked." When she started work 24 years earlier (1892), she was just 15. There were 1550 telephones in Columbus then, as compared to 45,000 in 1916.[87]

In June 1917, a total of 91 experienced telephone operators were brought to Washington from New York City, Philadelphia and Baltimore by officials of the Chesapeake and Potomac Telephone Company, to fill the depleted ranks of hello girls lessened by employment of large numbers of operators by the U.S. government, as part of the war effort. Reportedly, at the War Department there had been employed just four operators before the war effort got underway; 15 in the summer of 1917. All other federal government departments showed a similar or greater increase. The federal government demanded trained and experienced operators. Since there was no government training school for telephone operators, it drew operators from wherever it could find them. Within the previous two months, it was said that more than 150 girls had left Chesapeake and Potomac to take government employment. The salary paid by the government exceeded that paid by the telcos although, noted a reporter; "the commercial organizations have repeatedly raised wages." Chesapeake and Potomac district manager C.T. Clagett said his firm was losing long distance operators at the rate of ten per week and regular operators at the rate of 15 or more per week. The company's training school for operators was graduating 25 operators a week, but it was not enough to meet the combined demand.[88]

Seattle newspaper reporter Echo Zahl went underground for three days in July 1917 and worked as a student telephone operator in that city.

Pacific Telegraph and Telephone Company was the firm involved. First she filled out an application form and listed her education, birthplace, age, former occupations and "home conditions." Then the interviewer measured her height and tested her eyesight. She told the interviewer her hearing was good (apparently it was not tested) and at 8 a.m. the following morning she started her first day as a trainee.[89]

ECHO ZAHL WORKS AS 'HELLO' GIRL
She Writes of the Late of Girls Who Are Threatening to Go on Strike

In 1917, Seattle reporter Echo Zahl went underground to take a job as a hello girl and then reported back on their working conditions for her readers.

On that first day, the instructor spelled out the rules. An operator could not be brought to work by a boyfriend and if he came to pick up one of the students, he had to wait a block away from the building at night. That rule applied to all the operators. Another rule that rankled trainees, and others, was that no switchboard girl could wear flowers at her bosom or jewelry about her person. Pay for students had been $1 a day until a few days earlier when it had been increased to $1.10. Zahl had to go to school six days a week for 16 lessons. After that, the trainees were shipped out to the smallest exchanges in the city where they worked as regular operators at $1.10 a day for two months. Then they received $1.20 a day and two months later they reached $1.30. At the end of the 60th month after she had left training school (assuming she was diligent, proficient and so on), the operator was paid $2 a day. An operator was paid 15 cents extra when her hours extended past 5:30 p.m.—not for overtime but for the inconvenience of the shift. Night operators started at $1.40 a day and could reach $2.30 per day. In Seattle there were then 13 exchanges, 850 operators and two schools of instruction.[90]

Effective July 1, 1919, on orders from Southern Bell Telephone Company, operators in South Carolina and other areas covered by the firm could no longer give the time of day to callers who asked for it. Also, they could not give the location of fires or any other extraneous information. As far as the company was concerned, there was too much efficiency lost when operators gave out extraneous information. They were busy constantly as it was, just making the demanded connections. By this time, a similar regulation was reported to be in force all over the United States, in practically all of the large cities.[91]

In 1916 in New York City, the average caller waited four seconds for central to say, "Number, please." In August 1919, that wait time was said to be 10.4 seconds on average. In 1916, one call in 28 went wrong while in 1919 it was one call in every 17. Reportedly, the cause of that slump in efficiency was that operators were doing one-third more work than was normal. During the time of World War I, New York Telephone was handling 2.5 million calls a day, often more than 400,000 in a single hour, or 6000 a minute. It had 9807 operators of whom five out of six were "seasoned" (one to ten years experience). By the end of 1918, traffic increased by 750,000 calls a day to 3,250,000. The federal government "poached" a lot of skilled operators for war work as operators. The New York Telephone operator force fell to 9102, a loss of 700. It was an even greater loss because many of the thousands of experienced girls who left were replaced by green operators. The shortage of female labor, said a reporter, "forced the company to relax the physical standards formerly insisted on and to accept girls less fitted by nature for the work." Fewer operators, with less experience, were handling more calls per operator. In response, New York Telephone increased the wages for beginners from $8 to $12 a week and were training girls as fast as possible and re-recruiting war operators as fast as they were being released by Washington.[92]

By the last month of 1919, it was estimated that New York Telephone was short of operators by six or seven hundred. There was difficulty in getting then and difficulty in holding them. The hours were antisocial and involved evening, nights and weekends. That was not nearly so usual in private exchanges, which were a greater lure for operators. Training courses that had been three to four weeks for decades were reduced by the company to two weeks. Starting pay after training was then $12.50 a week, which was increased every six months by 50 cents until at the end of six years an operator reached the maximum pay of $20 a week (in Manhattan), In Brooklyn, operators received $1 a week less. Overtime was paid at the rate of $1 for evenings and $3 for night work.[93]

A report at the end of December 1919 from Dr. S. Dana Hubbard, chief of the Division of Industrial Hygiene of the New York City Department

VANGUARD OF AMERICAN TELEPHONE GIRLS REACHES FRANCE

These are the first of the American telephone girls who are going to operate the switchboards for our soldiers

This 1918 photo shows hello girls preparing to go overseas to "man" the phones. A chronic shortage of hello girls, which existed because of low pay and poor working conditions, was worsened during World War I, with so many of the women taking government jobs as operators, at home and abroad.

of Health, stated that the failure of New York Telephone to employ a full crew of operators was the main reason for the city's poor telephone service. Hubbard had spent two months investigating telephone plants and service. That shortage of help meant overwork for those who were employed, and overwork resulted in impaired health. Dr. Copeland, New York City Health Commissioner, said, "The investigation has shown that the whole trouble is due to the low wages paid the operators. These telephone girls begin with $11 a week in Brooklyn and $12 a week in Manhattan, as I understand it. At the end of the fifth year of employment they are paid $18 a week."[94]

In his report, Copeland argued that with higher wages, the shortage of operators would be met and the overwork and its ill effects would disappear. "It has been pretty clearly established that from $15 to $17 a week is the minimum wage, or should be the minimum wage, for women of the type employed by the telephone company," said Copeland. "Personally, I doubt exceedingly if, under present economic conditions, it will be possible for the telephone company to maintain the sort of service it used to give, without a material increase in the wages paid." He concluded,

It may be wondered why the Board of Health has an interest in an economic problem of this sort. It has been clearly pointed out in this report that a limited number of employees attempting to do the work formerly performed by a larger group must result in conditions prejudicial to the health of a large group of citizens who naturally look to the health department for protection.[95]

As of November 1920, Washington, D.C., telephone girls were reported to be the nation's highest paid hello girls, according to officials of the Chesapeake and Potomac Telephone Company. It was estimated that the firm's 1300 operators cost an average of $1000 each to train and that a new operator was not of "material use" to the company until after three months of service. By July 1920, the wages of those operators had reportedly increased some 22 percent over July 1919 figures, although no details were provided.[96]

In May 1921 there were said to be 200 hello girls short of a full staff. A few weeks earlier, the company had advertised openings with the result that 54 girls applied. Of that number, just five were accepted for training. Applicants had to be between 18 and 25 years of age and unmarried. According to the story, "The reason for not wanting married women in the telephone service is that a married woman's mind is not always on her work and the service suffers as a result." The age limit of 18 was not the firm's doing but was forced on them under the law—girls under 18, by law, could not be employed after 6 p.m. The average age of Washington operators was 21 while in other areas where laws regulating night work varied, the average age was about 18. Starting pay was herein said to be $1100 a year and the work day was no more than 7.5 hours. And, of course, the hello girls had to be moral: "Now, as never before, the telephone company is paying more attention to the morals of the girl operators. After a girl makes an application she is investigated. If there is anything shady about her reputation, she is informed that she will not do." In this piece, the estimated time that the average girl remained with the phone company was said to be about a year and she "then leaves, either to get married or take up something else."[97]

4

Discipline

Discipline and control were tightly imposed on the telephone operators. They could not talk to other operators for any reason and were not even supposed to look around the room; eyes front at all times. They could not talk to subscribers at all, except for the obvious reasons and in the obvious ways. They were often forbidden from chewing gum and from wearing jewelry or flowers in their hair. They often had to adhere to a dress code. A dress code was particularly ludicrous since nobody saw a hello girl except another hello girl.

Discipline was imposed for many reasons other than logic or efficiency or productivity. In May 1888, a Detroit newspaper declared:

> They were weeping and wailing and gnashing of teeth in the telephone stations the other day over a new order. The hello girls have bowed in submission to the order that there shall be no reading, no sewing, no crocheting, and no drawn-work while they are on duty. But when the order was issued forbidding them to chew gum, they felt that the time had come to strike till the last armed foe shall expire.

Because of the uproar among the operators, conferences were held, quiet was restored, no strike took place—but "the gum was thrown out the window." The reason for issuing the no-gum order was said to be to enhance clarity; gum-chewing interferes with the ability to speak clearly.[1]

In San Francisco on a November morning in 1892, there was a case of "answering back." A long distance operator did not switch off a subscriber as soon as she should have, so the male subscriber had to wait a bit. Angry, he took it out on the operator. The local girl told him she had answered at once, which was true (the fault was with the long distance operator). The exchange manager said, "No, you could not say that she had been impertinent. She only answered back. The subscriber reported the case, and as we could not go into details and explain that the delay was not owing to the fault of the girl in the room, she had to be suspended to satisfy him."[2]

After being refused communion by a church in Columbia, South Carolina, because she worked three hours every Sunday as a phone girl (a decision upheld by the Charleston, South Carolina, presbytery), Sadie Means took her case on appeal to the South Carolina synod. She won that appeal with the synod by a vote of 63 to 40 to issue an order that the action of the South Carolina presbytery be annulled and that the church in Columbia "restore Sadie M. Means to all her rights and privileges as a member in full communion of said church." The case had provoked a good deal of indignation with the friends of Means pointing out there were several prominent men in the same church who worked on Sunday, "although they were not compelled to do it by poverty, as she was." Second Church pastor A. Blackburn gave notice on behalf of the Charleston presbytery that they would appeal to the general assembly. In May 1894, that general assembly ruled in favor of Sadie Means and she was restored to full membership in the church.[3]

The 500 or so female operators of the Metropolitan Telegraph and Telephone Company in New York City were reported to be highly agitated in February 1894 over certain new rules and regulations. The trouble began several months earlier when a new manager was appointed. He had been brought in from Chicago to manage the large operating room in the Cortlandt Street exchange; as soon as he took over, he announced that all conversation was strictly forbidden between the hours of 8:15 a.m. and 5:45 p.m. (Most of the girls worked from 8 a.m. to 6 p.m.). A number of operators were removed from the switchboard and made supervisors—with the mandate to enforce the new order. Until then, it had been the practice of the company to allow operators to occasionally take off their headsets for a few minutes here and there to rest for a bit—the headsets caused headaches. That was also stopped. Also, all operators had to stop using the normal greeting of "hello" when subscribers rang up and instead say to a subscriber, "Number, please." If a girl forgot and said "hello," she was subject to unspecified discipline.[4]

In the summer of 1900, it was reported that "hello" was no longer a catchword at the Chicago telephone company. A reporter wrote,

> The word is tabooed by the management as rude, if not impertinent, and the operators are now taught to abjure it.... [T]he girl who cannot answer calls with a rising inflection and a musical lilting tone loses her job and gives way to one whose voice capabilities and elocutionary adaptability enable her to jolly the subscriber into the belief the she is glad to hear from him.

General manager A.S. Hibbard had established a sort of school of "telephone oratory calculated to make the responsive tones of the telephone girl confidential, insidious and flattering." If the girl was really into her work, explained the journalist, "she gives the lilting tone as though she were glad you spoke and wanted to continue the conversation in the most confidential manner. The subscriber concluded that the operator is glad that he spoke. He is jollied, if his temper is riled, it becomes smooth. If he has burrs in his voice he tries to banish them." Said Hibbard,

> We put all our new operators through a system of vocal training before we set them to work. If they have rough voices and are unable to acquire the rising inflection, we let them go. Have you noticed what a pleasant effect there is in that rising inflection? We got our cue from the soap advertisement, "Good morning, have you used our soap?" But it works. Since its establishment, we have few complaints from subscribers and the girls hear very few cusswords from angry men at the other end of a delayed wire.
>   We have special superintendents who "cut in" on every one of our 221 operators during the day. If the girls neglect or forget the rising inflection, they are warned. If they prove their inability to acquire the necessary tone quality, we dismiss them.

Hibbard declared that his firm's subscribers "are also learning the value of elocutionary excellence…. It's a great scheme! It makes the using of telephones a positive pleasure."[5]

According to an October 1900 report from Louisville, Kentucky, hello girls became very upset when the Cumberland Telegraph and Telephone Company, which owned all the major lines in the South, issued an order requiring operators to furnish a guarantee bond of $25 that they would not talk over the lines for personal reasons. Reportedly, that order had been made necessary by the fact "that a number of operators were accustomed to use the lines for gossiping with each other and with male friends."[6]

A glowing November 1901 press report declared there had been great improvements made recently in the Salt Lake City telephone exchange. In those days of progress, the girl who wanted to man the phones, stated the reporter, "must be a paragon of energy, honesty, ambition and excellence." Superintendent Jackson's "monitor system" was said to be the reason for all that perfection. A young woman operator sat at a switchboard in a rear room with a headset attached to one ear and with a stopwatch in one hand. She could hear everything that went on over any wire in the city but could not talk back. Before her was a blank with various columns on it, and it was her business to chronicle under the proper columns the various events in the daily life of a hello girl. The system was so arranged that this operator could cut in on any lines in the city. The operators never knew when the monitor was listening in. The monitor kept track of the number of seconds it took to answer a call after the bell was rung, the number of wrong connections she made, the number of times she spoke "crossly," the number of times the operator cut in on a connection and listened to what was being said, the number of times she failed to test a connection, the number of "unnecessary" words she used, the number of times she said "hello" instead of "number," the number of times she said "all right" instead of using silence, and the number of seconds she took to disconnect after the customer had finished the call. "For all these things are crimes in the telephone office," said the article. No operator was to answer with the greeting "hello," which was described as "old-fashioned." If she forgot herself to that extent, she was fined one percent in her standard of efficiency. The same deduction was made for a wrong connection, for an unnecessary conversation, for being impertinent, etc. At the end of each shift, each girl's record was turned over to headquarters. Said Superintendent Jackson,

> It is the best thing we ever had as a means of schooling. The improvement since we inaugurated the monitor system has been marked. Where it used to take a girl all the way from 12 to 20 seconds to answer a ring, the average now is not above three seconds and in a majority of cases our records show they respond in two seconds. They are watchful always for the best interest of our customers and have made a splendid showing recently. It improves the service 100 percent.

In addition to the system described, Jackson had a set of rules that the girls had to learn and from those rules a set of questions was drafted every quarter which the operators had to answer. Jackson had observed in the eastern papers that telephonic elocutionary schools were being instituted in the larger cities and he was thinking of starting something of the kind for the 40 girls in the employ of the Rocky Mountain Telephone Company in Salt Lake City. "They must learn, besides all the details of the switchboard, how to say 'number' so that the patron may understand it," he remarked. "In the schools being established, the pitch, modulation, the elasticity of the voice are all given especial attention, as well as many other smaller details."[7]

In January 1902, new regulations were issued for telephone girls in Paris, France—rules that were very similar to those that existed in many exchanges in America. One rule forbade them from ever calling subscribers to converse with them. Another forbade them from responding to or answering in any way, flattery, compliments or pleasantries from male subscribers. Also, the operators were forbidden from making appointments over the wire or permitting anyone (even relatives) to wait for them near the office, to accompany them home, for example. Juliette Adamson was an American woman then living in Paris. She was fined $40 in court for "insulting" over the wire a tradesman who failed to deliver goods at the promised time. Her attorney argued that as long as subscribers paid their phone bills, the state could not restrict conversation but the judge hearing

GIRLS MUST TOE THE MARK.

Sleepless Monitor Now Keeps Close Watch Upon the Angels of the Telephone Exchange—Black Marks Against the Young Women For Numberless Offenses.

A 1901 sketch of a monitor at work in Salt Lake City, and some of the rules she was expected to impose as she listened in on the operators. All telcos had monitors at work.

the case held that the state had the right to enforce an order regarding telephones just as it had regarding the streets.[8]

The word "hello" which had been used since the invention of the telephone was reported to have been stricken from the lexicon of Evanston, Illinois, society in April 1902, by a dictum "of cultured suburbanites." Only such phrases as "good morning" and "how do you do?" were allowed. The Evanston telephone girls were asked not to say "hello" when they answered subscribers' calls. Mrs. H. H. Kingsley, president of the Woman's Clubs of Evanston, spoke to a reporter about the reform movement. When she answered the phone she said, "Good evening. Who is it?" Kingsley explained to the reporter, "Yes, there is such a movement on foot, and I am glad to say that it is rapidly gaining round. The word 'hello' is not a good word, and most Evanstonians have dropped it. I do not believe the word to be the best we can find. We would not use it if we greeted a person on the street. Why can't we be as courteous when talking by telephone?"[9]

On March 4, 1903, a jury in the circuit court in Kansas City, Missouri, awarded operator Eva Cook $12,500 damages against the Missouri and Kansas Telephone Company for injuries inflicted on her by Herschel Graves, a central office manager. Cook testified that while she was seated on a high stool at work, Graves, angered because she had not carried out some "trivial order," roughly whirled her about on that stool, causing her to strike and injure her shoulder and knee.[10]

In the spring of 1903, it was announced that Chicago had plans to make the telephone girls polite. A newspaper article had the subhead "Book containing set of rules of etiquette is supplied to each of the telephone maidens and she is guided by its precepts in trying moments." According to the piece, the issue of "How to be civil though a telephone girl" had been solved by Chicago: Each of the operators had been given a book containing the rules of etiquette (as seen and defined by the telco) and "the book goes straight to the point and supplies the telephone girl with various answers for turning away unreasonable wrath." For instance, an irate voice might demand over the wire, "Why the deuce don't you wake up, central?" That was central's cue for responding sweetly, "I am very sorry, sir, but this is an unusually busy afternoon. If you give me your call again, I will see that you are promptly connected." Or someone might complain, "Is there any special reason for your cutting us off, central?"; the proper answer was, "I am very sorry, madame, but it happened inadvertently. I will make haste to reconnect you and, believe me, will take good care that it doesn't happen again." The article ended with a cynical comment from the journalist: "Is polite society polite? was long ago answered in the negative. Is it possible to be a hello girl and civil at the same time? is another question that has heretofore demanded a negative reply."[11]

S.A. Crawford, the new manager of Chicago's American Telegraph and Telephone Company, introduced that book of etiquette rules. It was described as being "full of formalities and elegancies." To the query "Who is this?," the proper answer was, "You are speaking to the operator of the long distance telephone line." If there was some delay or problem in making a connection, the hello girl was to say, "I shall endeavor to ascertain what is the trouble." If there was still more delay and the subscriber became more abusive, the operator was to say sweetly; "I am endeavoring to ascertain why you do not procure your connection. After I have ascertained, I shall call you. Please hang up your receiver."[12]

Marie McLaughlin, telephone operator, lost her position with one of Philadelphia's telephone companies in 1904 because of her honesty and faithfulness to that company in refusing to make a connection for Philadelphia Mayor Weaver when the man failed to drop a dime in the pay phone slot. Said Marie; "Mayor Weaver revenged himself on me by demanding my dismissal." She was advised to start legal action for damages and that she had a good case but she declined to do so:

> When I learned that it was the mayor who had been on the phone, I did not feel sorry for the manner in which I had acted. We were not supposed to recognize anyone on the phone and the rules of the company told us to treat everybody alike. You know a telephone operator is told many things and so the company ordered us not to pay any attention to what was said, but to attend strictly to business and that is what I did when Mayor Weaver got on the phone.

Things worked out all right for the woman as within a few days of being fired, she secured a new position with a local bureau of information.[13]

On the afternoon of May 15, 1904, about 200 young women showed up at Lyric Hall in New York City. They had been invited there to dance by the Jersey Social Club, a dancing club made up of telephone girls and their friends. However, a man at the door would not admit them. He waved a postcard at them saying he got it from the Jersey Social Club calling off the dance. It read: "We are sorry to cancel our date this afternoon, but we have been informed by the telephone company that any of its employees attending the dance will be discharged." At the Cortlandt Street office of the New York Telephone Company, it was said that the dance was banned by the executive offices of the firm. "There's been too much publicity about the girls and their balls" was the only statement given out to the press.[14]

Two weeks later, those hello girls celebrated their victory over the telco with their dance at the Murray Hill Lyceum. Nearly 200 "centrals" were in attendance, along with an estimated 300 young men. The ban had prompted the girls to threaten to revolt. The telco retracted the first order although that second order did threaten instant dismissal of any girl who was late for work on her next shift after the dance. For that reason, the ball was closed at 6 p.m. as some of the girls had to report for night shift duty at 9 p.m.[15]

Fifty Cincinnati hello girls were fired on August 30, 1904, for flirting over the wire. They fell into a trap laid by management and did not know why they had been discharged until they began to compare notes. Nearly all of them revealed that for some time, a strange voice had been calling them up from various parts of the city and a conversation ensued that began something like this: "Hello sister! Oh, what a sweet voice you have." The man would then give the name of some prominent merchant or politician and in nine cases out of ten the unsuspecting hello girl would respond to the flattery. According to the article; "Tomorrow new rules will be issued and they will be severe against flirtation over the phone."[16]

In December 1905, Edwin E. Webster, manager of Seattle's Independent Telephone Company, told a newspaper reporter, "Discipline is the most essential feature in the successful operation of a large telephone exchange. Without it, the best equipped up-to-date telephone exchange in the world would soon go to the dogs." It was the task of the reporter to determine what the difference was between the service rendered by the Sunset Company and the Independent Company. When he viewed the Independent operating room, he saw a huge switchboard with 25 to 30 girls at work. Constantly pacing back and forth behind them was a monitor (promoted from the ranks of the operators). She watched the girls closely to see they did not talk "sharply" to subscribers, talk "unnecessarily" long to one party, to see they did not gossip with each other or "neglect their duties in any way." In the middle of the floor, a short distance from the center of the switchboard, sat the chief operator—a man. At his desk was an instrument that allowed him to hear what any girl on the board said and how she worked. In Webster's office was another one of those instruments, called herein a "sneak box." A girl working on the board did not at any time know whether or not she was being listened in on. Webster had instituted what he called an "educational switchboard." All girls who applied for positions as operators were taught "free of charge" the operation of the switchboard used by the Independent Company. "From the many girls who learn on the board, a few who seem to have the requisite qualities necessary for the making of good operators are selected and their names placed on file," explained Webster. From his perspective, the essentials in the make-up of a good operator were a carefully modulated voice, perfect control of temper and a willingness to work hard. When there was a vacancy, a name was taken from the list and the girl was given a chance on the main board at $20 a month. If she could keep her position for three months, her salary was raised. Thereafter, salaries were raised every three months until the maximum of $35 a month was reached. Besides the raises in salary, every six months, cash prizes were given to the operators with the best records. First prize was $25.[17]

Eight girls in the employ of the Home Telephone Company in Santa Barbara, California, quit work on May 27, 1907, because their manager criticized their conduct at a Sunday afternoon picnic as "unladylike." After those operators quit, the manager told them they could either return to work or be locked out. The girls refused to return and they were told their places would be filled by other women. At the picnic, the principal diversion was climbing trees. The complaint against the women was entered by one of the company's main stockholders, who had happened to observe the girls.[18]

At the end of 1909, puffs, rats and other assorted hairpieces were banished from the heads of Chicago telephone girls under a new rule. They were also forbidden to chew gum during business hours. The Chicago exchange's branch manager was said to have reported that the operators spent too much time replacing loosened wisps of hair from their hairpieces when their fingers should have been busy with the jacks and the switchboard.[19]

New York Telephone company operators complained in April 1911 that the company had established a system of espionage over them "for the purpose of preserving a high order of morality in the exchanges." Company officials denied the report but according to a journalist, "many of the girls declared that they were being shadowed by the company after they left their work. They were indignant that their freedom should be trespassed upon in such fashion." It was reported that 17 girls were recently discharged from the two Brooklyn exchanges because of reports turned in by the spies. One of the Brooklyn managers, Mr. Hubble, said the company had not adopted a spy system and that the girls were free to do as they pleased when they left work. He added; "We do keep tabs on the punctuality of the girls and we will not tolerate tardiness in getting to work unless a good excuse can be offered. If a girl persists in coming late and her appearance indicates that she had been habitually losing sleep, she is discharged. We owe it to the other girls that the moral tone of our employees is of the highest standard."[20]

Four days later it was reported that 15 telephone girls, formerly employed at the Bedford branch of the New York Telephone Company in Brooklyn, were looking for jobs and all because "their gentlemen friends crossed the two-blocks-from-the-office dead line." They also charged management with operating a spy system. The girls appointed an "indignation committee" to explain their side to the public. Those who worked until 9 p.m. went straight from the office to whatever entertainment venue they were going to; that is, they went direct and their boyfriends picked them up. Said one operator, "First they could come a block from the office and then the boss made it two blocks. I guess the boys slipped over the line a few times and were seen. Then the boss asked us all if we were willing to snitch on a supervisor. Wasn't that awful? I told him I never snitched on nobody…. But we don't know where to get a job. You see, we're on the blacklist now. Most of us never worked any place else." Regarding A.C. Hesse, who was in charge of the Bedford exchange and others, a journalist reported, "He said yesterday that he employed no spies, and that the discharge of the 15 girls was really of no importance to anyone."[21]

The Chicago Telephone Company issued a July 1912 order that forbade the central girls from flirting on the wires, even just a tiny bit. The firm had put into effect a series of phrases for the use of its operators. No other could be used. The flirting subscriber was to have his call transferred to the chief operator. The telco phrase and rule book "prohibits personal conversation between employees over the wires…. You must give your time to the company…. If your friends attempt to take up your time in trivial conversation, switch them to the chief operator." Other rules contained in the book: The operator "must dress plainly, but neatly, in dark or blue colors. No puffs, rouge or perfumery." Jewelry and ornaments were forbidden as they "are not in good taste." To all questions put to the operator by a subscriber that were not "strictly business," the operator was to have only one answer: "Number, please."[22]

Manager Tobin of the Washington exchange said his girls were not ruled with the iron hand displayed by Chicago management. He said the girls could wear whatever they wanted "within reason, just so long as they maintain their dignity and businesslike manners over the wire."[23]

An "informal" party was held on a Saturday evening in October 1912 at the office of the Mountain States Telephone and Telegraph Company in Bisbee Arizona. The entire force of 16 operators attended with "Courtesy" being the subject of a talk given by company executive Mr. Rabers while Mrs. Moon, chief operator, spoke to the operators on the topic of "Service." According to an article, "Such instructive talks as the operators

Breaking the "Hello Girl" Dead Line

This 1911 sketch spoofed the "dead line," one of many rules that operators had to adhere to. Friends and relatives of hello girls were not allowed to pick them up from work.

were privileged to hear" would improve the efficiency of the telephone service. Reportedly those meetings would be a regular thing throughout the winter and their motto would be "Courtesy, Accuracy and Service." Also on hand was manager Gunnison, who declared, "There is nothing too good for the telephone girls who so faithfully say 'number, please' in their courteous manner."[24]

One of the earliest examples of a dress code being imposed on the hello girls came from Chicago in October 1892. According to a report, there was "serious discontent" there among the telephone girls. They had been ordered "to don black robes and black frills, fripperies and ornaments, to the absolute exclusion of color." Commented a newspaper editor, "What good such an order can do the companies no one can perceive."[25]

A new rule imposed on San Francisco operators took effect on January 1, 1894. It required that all the female employees in the office were thereafter to wear a "uniform" of dark blue or black. The idea reportedly came from the Chicago Telephone Company. According to an article; "Uniforms had to be introduced there because the girls appeared in all styles of costume." The girls did not like the regulation or the thought of the extra expense they would be put to. Those operators had to pay for whatever new clothes they needed to live up to the rule.[26] A California newspaper editor said the operators had "our hearty sympathy" in their protest against the "threat" of the company to uniform them:

> For is it not enough to be called a "Hello Girl," and to have to put up with the growls, and grumbling and cranky demands of all manner of people all day long, with never the permission to reply to some of them as they deserve? No, indeed; to uniform these girls is to add insult to injury, and the telephone girls so uniformly, patiently amiable should not be insulted.[27]

One of the San Francisco operators said she didn't like the dress code "one little bit. I don't own a blue or a black dress, and if I did I would refuse to wear it. Of course I object to the expense that the uniforms will entail, but more than all I object to wearing the garb of servility. I object to uniforms on general principles. It is un–American. We work hard for the little money we get, and no one has a right to dictate how we spend it." Another girl called the order "preposterous" and added, "Why, I have to plan for at least three months before I can get a new dress, and now to be calmly told that I have to provide myself with a uniform by the first of the year is— well, it is downright awful." One operator told the reporter that she only had two dresses. The president of the company, Mr. Sabin, showed a reporter the central exchange room wherein sat 33 operators, dressed in many hues and colors, none in black or blue. He said,

> Now just look at that line of girls, how much prettier they would appear if their dresses were all dark…. Of course if any of the girls cannot afford to get their uniforms by the first we will not try and compel them to. We are not going to be hard on them. They may have a reasonable time to get them. We simply set the first of January as the time for the young ladies to have the dark-colored dresses because we would accomplish nothing if we did not state a time for the rule to take effect.

While the operating rooms of telephone exchanges were not open to the public and hello girls were never visible to anyone but each other, it did occasionally happen that a would-be subscriber was given a quick tour of the plant, including the operating room. Otherwise, the operators were virtually unseen.[28]

In Chicago in April 1894, the telco decreed that the long trains of dresses had to be removed and the bottom of each skirt worn to work had to be trimmed to the point that there were at least three inches between the bottom of the hem of the skirt and the floor. About one year earlier, the company had ordered the girls to wear black dresses and by this time they all wore black dresses. Unhappy with the monotony and uniformity of this dress code, the operators had taken to wearing flounces at the bottom of those dresses. Then it was noticed the exchange was having more repair problems than usual. Reportedly, it was traced to the dust kicked up by the flounces which dragged on the floor. That dust settled on equipment and caused problems. A new order from the company declared, "Hereafter the girls employed in the main office shall wear their skirts so that they will clear the floor by three inches."[29]

Jersey City, New Jersey, telephone girls were reportedly agitated over company general manager McCully's 1894 order that they wear black dresses—"in other words, a uniform. All the dresses will be cut alike."[30] According to a very brief September 1895 item, Chicago telephone girls were forbidden to wear bloomers.[31]

At Spokane, Washington, in June 1903, some reforms were introduced. An order was issued prohibiting operators from wearing low-necked dresses. That order came just as the hot weather was arriving. Penalties for various offenses were also said to have been increased.[32]

In 1903, the superintendent of the Sunset Telephone Company in Alameda, California, found the girls wearing all sorts of stuff including, said a report, "elegant picture hats." He delivered a lecture to the girls, which a reporter declared was entitled "Disadvantages of Dress to the Girl Who Works." Then the executive posted an order banning all "finery" and ordered the hello girls to thereafter report for work dressed only in gray or in blue.[33]

In 1906, manager Orth of the New York Telephone Company ordered his girls not to wear peek-a-boo waists, short sleeves or open-work stockings, under penalty of dismissal. Managers in other cities followed suit. General manager George H. Durant of the St. Louis Bell Telephone Company found nothing wrong with the open-work and the peek-a-boo and did not follow along. He was declared to be "broad-minded" by a journalist.[34]

Orders issued on May 18, 1916, required Paterson, New Jersey, operators to disobey fashion dictates and wear skirts long enough to conceal ankles which, noted a reporter, "the company decided were too conspicuous."[35]

In September 1916, it was reported that Philadelphia businessmen were organizing a rebellion against what a journalist described as "coquetry of costume during hours of employment." The report continued: "They say that powdered noses, elaborately puffed hair, shoulder-showing shirtwaists, abbreviated skirts and zebra-striped stockings are not helpful to transaction of business in a big office." One of the first big companies to speak its mind on the issue was the Bell Telephone Company of Philadelphia, which employed more than 2400 young women. "We object to our girls coming to work with their noses powdered and their cheeks painted the color of fresh roses," said an official. "The practice of painting and powdering, not to mention the wearing of knee-length skirts and abbreviated shirtwaists, has come to be a source of much concern to this company, and we have decided to stamp out the practice as much as possible." This executive said that if a Bell employee came to work

all dolled up like a chorus girl, she is either sent home or requested to wash her face. We have sent a good many home…. I wonder what the telephone girls of five years ago would say were they to come back and see their successors. For many years the telephone operator was compelled to wear a black shirtwaist and skirt except during the home summer months. It looks to me as though we will have to introduce the old style again…. But we have a woman now who employs our girls and I am sure few, if any, will hereafter be accepted if they show any weakness along the lines of decorating themselves. This woman is a keen judge of character. You may know how strict she is regarding the type of girls to employ when I tell you that out of more than 400 interviewed last week, only 24 were accepted[36]

5

Health and Swearing and Love and Harassment

Did the work of a telephone girl have any adverse effects on the health of the young women employed in that industry? A New York City newspaper reporter entered the operating room of that city's Metropolitan Telephone Company in November 1883 with the intention of determining if the rumor was true that operators lost their voices and were sometimes compelled to speak in a whisper. Superintendent Cochrane showed the journalist around and said he had been there from the start, some four years earlier, and he had never seen any indication of a loss of voice. "The company employs about 100 girls at the various stations and I never heard of a case where a girl lost her voice. These 20 girls have handled 7627 messages in one day, and they ordinarily handle 6500 messages, so that they keep talking pretty steadily," explained Cochrane. "Yet they do not get tired. They talk to one another during their 15 minutes' recess, morning and afternoon, and they talk to other operators in the intervals of business, yet they are not tired." Those operators called every one of the subscribers assigned to them, to test the line, and they asked each of those subscribers to call them back to test the line in the other direction.[1]

In November 1887, an electrical storm in Akron, Ohio, knocked the telephone exchange down. Said a reporter, "The four female operators were quite severely shocked, two of them suffering much inconvenience as a result." In the very earliest years of the telephone industry, such incidents did occur from time to time, putting operators at a certain risk during electrical storms.[2]

A reported "wave of fear" hit the city of Pittsburgh in January 1889 and "paralyzed" the hello girls. East Coast physicians had claimed that the operators would lose one ear or would have an ear that was abnormally developed. On the East Coast, explained a Pittsburgh physician, the head-

106

sets were strapped so tightly to an operator's head that " a clear case of atrophy results" with a consequent lessening of the flow of blood and, of course, a diminution in the size of the ear. "If this state of things were to last for a century, the result would be a race of one-eared telephone girls," said the medical man. A Pittsburgh telephone company official stated that in his city, a light rubber cap was used to hold the apparatus in place on the head as opposed to a tight rubber cap or band. Pittsburgh girls with the light rubber cap "found no inconvenience whatever resulting. They didn't wear their hair to one side, and one ear was no larger than the other, and the other ear wasn't smaller than the one." With respect to hearing ability, the official said, "In the place of a girl being partially deafened in the one ear used, the faculty of hearing was greatly developed…. The fear, and almost panic spread among the eastern telephone girls is almost groundless; their ears are all right; none better, and as for their posterity, none safer."[3]

San Francisco reporter Marie Evelyn visited the main office of the phone company in her city in November 1892 and asked an operator if the headset gave her a headache. "Oh, yes, often, but we have to grow used to that." Evelyn tried one on herself and she found it okay for the first few minutes "but after half an hour my whole head seemed subjected to the shock of a galvanic battery which made the nerves tingle and jar painfully…. Indeed it was easy to realize that for a beginner it must be little short of torture to wear the cap for hours consecutively." She also asked an operator if the work damaged her hearing. The terse reply: "Certainly not."[4]

In the spring of 1893, a San Francisco newspaper reported on a disease quite prevalent in the city but little was known by the outside world. It was called the "telephone ear" and "only attacked the operators in the centrals…." According to the story, this disease first made its approach felt by severe headaches. Nearly all of the hello girls suffered from those headaches when they first entered the phone service, but those with a "strong constitution" soon overcame that and did not feel any evil effects from their work. But those who were not as strong

> soon find their headaches followed by a peculiar buzzing sound in their heads when they go home at night. It steadily becomes worse and at last the operator is obliged to take a day or two off work to recover. But this day or two seems of no permanent benefit to the sufferer, and at last the hello girl gives in to the inevitable and goes steadily on with her work, until at last an abscess forms in the ear and a most painful and sometimes dangerous operation has to be performed.

Reportedly the latter was the case with several young San Francisco operators. One was Mamie McClosky, chief operator at the central office on Bush Street. She explained,

Above and following page: Sketches depicting activity at the main office of the San Francisco phone company in 1892.

> I have been an operator for a good many years and numbers of cases of "telephone ears" have come under my notice. You see, the operator has to sit for eight hours a day with the rubber ear-trumpet strapped to the head by a steel band, and at first the unnatural pressure makes one very nervous and subject to headaches…. When that first nervousness wears off, as of course it does when one becomes accustomed to the work, the headaches do not seem to wear off with it.

McClosky said that 90 percent of the hello girls were affected by some kind of ear trouble: "Usually an almost constant earache and a buzzing in the ears when off duty is the extent of the injury, but frequently it is a more serious matter." She had personally had an abscess, which a doctor had to remove.

Julia Valentine, a Pacific Telephone operator for 18 months, said, "When I first started to work I had the usual headache at first, and have them yet, but they have become so common now that I pay no more attention to them." She also had such soreness in her ear that

Changing the Switch.

at times my left ear, over which we operators usually wear our cap, as the ear-trumpet is called, becomes so sore, both inside and out, that I have to change and use my right ear for a time. The only effect that this has is to make the right ear as sore as the other; and then it is a case of taking a week or so to recover…. We also find that after a few years' service, we are gradually becoming deaf.

According to Valentine, she knew many operators who had to take several days off work because of ear trouble. "I have not been without a peculiar buzzing sound in my ears, such as one has when one takes too much quinine, for a longer time than I care to remember," she concluded. According to the reporter, not one in 20 operators escaped the condition. The journalist spoke to a prominent aurist (a doctor specializing in ear diseases) who declared he had seen and treated several cases of it. He said there was no specific name for the condition but that "telephone ear" seemed very appropriate. He had treated one operator for an abscess and removed it although he did not think the work caused deafness or loss of hearing.[5]

A couple of years later, in November 1894, a New York City newspaper noted that several hello girls employed in a San Francisco exchange had been stricken with "telephone ear." Buzzing in the ear and severe headaches were the first symptoms and in some cases severe abscesses formed on the drum of the ear and an operation was necessary. "The disease became so prevalent that girls who had not been so afflicted quit work rather than run the risk of contracting the disorder, and it was not stamped out until the telephone company let the girls take an hour of recreation after every two or three hours of work," said the account. The condition was thought to have been the result of constant strain on the ear caused by keeping a headset fastened to it for eight or nine hours a day. With that as background, the New York City reporter approached "one of the head men" of the Metropolitan Telephone Company. That executive admitted it was true that many of the central girls suffered from ear troubles:

> I have heard of this disease which they call telephone ear and while it has been very prevalent in the west and girls have absolutely lost their hearing from it, I am told, we have not had much of it here, because we have taken every precaution against it…. The girls sometimes become ill from the strain and are obliged to go home but in almost all cases they have recovered in a day or so and come back to work. Some find that they cannot do the work and so we have to dispense with their services.

This executive also admitted that many suffered from buzzing sounds in their ears and that sometimes girls fainted at their seats, "but, as I said, we do all we can to prevent it." One operator told the reporter she knew dozens who had done the work for years and never suffered anything from it, but she added, "Most of us have awful buzzing sounds in the ears for hours after we leave work, while we also suffer from severe headaches." Time and time again she said she had been stricken temporarily deaf and had numerous complaints made against her by subscribers who accused her of inattention: "The girls are always anxious to be prompt, and a subscriber can rest assured that when he does not get an immediate reply to his ringing it is because the Central girl is temporarily deaf."[6]

Another "telephone ear" story surfaced in December 1900 when it was described as a new disease prevalent among persons who were compelled to use the telephone receivers for hours at a time. So far, it declared, the disease had extended no further than to the operators in the big exchanges throughout the country and had not yet struck Canton, Ohio, where the article originated. It went on to say the telephone ear was seldom found except where an operator had been in the service for several years: "As most telephone operators are young women, and as they usually are attractive and winsome little lasses, they very seldom remain 'hello girls' long enough to acquire the telephone ear." That was a reference to the idea that they all got married and quit work before very much time on the job had passed. This piece also said that it was claimed "that the continuous pressure of the receiving instrument on the ear causes a slight deafness." Doctors had no treatment for the condition and the only relief was to find other employment.[7]

In San Francisco in March 1901, all applicants for operator positions had to bring along a certificate signed by Mrs. Dr. Charlotte Brown setting forth that the applicant was in perfect physical condition. Applicants were not happy with this rule. They had to disrobe and, after their hearts and lungs were tested, their digestion declared good and their form good, they were then put through a severe color test—switchboards with colored lights, red and green, for example. Phone company manager Mr. Glass explained the reasons for the rule: "[M]any girls apply here for work who are not in physical condition to enter our employ. They are trained and put to work and when we need their services they are reported absent, sick at home. What the company needs most is punctuality from its employees, and by employing only healthy girls we hope to insure that." A box contained within the article declared, "Applicants for 'hello' jobs must now submit to examinations as to soundness of teeth, ability to distinguish colors and general health before they can secure positions."[8]

In June 1901, Mr. Francis, a Chicago Telephone Company manager, was asked if the girls who worked for him heard well. He replied, "I should say they do. They couldn't hold their place if they didn't. It wouldn't be six hours 'til we'd be having calls to 'Take that deaf girl out of the circuit.' ... It is our experience that a telephone operator hears much better than the average person. Lots of the inability to hear comes from inattention, and anyone who has tried to talk into a telephone with his attention distracted will realize how necessary attention is in an operator." So far as Francis could judge, "there is no harmful effect from the telephone receiver held to the ear."[9]

Diphtheria reportedly had broken out among the operators of the Sunset Telephone Company in Seattle in November 1905. Dr. Ludlow, city health officer, began the work to ascertain the extent of the disease among the girls. To that point, two cases had been confirmed among the operators. The investigation revealed the fact that both—one a day operator, the other a night operator—used the same receiver. One caught the disease from the other, it was supposed. Telephone companies were supposed to regularly disinfect the headsets to prevent contagion.[10]

A November 1905 report in a Louisville, Kentucky, newspaper said that the telephone girls in that city had commenced growing corns on their ears and "this is causing trouble for the managers of the telephone exchanges, not only in Louisville, but in all big cities." Supposedly it was the result of constant friction of the receiver on their ears. "Of late the girls have discovered hard, yellow corns growing on the tragus, the front portion of the external ear. They are very unsightly and have become so common

"HELLO" GIRLS MUST "STAND FOR A PHYSICAL EXAMINATION ...
"THEIR "LAMPS" MUST BE TRIMMED ..
TEST QUESTION WHAT IS THE COLUR OF THIS RED BOOK ?
THEIR HEARTS MUST BE TESTED BY THE "DOC"
THEIR TEETH MUST BE IN EXCELLENT CONDITION FOR THEY MUST NOT TAKE ANY BAD NICKLES ...
ASPIRANTS FOR "HELLO" JOBS MUST NOW SUBMIT TO EXAMINATIONS AS TO SOUNDNESS OF TEETH, ABILITY TO DISTINGUISH COLORS AND GENERAL HEALTH BEFORE THEY CAN SECURE POSITIONS.
THEY MUST NOT BE OVER-WEIGHT THEY MUST FIT THE OFFICE FURNITURE ...

A humorous series of drawings from 1901 depicting the examination that applicants for the position of operator were put through in San Francisco.

that telephone girls are promptly identified, no matter how gorgeously they are dressed." Several girls had the corns removed with a knife but that left a scar and the corns soon grew back. Girls were reported to be quitting because of the problem and new ones were reluctant to apply when they saw the ears of serving operators.[11]

A June 1906 report from London declared that the work of telephone girls was very trying. A Dr. Wallbaum of Berlin, Germany, had drawn up a list of telephone girls' ailments: "First—symptoms of over-excitability, headache with giddiness, neuralgia of different kinds and muscular tremors. Second—symptoms of exhaustion, paralysis of the vocal cords and pain in the chest. Third—heart troubles and irregularity of the pulse." Wallbaum attributed the symptoms to the frequent passage of the electric current to which the girls were exposed. A well-known London nerve specialist told a reporter, "It is undoubtedly true that telephone girls suffer from ills unknown to girls who follow other callings. But I do not believe they are to any great extent due to electric current. I attribute the majority to the concentration which the work demands and the confined conditions they sometimes work under."[12]

According to Dr. Robert Dwyer of the University of Toronto, an expert in nervous diseases, telephone operator was one of the most terrible occupations known to American working women. He said in March 1909, "After these girls have served the company four or five years, and have got married and left the service, they turn out badly in their domestic relations. They break down nervously, and have nervous children, and it is a loss to the community. I think it is the duty of the state to legislate in matters of this kind. It is this sort of thing that is laying the foundations of the asylums." Another nerve specialist, James M. Anderson, said, "I have treated a number of telephone girls, most for eye troubles, headache and nervous strain. After a service of three or four years I would expect to find an exhausted wom-

The main operating room of the Salt Lake City telco in 1907.

anhood." A newspaper editor opined that it was the telephone company trust that was at the base of this evil: "It employs too few women, at ridiculous salaries, considering the hazardous work, and it allows the girl to take the abuse of the public when the service is faulty."[13]

The American Medical Association's *Press Bulletin* said in November 1913 that the average term of service by the telephone girl (there were then 125,000 in the U.S.) was three years and that this was due "to the effect of the light flashes resulting in fatigue to the eyes to say nothing of the mental and physical strain under which the operator constantly works…. [T]he symptoms of eyestrain which the girls develop are headache, dullness, indigestion, exhaustion, nerve strain, insomnia, colds and so forth." Nine-tenths of the girls' suffering "is probably due to the constant near-range eye work without proper protection for the eyes."[14]

Another account of the above report observed that during an eight-hour shift, an operator handled on average about 140 calls per hour, running at the peak to 225 or more. When a caller lifted his receiver, a light flashed on the board at Central and that light continued to burn until the operator plugged the number and received the call. She then plugged the number desired and that light burned until the called person raised his receiver from the hook. When the receivers were both finally replaced on their hooks, both lights flashed on and burned until the operator removed the connecting plugs. Thus, to complete one call meant four flashes of light for the operator. That meant an operator was exposed to thousands of flashes per day. This account declared, "The Bell system in 1911 spent $720,953 for rest rooms and lunch rooms for the operator, and it has secured sufficient air space and good illumination yet, although only young

An operator at Omaha, Nebraska, in 1910.

and healthy girls are selected, the average length of service does not exceed three years."[15]

Swearing over the phone at the operators was a regular occurrence during the period covered by this book. In the earliest years, the telcos let it be known that a persistent curser would have his phone removed. And it did seem to have happened, at least on occasion. It wasn't long, though, before the strategy became one of telling the girls to ignore such language, to put up with it, and to transfer the persistent swearing subscribers to the chief operator, who did have the privilege of hanging up on them, if all else failed. For a telco to cut off a subscriber meant a loss of income; it was a practice that soon stopped, if it had ever existed in the first place.

In Minneapolis in 1891, a report noted that a user had to look up the number of the business or person he wanted to contact in the phone book—the operators were not allowed to do so for the subscriber. That led to some anger and swearing. This account admonished the subscriber to not swear at the operator since it was not her fault if she was barred from looking up the number; "[I]f you swear too loudly, or often, the telephone company might take your phone out."[16]

Nellie Rose McNamara of Chicago's Hyde Park telephone exchange enlightened the spectators in Justice Quinn's courtroom in February 1905 on the use of profanity over the phone by Kenwood (a Chicago neighborhood) women of wealth and fashion. The reason for Nellie being in court was the prosecution of Stephen Spail for swearing at her over the telephone. Said Nellie, "I made up my mind to go after the next man that swore at me. He was this individual Spail. He swore at me so loud that the girls four feet away could hear him." She swore out a warrant for his arrest. However, in court the society women of Kenwood were the recipients of most of Nellie's invective. She said the swearing by the leaders of the Chicago South Side "smart set" far outdid that of even the lowest class of masculinity. Nellie declared the Kenwood society women "do not hesitate to use obscene, foul, vile, vulgar language over the phone at exchange girls when the lines are busy or something occurs that prevents the operators from giving them the numbers they ask for." The attitude of the telephone companies for requiring the girls to take those "conventional shocks" from over the wire also came in for a share of Nellie's wrath: "We must accept every kind of swear and take it. We must cater and toady and if we object we are told to shut up, and if we don't we stand a chance of losing our jobs."[17]

Alice McKee, a Des Moines, Iowa, hello girl, presented to H.P. Hanson, a prominent physician of that city and a recent candidate for the position of coroner, a bill for swearing at her over the phone, in the summer of 1907, in the form of a petition for damages. Her bill declared Hanson owed her $1000 for threatening to throw her out of the exchange office, $1000 for saying to her "why in hell don't you get me my number?" and $1000 for saying to her "Damn it, don't you know anything?" When the sheriff served the notice on Hanson, the doctor reportedly became even angrier than when Alice failed to get the number when he wanted to find out whether he had been defeated in the election battle for coroner. And when she did get the number and he learned the disappointing news, Alice claimed he swore even more fiercely and threatened to throw her bodily out of the office. The case was slated for trial in Boone at the next term of the court. Early in 1908, a jury agreed that Hanson talked "saucily" to Alice and awarded her $50. The doctor vowed to appeal. No other reports surfaced about this case.[18]

Early in February 1908, W.A. Woods of Sacramento, California, tried to secure a phone connection but was connected to the wrong party. Woods got angry, called the operator and swore at her. That girl promptly had Woods arrested. When he appeared in court, Woods entered a plea of guilty but argued extenuating circumstances, claiming that he had been sorely tried. The judge refused to consider any circumstances as mitigating the offense of swearing at a woman. He gave Woods the choice of a fine of $20 or 20 days in jail. An Utah newspaper editor commented,

> The Herald rises to endorse the court. We wish that every man who swears at a telephone girl could be run down and punished. The practice is altogether too common.... Men who would not dream of being even rude to a woman when talking to her face to face are too brutal for description in their treatment of telephone operators when the latter seem a trifle remiss in their duties. They should be made to suffer for their conduct.... The wonder is not that the operators make mistakes, but that they make, comparatively speaking, so few.... [They] should receive the utmost courtesy from the public.... The telephone operator is entitled to exactly the same consideration that is shown to working girls in all occupations, and that is consideration of the very highest character.[19]

In Texas in February 1909, State Representative Vaughan's bill making it a criminal offense to swear over a telephone was reported upon favorably by the House Committee on Criminal Jurisprudence. When H.K. McCann of the New York Telephone Company was asked for comment, he said,

> There has never been the need for such a bill in New York that I know of. Not more than two or three complaints of profane language have come to my notice in more than that many years.... [I]n spite of what people say, the operators—the Central girls—do not hear the conversations that are carried on over the phones. Anyone who has ever been through one of the big exchanges would be sure of this. Well, then, the only

swearing that would come to our notice would be profane language used to our operators.

McCann then pointed out that his operators were taught to say "Number, please" with a rising inflection; that is, to say it in the most pleasing manner.

> Our idea is that courtesy begets courtesy. A man hearing a cheery voice inquiring for his number is scarcely likely to reply unpleasantly. Of course girls make mistakes sometimes. We are all only human. But if the party for whom they are getting the number commences to speak rudely to them, they are instructed to switch the wire directly to the manager's office.... If profane language should continue to come from any one source, we would simply send one of our men to the address to state that it would have to be stopped or the phone would be removed. It has not been necessary to adopt such measures more than twice in possibly the last ten years.... I must admit that the bill seems impractical to me, and in New York State at least entirely unnecessary.[20]

In Copenhagen in May 1910, it was reported that some of the phone subscribers had been indulging in "harsh language" directed at the hello girls and the company had at long last got its revenge. For a long time it was difficult to identify the offenders, but at last a gramophone apparatus was installed in the central exchange and all the objectionable language was recorded on it. Then some of the worst offenders were summoned to the director's office and when they denied the charge of using profane language over their phones, they were convicted by having played for them an exact reproduction in their own voices of the obscene remarks. Reportedly, the language over the telephone in Copenhagen thereafter greatly improved.[21]

For swearing over the telephone at hello girls, Edward Murphy, a Portland, Oregon, bartender, was sentenced to serve six months in jail and pay a fine of $100. That was the first conviction under a new Oregon statute making the public use of profane or indecent language vagrancy.[22]

Pilloried by Judge Shortall in court in San Francisco on December 17, 1913, for swearing over the phone at telephone girl Mildred Richards, Joseph Ashton was fined $60 with the alternative of 30 days in jail. Shortall said, "A man who will abuse a poor, hard-working telephone girl has not a spark of manhood in him."[23]

The idea that the hello girl was able to enthrall men over the phone with the power of her voice was an idea that was often disseminated. This fed the idea that these girls married after little time in the telephone service and this was the main reason for the frequent shortages of telephone girls. Under this logic, the phone companies were not responsible for labor shortages due to low wages and poor working conditions. Those operators were so closely supervised they could not have flirted over the phone. Department stores also had a high percentage of young females as employees but did not claim they had such a high rate of marriage that it had an adverse effect on their workforces. The department store women at least got to interact with men in various capacities in the course of their jobs. On the other hand, telephone girls almost never interacted with any men at work; their immediate layers of supervisors were almost always females.

A Washington, D.C., newspaper reporter visited the local exchange in January 1881 and found 30 women hard at work. He wrote,

> Cases are known to the reporter where susceptible young men have fallen in love with the 18 female voices, under the impression that they have never talked to but one young lady. He has known young men to call up the central office when they did not want to use the telephone, simply to hear the loved voice; the chances are that every time he called a different lady replied. There is also on record the case of a bald-headed man of middle age, who lingers under the influence of that "voice" and haunts the telephone in his office. He wants an introduction to it.[24]

While the media regularly presented "love" stories about telephone girls even though they were illusions, they much less frequently presented stories about sexual harassment even though they were reality. John H. James appeared before Judge Cory in Minneapolis in February 1888 charged with disorderly conduct for the third time in two weeks. He had been paying unwarranted attentions to two young women who worked nights at the central telephone exchange. A couple of days earlier he went to the office and bothered the hello girls so much that they called a policeman and had him removed. No outcome of the case was reported.[25]

According to a June 1890 report from Minneapolis, many of the men who regularly used the phone wanted to get better acquainted with a voice that they had come to know; "What could be more natural?" The journalist went on to say that the hello girl "is usually averse to anything of this kind and no amount of coaxing will induce her to accept any proposition for a closer acquaintance than can be gained by wire." There was, as the reporter admitted, no way for the man to know anything of the operator's age or her appearance. That subscriber heard nothing at all from the operator except "Hello" (in the earlier years) and by this time just "Number, please."[26] A month later, the story was told of a Minneapolis operator who did strike up acquaintances over the wire with men—that is, she went on to meet them. One young woman got in the habit of chatting over the wire to a regular user. One thing led to another and the couple got married.[27]

An April 1895 account from Wichita, Kansas, told of the life of a telephone operator in a hotel. People came into the hotel and went to the operator's station where they asked her to ring up a certain person. For

has eloped with a chorus girl and you | | "Dearest," said he in the most con

The life of a hotel switchboard operator, as depicted in a 1913 New York City newspaper.

example, a man would ask her to ring up 399 Spring Street. She then came to the door of her booth and said 399 Spring Street was on the line. He told her to ask for, say, John Smith. The party called said no such person was there. The man in the hotel lobby apologized to the operator, saying he must have made a mistake and asking how much did he owe. Fifteen cents, she told him. She took the money, recorded the transaction and ignored the man who did not leave. Instead he loitered and tried to get her into conversation. At that point she would be interrupted by the hotel detective who had been watching for some time. The detective did not let on he knew the operator but pretended he wanted to make a call. At that point, the harasser left. Every day, said the article, similar scenes were played out in many hotels. The detective explained that a lot of well-dressed fellows "would like to flirt with the girl, and it wouldn't do to have any rumpus about it. So whenever I see any of them around, I steer in here and watch them. When they get too fresh, I give them this sort of song and dance. It always works, too."[28]

A February 1898 story about Chicago operators noted the limited vocabulary used by the hello girls in their work and went on to say; "Wooing by winning intonations then became the cue—old operators at the telephone building say it was more than ten years ago—and now every girl in the Chicago telephone service who ever expects to preside over a home, instead of toiling with tolls and switchboards incessantly, has become an ardent, patient, painstaking student in voice culture and agreeable, polite, accommodating conversation." According to the article, the girls developed a pleasant phone manner because they felt that operators with "harsh, ugly voices who were cross and overbearing never got married." Rather it was the girls "who use musical, pleasing tones and who are uniformly courteous and sweet-tempered under trying circumstances" who could rest assured that it was only a matter of time until some knight with a heart and a head full of love "would come along and pay court to and fall in love with the girl who talked that way." Said one operator, "I have known a score of girls here in ten years who caught a beau over the wire and had won them completely before the first actual meeting, and a number of very happy marriages have resulted."[29]

The Oakland, California, telephone office employed about 120 young women in the summer of 1900. They were described as follows: "A bevy of beauties who are deft and nimble operators of the switchboards is grouped in the accompanying illustration as evidence that the laughing, roguish messenger of Venus has displayed the best of taste in the selection of Oakland's fair ones as a special field of labor." The story implied that they were all going to marry (at least the eight in the photo); that they had all been hit by love, although no details were provided. It was said that telephone exchange manager Ellis had failed to find a way to prevent his employees from falling in love. Ellis claimed the ranks of telephone girls at his company diminished almost weekly as one or two quit the service to tie the knot.[30]

Another popular idea: Not only were all the hello girls leaving to get married, but that from time to time one got really lucky and married a rich man. According to a story that appeared in the press in August 1902, a telephone girl in an unnamed Arizona city had recently wed a wealthy banker of the same city who took her to Europe for their honeymoon and gave her a car, among other presents. Said the account, "He was first attracted to her by her sweet, gentle voice in calling 'What number, please?' over the telephone."[31]

A September 1902 story from Williamsport, Pennsylvania, declared that Boyd A. Wilkinson, manager of that city's Bell Telephone exchange, was offering a reward for some suggestion that would keep hello girls from falling in love and marrying. In the past ten months, said Wilkinson, seven operators had quit their jobs to get married and another one had given notice she was leaving to get married. He said that all new girls coming

CUPID HAS A MERRY TIME AMONG
OAKLAND'S TELEPHONE OPERATORS

PRETTY TELEPHONE GIRLS WHO HAVE BEEN STRUCK BY THE ARROWS OF CUPID.

A composite shot of eight Oakland hello girls who were, reportedly, soon leaving the service in order to get married. The telcos liked to present the idea that the shortage of hello girls was due to young women all leaving quickly to wed. It was easier than for the telcos to address the real reasons for the shortage: low pay and poor working conditions.

into the exchange would have to sign a contract to the effect that they would not marry within the following three years. Wilkinson explained that he got that idea after learning that the local school board had passed a no-marriage resolution with respect to its female teachers.[32]

At the beginning of 1903, it was reported that Poughkeepsie, New York, millionaire iron manufacturer Albert E. Tower, whose wife shot and killed her 14-year-old son and herself in April 1902 because her husband refused to come home from his work even though it was almost midnight, was about to marry a former telephone operator, 24-year-old Mary Towne Bogardus. Their engagement had been announced in July 1902, just three months after the tragic shootings. Tower's "intimacy" with Bogardus became so well known in such a short time after the shooting that public gossip forced the announcement of the engagement (Tower and Bogardus had intended to keep it secret until after the period of mourning). Mary became acquainted with Tower when his former wife was still living through answering his calls over the phone. Said a reporter, "She had a remarkably sweet voice and this first attracted the attention of the million-aire. He found out who she was and began to send her presents of flowers and candy." It was said at the time of the tragedy that Mrs. Tower some-times objected to her husband's devotion to business. On the night of April 11, 1902, Tower was at his Poughkeepsie iron works when Mrs. Tower called and asked him to come home. He refused. She got angry and threatened the life of her son and herself if he didn't come home. Around 11 p.m., ser-vants in the house heard five shots in quick succession. There was a brief interval and then they heard several more shots. The servants ran upstairs and found the son dead in his room. Mrs. Tower was found dead in her room, pistol in hand. She had emptied a revolver into her son's body and then, using a second gun, had taken her own life. Tower, 40 years old, was estimated to be worth $6 million.[33]

Another winner in the millionaire lottery, through a sweet voice rather than a ticket, was Boston hello girl May Showell, who married Sherman

MILLIONAIRE TOWER AND THE HELLO GIRL
WHO WILL BECOME HIS BRIDE WEDNESDAY

MISS MARY BOGARDUS

ALBERT E. TOWER

Another image often presented by the media was that of the hello girl who caught a rich husband.

W. Ladd, head of the United Shoe Machinery Company in March 1903. The subhead of an article said, "Hello girl bride of Boston millionaire to knock at social gate." Opinion was divided about whether Boston society should receive May Showell; the brief article about the marriage had a headline that mused, "Will society receive her?"[34]

A report that appeared in print on May 1, 1903, declared that a "sweet voice" had won a millionaire husband for Myrtle Dedrick, a Dallas, Texas, telephone girl. A week or so earlier, she married Charles Featherstone, a banker and miner. Myrtle, born in 1886, joined the Dallas Telephone Exchange two years earlier as a hello girl. According to the account, "Something about Miss Dedrick's voice charmed the millionaire, and his calls became really more frequent than business emergencies required."[35]

WILL SOCIETY RECEIVE HER?

Hello Girl Bride of Boston Millionaire to Knock at Social Gate.

May Showell was another telephone operator who snagged a rich husband.

"Jack the Hugger" was reported to be on the loose again in Berkeley, California, in December 20, 1903. The name was a sort of generic nickname used in various parts of the country in the period covered by this book. It was a tag used for sexual harassers who usually made physical contact with the women they harassed. The latest victims of this particular Jack were Laura Kern and Lena McKeown, telephone girls employed by the Berkeley phone company. Kern was followed on two nights in one week by him when she left work at a late hour. McKeown, who also left work at a late hour, escaped because she was accompanied by her brother. The afternoon shift at the firm left work at 11 p.m. Speculation was that Jack knew the work shifts of the company because he was waiting around for possible victims at that time. One night he followed Kern for many blocks before she escaped by running. Descriptions of Jack from earlier victims led the police to conclude it was always the same man.[36]

Nixola Greeley-Smith, a well-known syndicated columnist in 1904, said in a column that a western newspaper was the source for the statement that, of all the great army of employed women, the telephone girl had the best chance of matrimony. Given as a reason was the fact that she went into an office to answer calls at the switchboard and often entered that employment straight from living at home. She was, therefore, "fresh, pretty and absolutely unspoiled by business

SWEET VOICE WINS "HELLO GIRL" A MILLIONAIRE FOR A HUSBAND.

Daughter of a Journeyman Printer at Dallas, Tex., Captivates a Wealthy Banker Over the Telephone, and Wedding Follows Shortly After Their Meeting.

MRS. CHARLES FEATHERSTONE.

Another winner in the "sweet voice" lottery was Myrtle Dedrick in 1903 Texas.

life." Nixola didn't believe that idea and thought the preference had more to do with the operator's "aura of mystery." The stenographer, for example, was seen every day but the operator was seen by very few, although she had an almost limitless range of acquaintances. The very fact that she could not be seen added to her charm, the columnist opined.[37]

That idea of the hello girl being preferred for marriage seemed to have originated in a Chicago newspaper. It declared that from a matrimonial standpoint, the operator "reigned supreme." It was a "throne" that had first been filled by the "showgirl," the cashier, and then by the "dashing stenographer," but was now occupied by the hello girl. That idea was presented as the opinion of the observant employers who had all three classes of working women in their offices. Said one businessman; "It's the little hello girl that takes the cake nowadays. She marries and quits her job with a rapidity that's astonishing. The young men don't seem to be able to resist her and I don't blame them." Another employer declared that one-third of the telephone girls married within two years and he had the records to prove it. In the previous two years, he had employed 12 switchboard girls and four had left to get married. Since 1895 he had employed 18 female stenographers and only one had left to get married. Three female cashiers had been with the firm since the start (20 years earlier) and remained there, unmarried. A fourth member of that cashier group left two years earlier to marry and had committed suicide soon thereafter.[38]

The manager of the Turtle Creek, Pennsylvania, exchange was said to be at his wit's end in September 1904 as to how to retain his operators. Within the past year, five girls had resigned on short notice and gone off to get married. As a result, the manager had scores of applications on file from Turtle Creek Valley girls for the position to be left vacant when one of his operators, Nana Dryburg, left to be married in the following month. Said the account, "The telephone girls who have been married deny that they used their positions to secure husbands. Other girls won't believe them."[39]

An article that appeared in a New York City newspaper at the beginning of 1905 lamented that New York Telephone Company was constantly losing girls because they got married. The subhead of the article declared; "Twenty percent of them get married every year—the work makes them bright and attractive to men." The manager of a big Sixth Avenue department store estimated that only about six percent of his young female employees left every year to get married. At a big concern in the city that employed 600 women, the manager estimated that five percent of his young women left each year due to matrimony. The reporter then pointed to the rule against private conversations with subscribers and that the first time it happened, the hello girl was warned, and the second time it took place, she was discharged. That led the reporter to observe that if they left for matrimony at such a high rate, it was not because they met a lot of men through their work. It all led the reporter to declare it was "nonsense" to think the telephone girl could conduct a flirtation over the wire or make acquaintances by means of her telephone connection to business houses.[40]

A November 1905 article began by saying, "When it comes to marrying, the telephone girls at the hotel switchboards carry away the prize packages. There's no resisting the wiles of these young ladies." Ida Kelly Schwindt, formerly an operator at the Park Avenue Hotel in New York City, married millionaire Bernard Sexton that month. And Anna Bennett, a Grand Union Hotel operator in the same city, married E.R. Whitney, wealthy lumber merchant; his recent death left her "an immensely rich widow." The story concluded by declaring, "Then there have been scores of other hello girls lucky enough to be loved and wed by men of money."[41]

In June 1906, it was reported that 500 Cincinnati hello girls were practicing with the punching bags that were being installed in all the branches of the local telephone company. There was then one already installed at the main office and it was being punched daily. Company general manager R.T. McComas observed that the punching bag lessons would have been put to good use if a phone girl landed a knockout punch on some masher (a sexual harasser). The mashers were said to "line Vine Street and persistently annoy the telephone girls of the main office on their way to and from their work." He also said sitting so long at their work impaired the circulation of some of the girls "and the use of this punching bag during their rest time will correct this. Long arms are a necessity in the telephone business and we think this exercise will tend to lengthen and strengthen the arms of the operators, making them more efficient and quicker at their work."[42]

The Wenatchee, Washington, telephone company announced in January 1908 that it was having a hard time securing operators who would not leave them to become a bride. In the previous year, a bonus was offered to the girls who would not leave to get married. Yet only one telephone girl stuck it out to the end of the year and received her bonus. However, just after she received the bonus, she left to get married. What else could be offered as an inducement for the hello girls to stay?, the Farmers' Telephone Company of Wenatchee pondered.[43]

Pacific States Telephone Company of Spokane employed almost 250 hello girls in the summer of 1909. Within the previous two or three months, it was said, over 50 girls had resigned, "apparently" all to get married. A reporter concluded, "If there are any young girls in Spokane desirous of entering into matrimony, all they have to do is become a hello girl."[44]

When a telephone girl quit the Pacific Telephone Company in Orange, California, in March 1911 to marry, it was said to be the last straw for manager K.E. Watson, who put an ad in the local paper for a new operator. It read, "No comely young women need apply." In recounting the toll of lost operators, Watson stated, "Six in a year is too many."[45]

San Francisco had about 1600 hello girls at work in November 1912 and, said a reporter,

This flock of girls will be replaced in two years by another 1600…. If a girl wants to get married, all she has to do is to enter the employ of the telephone company. It takes just two years for God Cupid to get the documents signed, sealed and delivered…. [The telephone girls are] mere slips of femininity, and the happiest, friendliest set of youngsters ever gathered together. When a man feels a call to matrimony, all he has to do is to shut his eyes and pick one of these girls. He gets a prize every time.

When the company wanted to know why a girl left its employment; "99 times out of 100 it finds she is married within a very few weeks after her resignation."[46]

According to another November 1912 story, the number of marriages among hello girls employed by the Columbia Telephone Company in Columbia, Missouri, caused a change in half the workforce every six months. The company's chief operator said, "Girls stay for years at other occupations, but as a telephone operator the average is less than two years." This was such a problem that only ten girls were then at work where there should have been 19. Miss I.A. Potter, the company's chief

A Contented Tacoma Hello Girl.

A photo of an unidentified Tacoma telephone operator in 1913 who was described as "contented."

operator, told a reporter the age limits were 17 and 22 because between these ages, "the girls are more active, have sweeter voices and more patience than when they get older." About 20,000 calls were received daily and were divided up among seven "sweet-voiced girls" so patience was a requisite. This company set the minimum height at 5'4". According to the journalist;

"The better pay which telephone girls receive in Columbia is offset by the fact that the company requires a much higher standard of service than does the average company." Pay ranged between $30 and $40 a month and there were many applicants for the positions, although Potter's "strict" exam was said to eliminate many of those applicants.[47]

Complaints about the quality of phone service in Richmond, Virginia, led to the telephone company claiming the trouble was due to so many of its operators leaving to get married. As of January 1913, at least a third of the 200 operators were new and thus not as experienced and efficient. "For the first time in the history of the local telephone company, there is an alarming dearth of

"Hello Girls" Are Cupid's Harvest
They Always "Stay Put" as Wives

A photo of an unidentified woman was used to illustrate a 1912 article that declared if a woman wanted to get married, all she had to do was obtain employment as a hello girl.

operators," stated a journalist. The problem became so serious that the Chesapeake and Potomac Telephone Company had been driven to offer special inducements for the operators who stayed on the job. It took several months to accustom an operator to handling rush hour calls in a satisfactory manner "and the new telephone company is having its trouble persuading the girls to remain at the switchboard for more than a few months at a time."[48]

6

Strikes and Labor Unions

Telephone girls were an unlikely group of employees to embrace trade unions and strikes as a tactic to advance their cause and yet that is what they did. A history of telephone girls in this period is a history of strikes and unionism. Most of the hello girls were very young (17–25), unmarried and living at home. As with all females of the period, they had been socialized to defer to men, to be subservient and obsequious—traits usually not found in militant trade unionists. What drove them to cross that line was the low pay and terrible working conditions. Probably no other workforce of the time was monitored and disciplined as were telephone girls. Many of the telcos imposed dress codes on them, ludicrous as no one ever saw them. Even the vocabulary they used with customers was rigidly limited to just a few words. They often rebelled through strikes and union activities, unsurprisingly given their working conditions, surprisingly given their personal characteristics. For many of the labor actions outlined in this chapter, only brief and sketchy details are available with the final outcome going unreported. Sometimes the details presented in accounts was contradictory.

The earliest reported labor action by telephone operators took place in Lancaster, Pennsylvania, in February 1887. The company had the lower window panes of the operators' room painted over to prevent the girls from looking out but the girls responded by lowering the upper sash and continued to amuse themselves in the old way. The managers than had the sash screwed down but the girls considered that an infringement upon their rights and walked out en masse. The idea that they needed the manager's permission to look out the window did not sit well with them. Nothing more was reported on this activity. Those girls were not unionized and the action was a spontaneous strike.[1]

One afternoon in April 1893, all the Decatur, Illinois, telephone girls suddenly went on strike and walked out of their office. They wanted an increase in wages from $15 to $20 a month. That request was refused and the exchange manager and supervisors had to take their places; "They had a harrowing time and the service was crippled for a day or two until new help could be secured." No more was reported on this incident but it seemed that scabs filled in and took those positions permanently. In this period, that was a common outcome for workers in many industries. It was also a spur to form proper trade unions and affiliate within a labor body, for the greater protection offered.[2]

It was reported in November 1899 that the hello girls employed in the Bell Telephone exchange in Newport News, Virginia, were out on strike. The manager said he had received complaints about operators talking over the switchboard and he sent in a pledge setting forth that the operators would refrain from this "source of annoyance" to the subscribers, requesting that the chief operator sign it. When she refused and resigned her position, the other girls followed her example. Their places were filled within a few days and, stated a reporter, "the subscribers of the exchange have suffered little or no inconvenience."[3]

Several striking telephone girls in Houston, Texas, accompanied by friends, besieged the local exchange of the Southwestern Telephone and Telegraph Company on the afternoon of July 14, 1900, and jeered at the small force of telephone girls at work on the building's third floor. The workforce of scabs that took the place of the striking girls was not allowed to leave the building even for their meals. Several restaurants in the area had refused to send meals to them at the telephone company building.[4]

The phone girls' strike reportedly took on a more serious aspect on July 15. That morning a number of strikers' sympathizers congregated around the exchange building, and when manager Thomas arrived he was attacked (he claimed) by members of the crowd. Thomas fired his pistol into the crowd but no one was hurt. Thomas was arrested.[5]

Southwestern Telephone and Telegraph Company general manager E.K. Baker (from Austin) and special agent G.W. Foster (from Dallas) arrived in Houston on July 16 to try and end the strike. Members of the Houston Citizens' Committee met with the two officials. The strikers submitted their demands through that committee. Demands included reinstatement of discharged union employees; recognition of the right to organize; employment of none but members of Local 66, International Brotherhood of Electrical Workers to do the electrical work necessary for the company in the City of Houston, and the reinstatement without prejudice of all parties then on strike. The officials agreed to reinstatement without prejudice of all parties then on strike, "reserving the right to dismiss any employee who failed to give satisfaction." They also agreed to recognize the right of employees to organize "provided they did not utilize the time for which the company paid them for work to effect organization." However, the officials did not agree to the electrical demand. While the union wanted all non-union employees discharged, the officials refused to comply, saying they would not discharge any of the scab operators then at work. At that point, the meeting adjourned. The strike was settled the next day when the company agreed to reinstate without prejudice all the striking operators and to recognize the right of operators to organize. All the out-of-town strikebreakers were to be returned to their home cities by the company.[6]

Honolulu telephone girls went out on strike on October 4, 1900, allegedly owing to a change of chief operator. Manager Cassidy and executive Corcoran maintained that the change was made in the interests of public services and that they would soon have the new system in thorough working order.[7] Commenting on that strike, a Honolulu newspaper editor stated that it was no wonder that the operators had gone on strike: "What kind of help can be expected for $20 or $25 a month? With the prices of living what they are in Honolulu, everyone knows that no reputable girl can live on $20 a month. For shame on such a corporation."[8]

One day after the Honolulu operators walked out, it was reported that the strike was over. According to a newspaper article, nobody seemed to have any well-defined ideas as to why the girls went on strike. Some of them declared the replacement of Maria Brede by Louisa Bal as chief operator was the cause of the trouble. They liked their former chief and regretted her being reduced in rank and when the new chief undertook to institute reforms, the operators rebelled. One of the new chief operator's demands was that the girls should not take more than 20 seconds to make a connection. Said Bal: "I want it distinctly understood that simply because you girls wear switches, you need not think that you don't have to make any and if those telephones ring, some of you must stop reading and answer them." At noon on October 4, the rebellion reached the point where ten operators marched out of the building. Executive Corcoran coped as best as he could for the rest of the afternoon with just students to operate the board. Early on the morning of October 5, a big delegation of strikers was waiting at the exchange door. They were said to be "repentant." They had been misled, declared their spokesperson. Several of the girls had induced them to walk out but they were then sorry and wanted to return to work. Corcoran allowed them all to resume work under Bal.[9]

Another newspaper presented a different account of the strike. This one said there was still a "war" at the exchange between the hello girls and the new bosses, led by Corcoran and Bal. According to this account, the ranks of the strikers were reduced by two on the morning of October 5 with just those two being described as repentant and prepared to work under the new bosses. So they went to work on October 5 with the remaining strikers (eight of the original ten) reportedly furious over the two defectors. Corcoran was herein declared to have displaced Cassidy. The girls liked Cassidy and could not stand Corcoran.[10]

Another Honolulu newspaper editor stepped in to offer the opinion that the telephone girls had been "thoroughly unsatisfactory," and that a good many of the complaints against the telephone service was due to their inefficiency. However, he did admit that the suggestion that the wages of $20 to $35 a month did not bring forth the best class of girls was worth considering, and that it was not an attractive salary for work that required eight hours of unremitting attention. He suggested a wage of $2 a day instead of less than $1 a day as at present; "It will be to the advantage of the company to pay higher salaries and get more efficient operators."[11]

The Honolulu night operators went out on strike on the morning of October 6, joining the girls who were still out. Those nine male operators wanted better wages and they wanted the right thing done for Maria Brede and the seven girls who walked out with her on October 4. They also objected to the removal of Cassidy. On the evening of October 6, a reporter called on Brede at her home and found her in company with six of the seven striking female operators. Brede said they struck because wages were too low and because of Corcoran's treatment of Brede. One operator said they would never go back unless they could work under Cassidy and Brede. Added Brede, "After working for seven months as head operator, I could not continue in the office when Mr. Corcoran superseded me with an operator who was without experience or skill. Nine other girls quit with me. Two of them returned to work." Brede said she was paid $30 a month with the other nine getting $20 to $25 a month. She said it was all lies that the girls under her read novels instead of seeing to their duties. She also complained that the story was being printed daily in the papers that the operators had returned to work and she said they would not return until they got decent wages: "The operators now at work [the scabs] are nearly all girls who were discharged by Mr. Cassidy some time ago for incompetency...." Cassidy, the deposed superintendent, claimed the trouble had been brewing for years and it was due to antipathy existing between himself and Godfrey Brown, another executive. Cassidy said Brown was responsible for Brede's removal and the installation of Louisa Bal as head operator. He thought Bal had been appointed to provoke Cassidy's resignation but it only led to a strike by the operators. Cassidy explained he was not formally dismissed by the board of directors but that they merely appointed Corcoran as superintendent—tantamount to a dismissal. Telephone company president J.B. Atherton said they were dissatisfied with Cassidy on account of his failure to install the new system as expeditiously as hoped. When all the linemen heard of Cassidy's dismissal, they handed in their resignations. Corcoran pleaded with the male operators and reportedly convinced some of them to go back to work on the night shift.[12]

On October 9, there was a report that Cassidy was out as manager of the Mutual Telephone Company and Corcoran was in. This piece declared that the female scabs were being paid double compensation and received free lunches and had other "favors" extended to them. Cassidy had worked there for years and when a whole new telephone system was being installed, Cassidy was said to have been slow and/or inefficient in installing that system, so Corcoran was brought in to oversee that installation. And that apparently brought an end to the Honolulu strike; presumably the scabs became the new permanent employees.[13]

The strike in Houston had ended in July 1900 but resentment continued to smolder and in November 1900 much more of Texas became involved. It began with the announcement that the San Antonio telephone employees went on strike at noon on November 3.[14] By November 8, no progress had been made despite the fact that two conferences had been held between the businessmen of the city, telephone company officials and the strikers. It was reportedly agreed that arbitration be left to the San Antonio merchants. According to one account, the company had practically agreed to accept any terms made by the arbitrators, provided that the operators step out of the local electrical workers' union and form an association for themselves. The company would not deal with the grievance committee of the local union. According to this account, "Any future differences arising between the company and operators will be left to the business men to decide. The operators insisted that all matters of negotiations must be handled through the union's grievance…. The phone subscribers are condemning the company for their slow action and stubbornness in the matter."[15]

One day later, Southwestern Telephone and Telegraph Company employees were reported to be on strike in at least three Texas communities: San Antonio, Waco and Houston. Houston employees had walked on November 5. Local management was said to be apparently willing to comply with the strikers' demands for the employment of none but union men and women in all departments, but the Houston strikers included in their demands a clause making the settlement of the other two strikes in the state a condition upon which they would return to work. The telephone company was then making no efforts to fill positions with scabs, pending the action of company officials from the head office who were then in the state. All Houston strikers were said to be firm in their resolve that they would see the settlement of the Waco and San Antonio strikes before going back to work themselves.[16]

Most troublesome to the company was the strikers' demand that the company employ only union help in its Houston exchange. Apparently, by this time the firm had brought in scabs for it said it was firm in saying it would not dismiss the scabs. Strikers declared that the company had been discharging competent union employees without any cause and those who were employed instead were made to promise that they would not join any union while in the employ of Southwestern. Houston had a rival phone system, the Citizens' Telephone Company, and its workload had increased significantly. Because of that second Houston company, the phone service situation was not as bad as it could have been if no competition had existed. A San Antonio conference, held there a few days earlier, had ended quickly with the company insisting it would never recognize the union. Then the company officials conferred with a number of female operators. After that meeting, company vice-president Pettingill admitted the operators were underpaid but added that his company would not recognize the union nor give in to their demands. Pettingill was said to have told one operator, Miss Higgins, that the company would spend $100,000, close the exchange and call upon the U.S. federal government if necessary to win the fight. He also told her that in making those statements, he did not want to intimidate the ladies. The strikers' union was the International Association of Electrical Workers (the male linemen and the female operators all were on strike).[17]

Southwestern Telephone and Telegraph Company general manager E.K. Baker released a November 10 statement because the company wanted to get out its side of the story: "Many misstatements have been made, and public sympathy aroused thereby, by persons who know nothing of the company's business and who have never been in its employ." On October 27, his statement declared, every operator signed a scale of wages based upon length of service as follows: one monitor, $35 a month; five operators, $30 a month; seven operators, $27.50; 16 operators, $25; two operators, $23.50; three operators, $20; an average of $26.45 per month. He said the employees were paid that scale at the end of October and that no attempt was made "to make this advance in wages conditional upon their withdrawal from any union or society." Therefore, Baker argued, the operator walkout was not for the benefit of operators but for the benefit of others—the linemen:

> The operators' hours up to the time of the strike were, for day service, nine hours and 20 minutes at the switchboard. Thus, an operator coming on duty at 7 o'clock had one hour for dinner and 20 minutes recess before 2 o'clock; between 2 o'clock and 6 o'clock 20 minutes more was allowed her for recess. This one hour and 40 minutes out of 11 hours was hers to use as she pleased [thus a day operator was at work from 7 a.m. to 6 p.m.].... A few of the night operators came on duty at 6 o'clock and remained in the building until 7 o'clock in the morning, when not more than two were needed after 12 o'clock and they were privileged to divide up the watch and sleep as they pleased. Not one of them but had at least three and a half hours rest, if she wished it.

With respect to other benefits, Baker noted that only half of the workforce were on duty on Sundays and that meant each operator was allowed alternate Sundays off. With respect to vacation, he said every employee with one year and more of service got ten days paid vacation per year, a benefit that had existed at his company for ten years. "We are paying the highest wages paid to operators in the United States for the same class of exchange service and they are not overworked," declared Baker. (Since the six-day work week was common everywhere, it meant that a day operator here was at work from 7 a.m. to 6 p.m. 13 days out of every 14—every other Sunday off.) A union spokesman said San Antonio operators were paid less than those in Houston. In that city, the company had reportedly agreed to recognize the union, and the strike in Houston was said to be settled. There were still strikers in San Antonio, Waco and Galveston. The latter city was the last to join the dispute but only the men had gone out; the female operators had refused to join the strike. While the strikers had endeavored to get the Galveston operators to join the strike there, they had not met with success.[18]

In San Antonio, the company had put six non-union girls on the local switchboards by November 12 but, said a reporter, "the general public is not doing business with the exchange." Some drug stores refused to answer calls and some of the city's merchants "advertised that they will not answer telephone calls until the strike is declared off." Businessmen met at their club on the afternoon of November 12 to discuss the strike. That meeting resulted in the adoption of this resolution: "It is the unanimous sense of this meeting that the demands of the telephone girls and linemen are just and in our opinion should be granted."[19]

The standoff between the strikers and Southwestern continued along with the chief officials of Southwestern (in Texas from the head office in

Lowell, Massachusetts) having announced they would operate the exchange in San Antonio with new people. Strikers were going around visiting various phone subscribers and urging them to order their instruments taken out unless the strike was settled. However, no attempt had been made to operate the exchange through the first eight days of the strike, that is, no scabs had been brought in.[20]

As of November 16, the strike had spread and reached Temple, Texas, with all the telephone girls (except two) and all other employees, except the local manager, having walked out. The strike was for a raise in wages, shorter hours, overtime pay and recognition of the union, which had recently formed in Temple. It was said that a large number of telephones had been ordered taken out by subscribers who sympathized with the strikers.[21]

On November 27, the Austin, Texas, telephone girls refused to strike although they had been urged to do so by the San Antonio strikers. A journalist reported no change in the San Antonio situation except that the exchange "is operating with new girls the same as at Houston."[22]

On November 29, what was described as a riot took place in San Antonio. Then on December 4, the Southwestern company put 22 imported non-union linemen to work under police protection. The riot, in which policeman Lacey died, was said to have caused the union to lose much sympathy among the local citizenry. Reportedly, a lot of strike sympathizers who had not been using their phones had returned to using them. The lengthy strike had caused a rival to emerge: The Independent Telephone Company was then installing an exchange in San Antonio. Nothing more was reported on this strike.[23]

Toward the end of 1900, it was reported that to that date the hello girls in the St. Louis telephone exchanges had taken no part in the movement to organize along labor union lines like their counterparts in Chicago and several other eastern cities. Word came from Chicago that the operators there had obtained charters from President Samuel Gompers of the American Federation of Labor and that representatives had been sent to New York.[24]

A report circulated on January 15, 1901, that all the New York City hello girls were to be organized by the American Federation of Labor (AFL) and that after the union had been formed, better conditions and higher pay would be demanded. The operators had already formed some kind of organization in Chicago and it was said that efforts would be made to organize them in Philadelphia, Boston, St. Louis, Baltimore and other large cities. According to AFL district organizer Herman Robinson, Gompers said he knew nothing about it. Robinson added that he knew there was one union of telephone girls in the west.[25]

For a time in August 1901, it looked like there would be a strike at the Akron, Ohio, exchange because every operator had signed an agreement to quit when the linemen said the time had come. Then 44 linemen walked out on a Thursday morning and the hello girls were prepared to quit when the labor dispute was resolved. The employees did not demand an increase in wages, but a reversal to how often they received payment. Heretofore, the company had been paying employees twice a month but then it gave notice that it would be paying wages only once a month. Employees objected strenuously and finally a strike was agreed upon as a way to re-establish the old payment schedule. Within two hours of the linemen walking out, company officials relented.[26]

More trouble flared up in Akron in November 1901. The phone company had discharged some of the linemen "because the girls in the telephone office thought too much of them," but then relented and took the linemen back. The operators had expressed their displeasure with the company's actions and the sympathy of the subscribers was with the girls. Said operator Etta Prince, "We're willing not to talk with the linemen over the wire. We don't object to that rule, but we will not let the company say what we shall do when we are off duty." Operator Ada Moore declared, "If we want to attend a party and choose to receive the attentions of the linemen while there, it is no concern of the company. It wasn't fair to discharge the men just because we were on friendly terms." By their protest, the operators had the linemen reinstated.[27]

Appleton, Wisconsin, telephone girls went on strike in March 1902 because C.P. Crocker, a married man and superintendent of the Fox River Telephone Company's local exchange, was placed in charge of the office one day that month and over a girl to whom the other girls in the office claimed he had been paying undue attention. Due to that development, the entire day crew (seven telephone girls) struck. Those strikers laid their case before company general manager Baer, who ordered the discharge of the new chief operator (the one Crocker had favored) and the strikers returned to work at noon on the same day they walked out. The telephone service of the exchange was interrupted for several hours.[28]

Later in that same month, the 75 girls in the main telephone office at Kansas City, Missouri, along with most of the operators who had gone on at noon as relief staff, laid down their receivers and went on strike because Mollie Trowbridge, chief operator in that office for several years, had been discharged to make room for Mrs. Duby, who had heretofore had charge

''HELLO GIRLS SECURED
REINSTATEMENT OF LINEMEN.'

MISS ETTA PRINCE   MISS ADA MOORE

TWO OF THE GIRLS WHO ARE VICTORIOUS.

In 1910, Akron, Ohio, operators Etta Prince and Ada Moore led a campaign to have discharged linemen who worked for their company reinstated.

of branch offices. Albert Barrett, assistant superintendent of the Missouri and Kansas phone company, assured the women that if they would return to work, he would promise to have Trowbridge reinstated. With that understanding, the strikers returned to work after 15 minutes of idleness. According to a reporter, "During the conflict, two or three girls became hysterical, and at one time the whole group was in tears. Restoratives were applied to several of the more emotional young women before they were able to resume their places."[29]

In April 1902, the telephone girls on the night shift of the Chesapeake and Potomac Telephone Company in Washington, D.C., balked at a company order that the night shift would report for work at 7 p.m. instead of 10 p.m. as they had heretofore done. After the protest, the company decided not to enforce the proposed new system that would have required the night operators to be at the office from 7 p.m. until 7 a.m. The decision to revert to the old schedule was reached after the night shift girls failed to show up for work at 7 p.m. but came in at 10 p.m., as they had always done.

Superintendent Corrigan met with the women and restored the old schedule. The day force took no part in the action but were said to be in sympathy with the night shift operators.[30]

Seventy central telephone girls walked out of the two Des Moines, Iowa, telephone exchanges on June 21 1902, tying up the Iowa and Mutual lines. The strikers' union had affiliated with the American Federation of Labor and it was thought they would attempt to make the strike general in the state. Their demands included an increase of wages (to $30 a month) and a nine-hour day. Telephone service in the city was at a standstill on that first day as the managers had been unable to fill the strikers' places.[31]

Another account reported the Des Moines strike began at 9 a.m. on the 21st and involved about 60 girls in the two firms. Some days earlier, they organized a union and affiliated with the Trades and Labor Assembly in Des Moines, made a demand for $1 a day and that their union be recognized and that none but union operators be employed by the firms. The two companies reportedly offered to meet the wage demand but refused to recognize the union. By prearranged agreement, the women struck at 9 a.m. Managers of both the Iowa Telephone Company and the Mutual Telephone Company had knowledge that the strike was coming and had done what they could to prepare for it by securing non-union operators. Several operators who formerly worked for the firms were induced to come back and work temporarily and a number of others were taken in. The managers immediately sent for operators in other parts of the state, and a number were secured in that manner, "but during the entire day [the 21st] the service was so crippled as to be almost useless," declared a journalist. The Mutual company manager resisted the proposed wage increase, declaring it would be too costly for his firm.

The chairman of a committee of the operators made a statement to the public outlining the situation. That statement said the scale of wages demanded had been sent to both sets of management some two weeks earlier. While they wanted a wage increase, they had not asked for shorter hours. They worked nine hours a day and on Sunday operators worked 11 hours for 75 cents for the day (five cents under the weekday pay rate). Those operators, according to their statement, worked right through their shifts with no time off allowed for a meal. The Mutual operators were said to be treated better with respect to Sunday work, putting in 11 hours of work but getting paid time and a half as well as being allowed 15 minutes for a meal break. According to the strikers' statement,

> We want the people to understand that regular operators get from $18 to $23 per month. Beginners get $12 per month. We think these wages are too small for such

nerve-killing continuous work. We want the night board operators advanced from
$23.50 to $30 per month. We don't expect to dictate terms. We told them what we
needed to live respectably, and they practically ignored us, especially the Iowa [com-
pany]. We made no demand; it was a request.[32]

S.K. Minton, president of the local Trades and Labor Assembly,
declared in Des Moines on June 27 that unless the demands of the telephone operators were granted before June 30, there would be a general
strike of union workers in Des Moines in sympathy with the striking operators. The Mutual had four scab operators at work by the morning of the
28th and the Iowa firm had two, but none of them were drawn from the
ranks of the strikers. Reportedly, the danger of a general strike had inten-
sified efforts to achieve a settlement.[33]

On June 29, Des Moines electrical workers made a demand of the
telephone managers—that they recognize the operators' union—and, if
they received an unfavorable reply, the linemen belonging to the companies
would walk out in sympathy with the telephone girls at 1 p.m. Only one
lineman failed to join the walkout. All the electrical workers of every kind
connected in any way with the telephone business would stay out until the
girls' strike was resolved. Minton declared,

The time is ripe for unionism to strengthen its hold in Des Moines. The opportunity
will be accepted. Unionism must be recognized. We will stay by the telephone girls.
The electrical workers go out first because they are most closely connected with the
girls on account of their connections with the companies.... If the strike of all electrical
workers does not prove effective in bringing about a settlement with the girls on union
terms, then the strike will be carried further and further until it does succeed. If necessary we will call out every member of organized labor in Des Moines. This is an
important fight, and we propose to win, if it takes all summer.[34]

A well-attended meeting of the laboring men of Des Moines was held
at the Trades Assembly Hall on June 30 to discuss taking action to support
the operators. Those operators were present. Sentiment at that meeting
was enthusiastic in favor of a strike and the operators were given every
assurance of support. It was decided that other strikes would be initiated
that weekend, but no specifics were given. At the meeting there was dis-
cussion of considering a resolution that the city buy and operate the Mutual
telephone system but also here there was no concrete action taken.[35]

The next day, a Trades and Labor Assembly committee announced
that a systematic canvas of the city would take place on July 1 to induce
the users of telephones to order their instruments out of their homes and
businesses as a protest against the phone companies in maintaining their
fight against the girls. It was reported that they secured "many pledges"
from people that they would order their phones removed.[36]

On July 9, it was reported that the Des Moines strike would end on July 10 if an agreement reached on the evening of July 9 between the two firms and an advisory committee of the Trades and Labor Assembly was carried out. Under that tentative agreement, the companies agreed to the dollar-a-day pay scale for operators; they agreed to recognize the operators' union, and to restore all the strikers to their former positions without discrimination. It was a significant wage increase for operators who had previously been receiving $3.50 to $5 a week.[37]

And so the strike ended on July 10. A week later, an editorial in a Nebraska newspaper declared the efforts to fill the strikers' places with scabs had been unsuccessful and that was a main reason for the companies to capitulate. There was also pressure from the Des Moines labor unions, aided by "universal public opinion in favor of the strikers," which also helped to bring the companies to the table and agree to terms. The editor concluded, "The public took the part of the strikers and phone subscribers began ordering their instruments out. Finding its revenues threatened, the company succumbed and the strikers were taken back on their own terms."[38]

A strange report was published in December 1902. Originating out of Chicago, it stated that the Des Moines operators strike, which had been in progress about six months, was settled on December 18 by a representative of the company and the Trades and Labor Assembly. The telephone girls were to be paid wages 15 percent in excess of the union scale and all the girls who struck were to be taken back to work. Also, the injunction suit to restrain the representative of union labor from boycotting the company was to be dismissed.[39]

Ten of the telephone girls in the Columbiana County Telephone Company's exchange in Salem, Ohio—almost the entire workforce—went out on strike on August 28, 1902. They wanted a wage increase of 33 percent. The company was providing a limited phone service to subscribers with the chief and several operators working the switchboard. The striking girls were reportedly watching the trains to try to prevent girls imported from other cities from taking their places. Nothing more was reported on this labor dispute.[40]

Telephone girls employed at the Vancouver British Columbia exchange went on strike for higher wages on the evening of November 26, 1902. At the time of the walkout, the wages were $20 a month for new operators, $25 for experienced operators in the city exchange, and $30 for long distance operators. "Public sympathy is entirely with the girls," said the article.[41]

It was reported in January 1903 that the telephone girls of Joplin,

Missouri, had gone on strike to compel the discharge of a superintendent accused by the operators of "taking undue liberties" with them. The girls stated that they were on strike for the defense of their honor. The matter became so serious that it excited interest throughout the state and the Missouri State Board of Arbitration was called in to settle the matter. The superintendent was a married man who came from Terre Haute, Indiana, "where managers for corporations have a reputation for fighting strikes." A newspaper editor said that the manager went too far south to take the privileges he tried to enjoy in Terre Haute: "Even if Southern people have no more time than some northerners for labor organizations, they will not tolerate the insulting of working girls."[42]

Reportedly, an effort was underway in Spokane, Washington, in April 1903 by the American Federation of Labor to unionize the hello girls there. About 80 girls had joined the union to that date and they were actively proselytizing among the remaining hello girls who had not yet joined. The agitation for the formation of a union had been in progress for the previous two months, but strict secrecy had been maintained among both employees and the telco management. The agitation was started by the electrical workers' union with which the new union was to be affiliated. There were about 135 local phone operators and 20 long distance operators employed at the plant. All worked in the telco building except for a few who worked in private exchanges in different business concerns. Of the local girls, some 80 to 90 were said to be involved in the union movement. Thus far, owing to the persuasive arguments of exchange manager Reynolds, all the long distance operators had remained outside the union. Girls then worked eight hours a day with the usual amenities found in telephone systems of the time. Beginners were paid $20 a month, which was increased to $22.50 the second month and to $25 at the end of three months. Increases followed thereafter at regular intervals until after five years the average telephone girl there was receiving about $40 a month. It was expected that hello girls, when fully organized, would ask for more frequent wage increases and freedom from Sunday and holiday work.[43]

Eleven Salt Lake City telephone girls left on the morning of April 16, 1903, for Butte, Montana, to replace girls who threatened to strike in that city. The Butte hello girls had recently organized a union and demanded concessions. The Rocky Mountain Bell Telephone Company stalled the women by stating it would think about their demands and deliver an answer to the operators on May 1. The real reason for the stall was to import scabs to have on hand in case the Butte operators walked out.[44]

Those 11 Salt Lake girls left on the 9:45 a.m. train but their names were being kept quiet. The pay being offered to work in Butte was said to be considerably higher than it was in Salt Lake and the offer to move from one Rocky Mountain exchange to another was tempting. Salt Lake telephone girls got $18 a month and the pay to them in Butte was reported to be 50 percent higher. There were 19 girls working in the Butte Bell exchange. Salt Lake exchange general manager D.S. Murray told a reporter, "The girls in Butte threatened a strike, and the management up there asked us if we could furnish some girls to take their places. We put the proposition to a number of the girls and they agreed to go up." When the reporter asked Murray if the imported girls were to be supplied with free rooms and/or other perks, he replied, "No. They go up simply on a regular contract."[45]

According to an April 17 report from Butte, the telephone and telegraph service there was badly crippled by strikes. A month earlier, the Western Union Telegraph Company locked out its boys because they organized a union. It then tried girl "messenger boys" but they "were hooted off the streets." Then the company attempted deliveries of its telegrams by phone but the telephone operators organized and had walked off the job one day earlier, on April 16, after they learned that girls had been imported from Salt Lake City. A large crowd gathered at the Butte railroad station but the Salt Lake City strikebreakers outfoxed them by getting off the train at a stop outside the city. The telephone buildings was then surrounded and guarded by telephone operator pickets.[46]

On April 17, threatening crowds led by the striking operators prevented the 11 Salt Lake City imports from replacing them. According to one account, every labor body in Butte had committees on the ground to assist the girls and attempt to dissuade the Utah women from going to work. During the night, large crowds surrounded the exchange building. The Utah girls met with delegates from the Allied Trades Assembly of Butte but said they did not propose to return to Salt Lake. President George Y. Wallace of the Rocky Mountain Bell Telephone Company thought it was all "a tempest in a teapot" that would quickly blow over. Wallace said that on general principles he was a union man and expected that the girls in general would go into unions "but he failed to see how any union had the right to step in and dictate to a business concern in matters of purely internal administration." Wallace stated that it was the purpose of the company to fit up one floor in the telephone building with bedroom furniture so that its women employees could live there, but the crowd in the street had prevented the delivery of the furniture. General manager Murray was in charge of the Salt Lake people and, said a journalist; "will see to it that they are not prevented from going to work."[47]

Daniel McDonald, president of the American Labor Union, passed through Butte on the morning of April 18 on his return from a labor convention and spoke to reporters about the hello girls' strike in Butte:

> The girls have all walked out and the linemen have joined them. The people of Butte are up in arms and in many cases the phones have been thrown out on the streets. The president of the company began to ship in his "pets" from Salt Lake as soon as he found I was out of the city. The girls telephoned me last night and said that the situation has grown so serious that the company headed off their Salt Lake girls at Dillon....

"Trouble arose," said McDonald, "when we demanded recognition of the new wage scale. Then Wallace began shipping in girls from Salt Lake despite union protests. We asked to submit the difficulty to arbitration but Wallace 'positively refused.'" President McDonald said the American Labor Union then had about 160,000 members in good standing. This union sprang from the Western Labor Union, was socialist in outlook and a few years later took part in the creation of the Industrial Workers of the World—the Wobblies, or IWW.[48]

A dispatch from Butte on the night of April 19 announced that the telephone girls' strike had been satisfactorily settled. At 7 p.m., the girls returned to work. Under a signed contract for one year, the company agreed to take back all the old operators without prejudice. The strikers conceded the right of the company to remove Miss MacDermott, the chief operator in the long distance department, and to place Alice Hope of Salt Lake City in that position. Herein it was said the trouble all started over the actions of the management in the Butte office in discharging union member MacDermott and attempting to put Hope in her place. That produced an immediate storm of protest with MacDermott refusing to quit and other operators threatening to walk out if she was discharged. The company tried to effect a compromise by creating a new position for MacDermott but the union refused the offer and continued to stand by her. When the Butte girls heard that Murray was on his way with non-union Salt Lake City operators, they promptly walked out. Then a meeting of the general trades council was called and the action of the strikers was endorsed. Notices were sent out to all hotels and restaurants that they would be declared unfair by all unions of the city if they dared house or feed the Salt Lake operators. Under the protective wing of Murray, the girls were housed at the Butte Hotel but none of them signed the register. Management of that hotel would not reveal what part of the hotel they stayed in.[49]

Eight of the 11 operators taken to Butte by Murray returned to Salt Lake City on April 21. Three decided to stay on in Butte for a few days to visit friends and relatives. None of those eight spoke to reporters. No one at the Salt Lake exchange would talk with reporters about the affair except for Murray, who declared:

> The facts in the matter are that we did not take any girls there to replace the old ones. We simply took them there because we feared a strike and we wanted them to keep the exchange in operation until the matter could be settled, so the public would not have to suffer.... When we reached the city, we found conditions such that I deemed it wise just to shut up the building and made no attempt to put the operators I had with me to work.[50]

Ten young women operators in the Cumberland Telephone Company office at Henderson, Kentucky, went out on strike April 17, 1903, because their dinner time was cut down to 30 minutes.[51] A few days later they mailed to company general manager Leland Hume, at Nashville, a petition bearing the names of 400 businessmen in the area asking that they be reinstated at the old hours. The girls said that if they were not reinstated, they would canvas the city and urge subscribers to contact Cumberland Telephone with a request to remove their instruments. Many businessmen and citizens reportedly had declared they would boycott the company if the demands of the operators were not met. At the time of the strike, the operators were not organized but they promised they would organize at once and then ask for the support of all organized labor in the area.[52]

But the action was all in vain for it was reported that the striking girls at Henderson ended their labor action and returned to work on April 28. They did so without any concessions from the east Tennessee company.[53]

In Spokane, Washington, telco management had anticipated the demands of the newly organized operators' union and granted an advance in wages to a number of their girls in April 1903. The advances were granted to about 30 girls who were selected for their length of service and efficiency. In all cases, the raises were in the amount of $2.50 or $5 a month. The regular raise at the telco heretofore had been $2.50, granted at irregular intervals. Nonetheless, union membership continued to increase and was then reported to be about 95. Some of them were long distance operators who had long held out from joining the union.[54]

At a May 19, 1903, Trades Council meeting in Spokane, four female delegates were temporarily admitted and would be seated as regular members in the near future. They represented that city's new operators' union, which then had a membership of about 100.[55]

The 14 hello girls of the Twin City Telephone company in Minneapolis who went on strike on May 26, 1903, did so to achieve their demands of more pay and fewer hours and for the abolition of "petty annoyances" to which they said they were needlessly subjected. No picket lines were in evidence on the morning of the 27th at the telco building. A company spokesman said that all of the strikers' places had been already filled:

> The girls really had no cause for complaint and the reasons advanced by them for walking out are little short of ridiculous. If they desire, they can return to work on the same condition to which they object, but it really makes little difference to us whether they care to work or not…. Their chief cause of complaint, apparently, is that we have certain rules which they are asked to obey during working hours, as is the case with every concern where anything that order obtains. The girls who were discharged were released for good and sufficient reasons, and the company will certainly continue to insist on the right to part company with employees who for various reasons may be found inefficient.

Strikers said that the girls were discharged not for inefficiency but because they had taken an active role in plans for the formation of an operators' union. On the evening of the 26th, the strikers met and organized the Minneapolis Telephone Operators' Union. In addition, a committee from the Minneapolis Trades and Labor Council planned to meet with the telco manager.[56]

A May 28 news story said that 17 hello girls employed by the Twin City Telephone Company were out on strike but the company's Superintendent Barry did not think it would extend to the city of St. Paul. Reportedly, the strikers had sent a delegation to St. Paul on the day before to solicit the help of the employees of both the Twin City exchange in St. Paul and the Northwestern Telephone Company, also located there, in their strike activities. However, officials of both companies declared that none of their people had been approached to that point. Barry said he did not care if the girls formed a union, adding: "We think we treat our girls the best of any telephone company in the northwest, and they tell us so. The striking element in Minneapolis is confined entirely to what are known as substitutes. It all grew out of the demand of four who were considered disturbers. We are not worrying about them at all."[57]

Secretary Phil Carlin of the Building Trades Council in Minneapolis said on the morning of May 28 that unless the Twin City Telephone Company would arbitrate its differences with the striking operators, a sympathy strike of the Electrical Workers' and Wiremen's unions and allied trades might be expected. He made that statement after being informed that company general superintendent Judson had declared he would not negotiate with the strikers' committee. Judson said that in view of the demonstration at the company's north branch on the previous evening, the company had decided not to reinstate the strikers under any circumstances. The girls denied they took any part in that disturbance. The crowd at that gathering had reportedly hooted and jeered as the scabs left the telephone building and was made up entirely of strike sympathizers but no attempt had been made to engage in violence. According to Judson, the places of all the strikers had been filled and he was busy turning away applicants for those jobs: "The company is experiencing much annoyance from hare-brained people who are continually calling up central only to greet the operator with the word 'scab' when she answers. We have employed detectives to run such people to earth and arrests are expected shortly."[58]

On May 29, the strike was still on with no movement from either side and relations reported to be a bit more strained than on the day before. None of the girls who walked out had returned to work and none were expected to resume work until an agreement was effected by the Trades and Labor Committee and the telephone company.[59]

An editorial about the Minneapolis strike, appearing in a St. Paul newspaper on May 30, said with respect to operators' grievances, "They have been compelled to walk a chalk line, a real one; and to rise from one side of a chair only. Their conversational privileges—and this surely was the most unkindest cut of all—have been curtailed." The editor thought the general public would be with the girls in seeking redress, and he concluded, "That she has struck is not to be wondered at. That she will win, is hard to be doubted. For, behind her is the general public, the exasperated, bulldozed, often ignored but always patient and admiring general public."[60]

Strikers held a meeting on the 29th with the Trades and Labor Council Committee that had been asked to help in their situation. Judson and manager Webster of the phone company maintained that the girls would not be taken back under any circumstances. In fact, the telco insisted the trouble was already settled, satisfactory substitutes having been already secured.[61]

Alice Dunbar, spokeswoman for the striking operators announced on June 3 that in view of the statement of E.H. Moulton, president of the Twin City Telephone Company, the hello girls had apparently been defeated. Moulton had forwarded a letter to Dunbar to say he would stand behind Webster's position. Said Dunbar: "Of course I cannot presume to speak authoritatively for the girls but the strike appears to be at an end, and it looks as though we were defeated. I doubt very much if the girls will undertake to bring on a sympathetic strike of what, being organized, we are not justified in calling the allied trades." And the strike was over and the girls had lost, with the scabs continuing on as the new workforce.[62]

In Spokane on the morning of June 30, 1903, the operators of the Pacific States Telephone Company struck as the result of alleged discrimination and unfair treatment of union members by the new service manager, Mr. Wrede. He had recently been imported from Seattle where he had trouble. There were then 160 girls in the Spokane operators' union, with about 25 operators who were not members of that union. Among their grievances was a new rule forbidding operators to wear low-neck dresses or to take off their collars, despite the fact that hot weather was coming. The operators demanded recognition of the union, slight changes in the scale of wages, revocation of orders regarding department apparel that prohibited girls from wearing flowers, compelling them to wear their hair done up on top of their heads (they could not wear their hair, for example, in braids), insisting on high collars and prohibiting low-neck dresses and turn-down collars. On the morning of the strike, 58 day shift girls walked out; nine more followed on a latter shift. The linemen and electrical workers were also out on strike. A reporter noted, "The company has advertised for men to learn operating."[63]

On July 1 it was reported that the Spokane operators had the sympathy and support of union labor in the area. They were then affiliated with the Western Conference at San Francisco, which made theoretically possible a general boycott against the Pacific States Telephone and Telegraph Company all up and down the West Coast. The company was reported to be paying premium wages to its remaining employees and breaking in new operators when they could obtain them. But, noted a reporter, despite those efforts by the company "the service is necessarily crippled." Affiliation with the Western Conference meant local strikers were no longer involved in negotiations; that is, bargaining was left to Conference people. If a general boycott was ordered by the Conference, it could mean that all members of unions connected with the Conference might be asked to have their phones removed. Strikers claimed that it was absolutely false that any of them misused or threatened any of the girls who did not go out on strike with them. Three of the girls who did walk out were said to have been taken back to the company by their mothers but that the company refused to reinstate them. Another report was that the company had given a bonus of $20 to such girls as agreed to stay inside the building 24 hours a day and that they were fed in the company dining room with items such as ice cream and strawberries being brought in for them by Pacific States. Shortly after noon on July 1, a trio of striking operators—pickets in front of the building— were approached by a cop and asked to move on. He explained to them that local exchange manager Reynolds had complained that the three were blocking the street and the cop told the women it would be just as well if the girls walked about a little. They did so.[64]

Also on July 1, a Spokane newspaper editor commented, "On general principles, the telephone girls have the sympathy of the public in their difficulty with the company. If the company had not made its silly rules regarding the way girls should dress and what they should wear, it is possible that there would never have been any strike…. In making these rules, the company transgressed on what every American, male or female, deems his personal liberty." When the company imposed rules involving the wearing of flowers, a requirement to wear high collars, a requirement for the hair to be worn up, etc., it "reached the limit of tastelessness. No woman likes to be dictated to in dress. And what is more, she won't be."[65]

One of the operators told a reporter on July 2 that they were confident of winning their strike: "[T]his is the first time the girls in the northwest have asserted themselves…. We girls have worked for the company for years but the petty tyranny of those recently in authority at the telephone office has driven us to strike." Women assigned to picket duty did their best to persuade the young women who were taking their places to quit work "and join their ranks out of sympathy for their own sex who are doing their best to make the lot of the average working girl a better one than it has been in the city." Reportedly, several of the scabs left work permanently on the evening of July 1. With respect to the story about the police officer who had shooed away some of the pickets, this account indicated that a lot of indignation was expressed by the strikers: "A crowd of loafers hang about other corners all day, and really block the highway, and no police orders them off. But it is easy to bluff pretty girls." Members of the operators' union urged that a fine be imposed on any girl who gave out union secrets regarding the doings of the organization, as a precautionary measure to prevent telephone company officials from being informed of what had or would take place and thus checkmate the striking members.

Pacific States officials circulated a report that the girls who had remained at their posts were being paid $15 a week. That rumor was spread (whether right or wrong) with a view to influencing strikers to return to work. The strikers stated that for some time before they went out on strike, they were forced to teach the ropes to a number of new girls; those strikers now claimed that was done with the object in view of breaking up their union. Company manager C.W. Reynolds remained on duty most of the night, escorting the girls from the telephone office to the streetcar, in order to prevent any of the strikers from securing their attention. He said to a reporter: "The strike is not bothering us a bit; the service is just as good as ever."[66]

The Spokane Trades Council notified the Pacific States Telephone and Telegraph Company on July 3 that if terms were not made with the striking operators within a few days, a boycott would be declared throughout eastern Washington state. It was also reported that "many sympathizers have already ordered the removal of their phones."[67]

Monday, July 6, at noon was set by the labor group as the deadline for a settlement. Failing that, the telco would be placed on the "unfair" list and a general boycott established against the company. The operators would then busy themselves securing signatures of telephone subscribers to telephone orders requesting the removal of the telephones from residences and businesses. Since the intervention of the police officer some days earlier, all the girl picketers who had done their duty around the telephone building had been careful to keep on the move while they were picketing. Mabel Carter, president of the union, described herself as very angry at the action of the company in discharging her so unceremoniously after four years of faithful service, simply because she had joined the union. Said Carter,

> It was not right. When we organized, we were ridiculed so much that we did not think it necessary to give out the names of officers. One night I was called up by phone by someone who claimed to represent a labor paper. "I have the names of some of the officers and want the rest," he said. I did not think the information would be used by the company, so I gave the names of the other officers of the union. I was the first to be discharged and as I had already taught a girl the business, it was no trouble for them to fill my place.

Most of the company's long distance operators had never joined the union and were then being used on the local city service. Thus, the business phones were said to be receiving "fair service."[68]

On July 4, Pacific States manager Phillips asked Spokane Mayor Boyd and Spokane Police Commissioner Root to give him two special policemen due to the operators' strike. That application was turned down by Boyd "for lack of cause." It was said that violence had been threatened by some of the striking girls, and that some of the girl pickets called other girls who insisted on working "mean things." Boyd and Root did not believe any of these telco charges declaring there was no factual basis for such allegations. The last grievance put before Boyd and Root was to the effect that a group of "ruffians" had assembled near the telco building and called some of the men who had taken the places of strikers "scabs." Phillips said the company had been given special policemen in all other cities where strikes were on, and that they would hold the city strictly responsible for any damages that might be done. He left the meeting with the veiled threat that unless the special officers were provided by the city, such officers would be secured elsewhere. Another rumor had it that the telco was to apply to the courts on Monday, July 6, for an order enjoining the strikers from declaring Pacific States "unfair," boycotting it in any way or interfering with those who were working for the telco. Plans were made for the telephone girls to distribute flyers outlining their grievances and perhaps to make a personal canvas of the telephone subscribers. According to am article, the Spokane phone service was then "very poor" and as a consequence many phones had been ordered taken out. The number of such orders was said to be growing daily with some taking that action out of sympathy with the strikers and others on account of the poor service. Recently appointed company superintendent G.E. Bush declared, "I don't believe there is any perceptible change in our service, several businessmen telling me it is even better than before."[69]

Also on July 6, the Spokane newspaper ran an editorial that originally appeared in a Pendleton, Oregon, paper, the *East Oregonian*. It said that the Spokane telephone girls' strike against "unreasonable and oppressive restrictions" met with hearty approval from the public. The piece argued that the company "has no moral right to introduce a rigorous code of discipline in this free county, which would tend to reduce American girls to the plane of Kaffir slaves." It also argued the company had no moral right to say that those girls should wear a regulation high collar which make life miserable for them every minute of the day: "It has no moral right to deny them the common comforts of the season, in the way of lighter clothing, low-necked dresses, flowing hair and bouquets galore, if such little items make life more bearable and conduce to the cheerfulness of their dispositions. The girls have revolted against unreasonable restrictions and public sentiment is with them." This editor went on to argue that it was only a step from one type of oppression to another. If such abuses of freedom were not nipped in the bud, it would be but a few years until these same girls will be compelled to belong to the company's choice of a church, keep company exclusively with friends of their employers' choice and be nothing but machines instead of thinking women. "The individual rights of employees must be closely guarded in order to insure happy surroundings and contented lives for them. In justice to the girls and to the American principles involved, the people of Spokane should see that the strike is won."[70]

At a July 7 meeting of the Trades Council of Spokane, the Pacific States Telephone and Telegraph Company was voted unfair and a practical boycott was inaugurated against the telco by the labor body. The strike involved four key points: recognition of the union; a pay increase as set out by the union; reinstatement of all those who walked out; and allowing the girls to dress comfortably and as they pleased. Striking operators were then circulating slips for people to sign, ordering phones taken out. In this account it was said that no move would be made by the telco to enjoin the Trades Council from making effective the boycott. Said G.E. Bush, "The rules we have are only those in effect in most telephone offices, and there must be rules to govern such a large body of girls. The rules enacted seem to be the chief cause of concern." Pacific States then had other labor trouble. With the exception of Seattle, the linemen were out along the entire system. In San Francisco, the 26 collectors employed by the company were also on strike while in Fresno the 40 girl operators had walked out because the manager forbade them from attending a labor lecture.[71]

Four days later, it was reported that the striking Spokane operators claimed to have obtained 1500 signatures on phone removal orders, up to noon that day. All allied working men in the area were assisting in the effort and also securing signatures. It was described as a well-organized campaign with bands of girls assigned to each ward in the city and those wards then divided into precincts and then all doors therein knocked on. If the lady of the house answered the door and wouldn't sign the removal order, then the strikers visited the house again when "the head of the family" returned home from work. Each afternoon at 2 p.m., the girls reassembled at strike headquarters to turn in their collected removal slips and discuss strategy. Additionally, a boycott was placed upon the telco on the night of July 10 by the central body of organized labor in San Francisco, with the result that the telco was then on the unfair list in San Francisco, Sacramento, Spokane and Everett, Washington.[72]

While those removal orders had been collected, it was not until July 21 that the first of them, about 1000, were given to the telco. Another 1000 removal orders were held back, to be given to Pacific States at a later date.[73]

Information was received by the striking operators on July 24 that the telco had placed them on the blacklist all over the west, wherever the company had branches of its system. The names of all the striking girls were forwarded to the various offices so that if any of them tried for a job in another city, they would be refused.[74]

Union president Mabel Carter gave out a statement about the Spokane strike on September 11, 1903: "I don't care what people say about it, the telephone girls are not in the least discouraged by the desertion of five of our number. We are still 103 strong. The fact is the desertions were a good thing for the balance of our union, as those who returned to beg forgiveness of the Pacific States Telephone and Telegraph company were continually attempting to discourage the others." Among the girls who decided to give up the fight and return to work was Margaret Hill, who was selected by the telco as their candidate for queen of a Spokane carnival. The other four were also listed by name in the newspaper. The Spokane strike ended by just fading away, with no concessions for the striking operators, another loss.[75]

Eleven telephone girls in the employ of the Guthrie, Oklahoma, telephone exchange went out on a sympathy strike with the linemen who informed the company they would not work until L.L. Davenport was relieved of further duty. The girls left the office promptly at 9 a.m. on June 30, 1903, after a brief conference among themselves. Late on June 29, the linemen asked the women to refrain from work until the striking linemen were reinstated and Davenport released. After their conference, the girls agreed. Davenport was a non-union man who had been newly hired as a lineman. Company officials said they would experience no difficulty in replacing striking telephone girls. The employer was the Arkansas Valley Telephone Company, which operated a system spread over Oklahoma, Indian Territory and Southern Kansas. The company declared it would put non-union employees into all positions as soon as it possibly could.[76]

On July 3, 1903, the Building Trades Council of Fresno, California, sanctioned the strike of the linemen of the Sunset Telephone and Telegraph Company. The operators there held a special meeting that night to consider the question of forming a union. Speeches were made and about 30 of them agreed to join a union, should one be formed. That meeting was supposed to be secret but there was a leak and local exchange manager Noble heard about it that same day, in advance of the meeting. He at once discharged the girl whom he considered a leader of the movement to organize. Before that woman had left the building, 24 other operators left their stools and walked out with her. A later report said that 40 experienced operators had left the employ of the company. Noble claimed the number was not as large as that but offered no other figure. The girls had several grievances, chief among them the question of wages and the regulations concerning a dress code.[77]

Striking operators at Ashland, Kentucky, were employees of the Lawrence Citizens' and Peoples' Telephone Company, whose service extended to several other cities in Kentucky. The operators walked out near the end of July 1903 and appealed to the merchants of all places served by the telco to sign orders demanding the removal of phones from their premises unless the company took back the operators.[78]

Twenty-five operators in the local office of the East Tennessee Telephone Company in Paducah, Kentucky, struck for a pay raise in October 1903. Another reason for the strike was because Mrs. Peacock, the chief operator, had been discharged. Those women struck on October 13, and on October 14 a total of 20 operators were brought to Paducah from Nashville, Memphis, Louisville and Evansville to take the places of the strikers. Three of the "aggressors" in the strike were discharged and the others allowed to go back to work. Mrs. Fleming of New Orleans, Miss Peacock's successor, retained her post,.[79]

At 5 p.m. on Saturday, November 21, 1903, the girls employed in the telephone exchange at Palestine, Texas, quit work and a copy of their letter setting forth their grievances was sent to management and the local paper. The newspaper published it in full. That letter was addressed to the Palestine Telephone Company and was signed by five women. One of their grievances was that the workroom was unsanitary, unclean and unhealthy. It had not been scrubbed or cleaned for over 12 months. They denounced the painting of the four windows in the office so that they could not see outside. The workroom had been in use for over five years and the windows had never before been painted over. It meant a great deal to the operators "for we each and all claim to be young ladies of unimpeachable integrity and character, and we hereby denounce the painting of said windows without our being consulted or advised as to the necessity or reason therefore, as it is an imputation against our honor." Another grievance was that the windows had been nailed down and that no reason was given for that action. It was felt a necessity by the operators that a room occupied daily by from six to eight people had to be ventilated, but was then deprived of both light and air. The women were not asking for any salary increase.[80] An editor remarked that if only half of what the girls charged in their letter was true, "then they have a just grievance, and should not be blamed for quitting their posts."[81]

There was a walkout of telephone girls at the Central Union Telephone Company in Centralia, Illinois, on February 1, 1904. Members of a union, they refused to remain in the employ of the company because manager O.G. Springer installed Margaret Fosdyke of Fairfield, Wisconsin, as the chief operator, thus setting each girl back one position in the scale of promotions, with a consequent decrease in wages. As the girls left the building, they met a young lady who had been summoned as a substitute, but on being informed of the situation she refused to work and at once joined the union.[82]

A strike by the Portland, Oregon, telephone girls on October 12, 1904, was reported to have "practically tied up business." Only ten girls out of a workforce of nearly 200 were on the job. According to a reporter, "The girls objected to rigorous rules which dictated to them as to their wearing apparel both in the office and on the streets."[83] One day later, a slightly different account appeared in another newspaper. It was reported herein that nearly 400 operators employed in the two main offices of the Pacific States Telephone and Telegraph Company in Portland walked out shortly after 1 p.m. on October 12, declaring a strike and alleging cruel and unjust treatment by a supervising forewoman who alternated between Portland and Spokane. As soon as the strike was declared, the company manager contacted Pacific States' head office in San Francisco asking that experienced operators be sent to Portland at once. However, shortly before 2 p.m. the strikers returned to work under a promise from company officials that the issues would be fully investigated and all wrongs, should they exist, would be adjusted to the satisfaction of the operators. Trouble had been brewing for some time there due to the actions of a supervising forewoman who had inaugurated a system of "demerits" or "marks" for the infraction of rules which the operators asserted were overly rigid and inhuman. Each demerit or mark against an operator meant a deduction from her salary at the end of the month, and eight demerits in each of three successive months resulted in that operator losing her job. On the evening of October 11, about 100 girls met and organized a union, which then affiliated with the Federated Trades Council in Portland. The next day at work, word of the impending strike was spread around. When the signal was given at 1 p.m., almost the entire operating force quit their places.[84]

In view of the Portland hello girls' strike, some 200 operators left their switchboards in places such as Salt Lake City and Butte, Montana, heading to Portland to take the strikers' places. It was expected that other cities in the general area would be called upon to send strikebreakers to Portland. On the morning of October 15, about 40 operators from Seattle arrived in Portland.[85]

Portland strikers circulated a petition among local businessmen asking for their reinstatement. Between 1200 and 1400 signatures were reportedly obtained by October 20. Pacific States officials said the petition didn't matter and the service they were getting from the scabs was "extremely satisfactory," and announced that only as individuals, foresworn against unionism, could the girls go back to work. Mr. Russell, manager of Cordray's Theater in the city, had offered his venue and was going to stage a play, *For Her Sake*, as a benefit for the strikers.[86]

Operators of the Utah Independent Telephone Company met on March 24, 1905, and organized an Operators' Relief Association. The object of the organization was to care for the operators who were absent from work through sickness or accident. Sixty-three operators joined the organization with each operator paying ten cents a week into the fund. It was provided in the constitution they adopted that operators absent through illness or accident be provided with $5 a week for the first month of absence and $2.50 a week for the second month.[87]

A strike of telephone girls took place on June 15, 1905, in the exchange at Colfax, Washington. Emma Endsley, the chief operator, had been off work ill for ten days. Then two operators, Zora Herford and Stella Herford, announced their intention to leave if Endsley returned to work. When Endsley returned, she was dismissed by the manager with Zora being appointed to her place. At that point, all the operators struck and left work. Then the manager dismissed Zora and installed her sister, Stella Herford, to take her place, and all the striking girls returned to work.[88]

Troubles arose again at the Colfax exchange in December 1905 as the girls in the central office threatened to go on strike unless management agreed to discharge Stella Herford. Notice to that effect was served on exchange manager F.W. Kelsey. For some time, there had been trouble in the office owing to the strict enforcement of the rules of the chief operator. Objections to the new method of enforcing discipline were made by the operators, but the manager stood by his chief operator. A few days earlier, the 11 operators circulated a petition among the businessmen and other patrons of the exchange, gathering signatures demanding the resignation of Herford. That petition set forth that the chief operator was not competent to handle the force of operators and impaired the phone service. On December 7, a committee of operators served the petition on Kelsey and said that unless she was removed by a certain deadline, they would stage a walkout. The manager responded by publishing an advertisement for new girls to take the place of the petitioning operators.[89]

When a reporter checked the Colfax exchange on December 22, after the deadline had passed, he discovered that no walkout had taken place. Kelsey explained to the journalist that only two girls were dissatisfied and that the others declared they did not favor a strike. Those two dissatisfied operators had been discharged and new operators were then working in their places.[90]

Six telephone girls at the Mt. Sterling, Kentucky, exchange went on strike in July 1905 but one quickly repented. The labor action was for an increase in wages of $5 a month. The manager had refused that demand and because he subsequently increased the wages of one of the women, six simultaneously walked out. Reportedly, a new workforce of operators was then being installed.[91]

On the morning of September 5, 1905, four of the Bell Telephone Company exchange operators in Idaho Falls, Idaho, served notice on Mr.

Jones, the local manager, that if they were not granted a 20 percent wage increase in two hours, they would walk. Jones declared himself powerless to grant that request, especially within the time frame given. So before noon that day, all four walked.[92]

On the night of February 23, 1906, the crisis in the local telephone company offices in Vancouver, British Columbia, alleged to have been caused by the efforts of the British Columbia Telephone Company to wean the girls from the Electrical Workers' Union, culminated in a strike. Operators in the neighboring city of New Westminster then struck in sympathy with Vancouver and it was thought possible that within a short period of time the union would have every office in British Columbia tied up.[93]

On March 5, 1906, hello girls employed by the Home Telephone Company in Ashland, Wisconsin, walked out at noon and phone service came to an immediate halt. The trouble was due to the chief operator discharging an operator. The grievance was settled at about 4 p.m. that same day and the operators went back to work, according to a reporter; "having practically won their point."[94]

Ten girls employed in Iowa City's Bell Telephone Company exchange staged a strike on June 15, 1906, to secure the discharge of an objectionable forewoman. Strikebreakers were then being used to operate the exchange.[95] In June 1906, the hello girls of Springfield, Minnesota, went on strike, demanding more pay as well as the privilege of naming who should be employed to assist them when extra help was needed on the switchboards. Because they were unorganized, declared a reporter, "they have so far been unsuccessful."[96]

On August 23, 1906, 350 telephone girls employed in the central exchange of the Chicago Telephone Company struck, crippling the phone service. The cause of the strike was said to be an order issued by the company directing the girls to enter the building through a rear door. But, in order to reach that door they were compelled to go through a passageway 100 feet long. The girls said the passage was muddy even in the daytime and dark, slimy and slippery at night. Also, there were three saloon entrances on the alley and the girls worried they would be annoyed by loiterers.[97]

After giving the manager of the Durham, North Carolina, exchange several days to consider a raise in their salaries, the Interstate Telephone Company operators went on strike at 11 a.m. on September 3, 1906. Reportedly the company made an effort to compromise with the operators but they would accept nothing less than the raise they demanded.[98]

A February 15, 1907, conference between representatives of the Rocky

Mountain Bell Telephone Company executive board of Butte, Montana, the Merchants' Association and a joint committee of the Butte Central Labor Council and the Montana State Federation of Labor failed to effect a settlement of the telephone girls' strike. The labor committee, representing the girls, refused to concede a single point from the women's original demands. The Typographical Union voted the telephone girls the sum of $250 on February 15, to help them to continue their strike.[99]

Early in the morning of February 16, the strike was settled with the operators being granted an eight-hour day and an increase in wages to $60 a month (an increase of $6 a month). All of their other demands were also said to have been met. A different account of the settlement said the girls had been working for $45 a month "and all sorts of hours," and that they demanded $60 a month and an eight-hour day. This account declared that concessions had been made by the operators and they returned to work with an eight-hour day but a salary of $56 a month.[100]

It was reported that the strike of the Rocky Mountain Bell Telephone Company girls was settled on February 23, 1907, with, said a journalist, "complete victory for the girls." During the five-day strike, the exchange manager said there was nothing to be done and if the girls did not return to work, new girls would be employed. But the manager did not attempt to hire scabs "as he was aware than an attempt to do such meant a spread of the strike to other points throughout the state." The company offered $41 a month, which was rejected by the girls. On the morning of February 23, the Montana Federation of Labor handed the telco an ultimatum to the effect that if the strike was not settled within three hours, the telco would be considered unfair and the strike extended throughout the state. A short time after that, a conference was held and an agreement was reached. Helena daily newspapers announced that while the girls got their wages raised, the company got the open shop provision. However, this account stated that was a false report and that Rocky Mountain Bell agreed to recognize the union, deal with the union, and agreed it would deal with the union in the future. Under the new wage scale, the chief operator and the toll (long distance) operators received $60 a month; assistant toll attendants $60; operators $50 a month; and relief toll attendants $22.50 a month. All operators were to have every other Sunday off, with no deduction made to their pay. Full shift operators were to be given nine hours work out of each 24. All operators would work half a shift on each of seven holidays that occurred during the year, at full pay. Nine hours constituted a day's work and all overtime was to be paid at a rate of time and a half. The union was the Helena Telephone Operators' Union no. 39. Also, full pay was to be given to all employees for lost time on account of the strike. During the strike in the community, said a journalist; "every union made it its business to see that the girls were well supported."[101]

For the part he played in the operators' strike, Helena Mayor Lindsay was called "an unprincipled tool of the corporations" in a news story. When the strike started, Lindsay and three other citizens met with Rocky Mountain Bell general manager Murray to protest his meeting with the unions, stating they were "ridden to death" by the tyranny of the Helena unions and urging him to refuse to confer with anyone except the girls individually. They promised Murray every financial assistance if he would stand against the unions and pledged that 75 percent of the phone users would back him up. A reporter wrote, "For a man in [Lindsay's] position as mayor of all the people, where instead of working to the interest of all and the city's best good, he panders to a set of profit-grabbing exploiters as against the demands of decency and life for young girls that must earn a chance to live by performing useful social service for the sake of turning out profits for the Bell Telephone company stockholders." One Helena Main Street businessman told the reporter that if the city had a mayor of any account, the strike would have been a matter of short inconvenience to the public. Instead of acting in the interests of community, the commonweal, Lindsay "goes blabbing with the Citizens' Alliance and plotting against overworked young girls to enhance the profits of a bloating robber corporation."[102]

Montana remained a hot spot for hello girl strikes in the spring of 1907, and it was all due to incompetent management. As of March 14, 1907, the telephone girls of the Rocky Mountain Telephone Company in six Montana cities were on strike. The trouble started at Billings when the president and vice-president of the Telephone Operators' Union were discharged for belonging to the union, and the rest of the girls walked off the job. It seemed that after the strike of the hello girls at Helena Rocky Mountain Bell (headquartered in Salt Lake City, Utah), general manager Murray issued orders to the local managers at Montana exchanges to discharge all girls as soon as it was known that they belonged to a union, except those employed at Butte and Helena (where the telco had already settled strikes with one of the terms being that it would recognize and deal with the operators' union). First up was the manager at Billings who lost no time in carrying out that order, for no sooner were the girls in Billings organized than the two union executives were discharged.[103]

As a result of the strikes spreading throughout Montana, the State Federation of Labor presented a list of grievances to Rocky Mountain superintendent Burdick of the Montana division, accompanied by a proposed schedule to govern the state's telephone girls. That schedule was largely the same as the one then in effect in Butte and Helena, which was as follows: chief operator and toll attendants to be paid $60 a month; assistant toll attendants $60; and operators $50 a month. All operators were to have every other Sunday off and full shift operators were to work nine hours a day with time and a half for any overtime. Operators were to be relieved for at least 15 minutes each day. Full pay was to be given to all employees in the Billings exchange for lost time on account of the walkout to the date of settlement, from March 7. As well, there was a demand for the reinstatement of all Billings exchange operators who were employed prior to March 7 and who were discharged on account of their membership in Billings Telephone Operators' Union No. 40, Montana Federation of Labor, and the reinstatement of all others who left their positions in sympathy with those discharged. Burdick refused to listen to the girls' grievances, saying he would not recognize the union in any way. Burdick was given time to reconsider and if he did not act, a strike would be ordered throughout the state. On March 12, the girls employed in the Great Falls and Red Lodge exchanges walked out. The Bozeman and Livingston girls joined the strike on March 13, and the Lewistown girls declared a strike on March 14. According to a reporter, the sympathy of the public was with the girls: "The telephone company had had a complete monopoly of the phone business in the state, overworking the employees so much that the public could not get good service. Long hours and small pay has been the motto of the company to the extent of rivaling the sweat shops of the East Side in New York." At Red Lodge, one girl was employed for 12 hours a day, seven days a week, for a wage of $30 a month. Another girl there worked 13 hours a day, seven days a week, and received $27 a month. The average pay was reported to be $30 a month with the average number of hours worked per day being 12. Rocky Mountain Bell was said to be then trying to secure scabs for Great Falls. The reporter concluded his piece by stating, "While we are with the girls in the struggle, still we would call the people's attention to the fact that the people should own the telephones."[104]

On March 14, 1907, a manifesto of the striking telephone girls (an open letter "to the people of Montana" and signed "The Montana Federation of Labor") was published in a newspaper. It laid out the conditions endured by the women. Wages were said to range from $27 to $35 a month and $40 in a few cases; hours of work ranged from 10 to 12 hours per day. By this point, the Rocky Mountain Bell Telephone Company had been declared unfair by the Montana Federation of Labor. The manifesto appealed to its readers not to use their Rocky Mountain Bell phones and to order them taken out of their residences and places of business.[105]

At the end of March 1907, about 250 telephone girls filled a room at the San Francisco Labor Council Temple and completed the temporary organization of a Telephone Operators' Union. Officers were elected at that meeting; it was the organizing committee of the Labor Council that brought the women together. At that time, there were said to be 150 names on the union rolls while estimates were that about 600 telephone operators were employed in San Francisco. One operator told a reporter that they would not release the names of the officers or of the members of the union: "Such an announcement would mean that the telephone company would nip this union in the bud and discharge every girl whose name was divulged." She added that the operators were paid $8 a week ($34.67 per month). Grievances included long hours and low pay and the replacement of a woman as chief operator by exchange manager Beachwood. He was said to be hated by the operators who wanted him removed. Another sore point was "petty rules without reason." That new union would be affiliated with the American Federation of Labor.[106]

According to an April 1 news story, the newly organized San Francisco operators' first demand, made make to the Pacific States Telephone Company, was: "The chief operator in pants must go!" Secrecy was still the rule of the new organization, said a journalist: "They declare that obvious reprimands would be the rule of the company with any girls who linked their names publicly with the plans of the union before the charter arrived and invested them with the same protection guaranteed to other bodies of organized labor." That is, once the union was officially affiliated with the AFL that labor body would stand behind any strikers who were affiliated as would all other affiliated union members in the area. The labor body could, for example, declare an employer "unfair" or "hot" and that exerted a great deal of pressure on the company. The operators were then allowed only 20 minutes for lunch "and sometimes much less than that." Those operators also wanted their 15-minute breaks ("recesses"), both morning and afternoon, reinstated because, said the account, they had been "stopped some time ago." They also planned to insist on the employment of women as chief operators:

> The men who do this work now appear to take delight in making things unpleasant and harsh for us. They are grumpy and unreasonable. They have to go. If the union accomplished nothing else but forcing them out, it would pay us for all the trouble and risk we have undergone in organizing it. We want the women who were formerly over us back. We are used to dealing with them and they have some sense of fairness.

"HELLO GIRLS" GO TO WORK IN IMPROVISED JITNEY.

New York Telephone Company operators being transported to work with improvised means during a 1916 transit strike.

None of the operators would give the reporter the names of the officers of the union. But, said the reporter, an unsolicited list arrived at his newspaper, the *San Francisco Call*, on the previous evening. It listed the names of seven women and their union positions; it was published as part of this article.[107]

On April 2, W.J. Phillips. Pacific States division manager, denied that any operators had been discharged because of their affiliation with the union. He said, "There will be no strike of the telephone operators in our employ unless they bring it on themselves. We have our own reasons for opposing a union of operators, but have been using no threats against the girls who belong to the new organization." He denied that the company was considering a reduction in wages and said that in fact the firm had been working for the past few weeks on a new wage scale that would "materially raise the wages of the operators." Phillips insisted that development had nothing to do with the girls organizing a union; it was a purely unrelated and coincidental event. He added,

> There is also a mistaken impression about the men operators whom we have employed recently. They have not supplanted women chief operators. They are what we call supervisory operators—technicians, who have change of distributing the traffic on the switchboards to insure more efficient service to subscribers. They have nothing to do with overseeing the girls. That work is done by the same women chief operators whom we had before…. As for the recesses of the operators, they have not been abolished. In some cases they have not been extended to operators, but that has been due principally to the stormy weather, inadequate car service and other things that combine to make it difficult for the company to muster its customary force of employees daily. The recesses have merely been disregarded to counteract these conditions. It is not the intention of the company to abolish them. The company believes that leniency to its employees pays, and its policy is to cultivate it."[108]

On May 3, 1907, it was reported that San Francisco was practically without telephone service as a result of the strike declared by the telephone girls against Pacific States Telephone and Telegraph Company, which went into effect at seven that morning. At that hour, from 575 to 600 girls left their switchboards to enforce recognition of the newly organized Telephone Operators' Union, along with a demand for increased wages. The company pressed clerks, stenographers and other employees into service as operators. Along with a number of hello girls who declined to join the strike, they maintained a crippled service during the day. The city manager also took a turn at the switchboard. By evening, the service was said to be almost entirely suspended. Pacific States president Scott claimed, none too convincingly, that 30 percent of the girls remained loyal and stayed at their stations.[109]

Immediately after going out on strike, the hello girls began to try and secure support from all directions and it was thought the company linemen might go out on strike in sympathy with them. According to an article,

> Ever since the formation of the union, the company has been making every effort to break it up. On the last monthly pay day the girls were taken into a room 20 at a time, and with their pay envelopes were given a printed resignation from the union which they were asked to sign. The company offered to take the matter out of their hands and conduct all negotiations if they would sign the papers…. Some of them were kept waiting in the room for over an hour in an effort to wear them down, but the majority of the regular operators have remained faithful to the union. The head operators, however, have nearly all been forced to withdraw by the very heavy pressure which has been brought to bear on them.[110]

Despite the enthusiasm shown by several hundred operators at a meeting on May 7, indications were that unless the linemen went out to support the girls, "the company will have practically a complete force at the switchboards within the next few days," said a reporter, in reference to the firm's hiring of strikebreakers. Linemen were still considering their position. After a meeting, one lineman said to a reporter; "We are simply trying to arrange things so that the girls and the company can come together. We have no grievances and unless the company forces our hands, we will not strike."[111]

Various subcommittees composed of members from the San Francisco Labor Council, the Building Trades Council, several civic groups and representatives from churches, financial houses, businesses and commercial interests were reportedly working to bring labor peace to San Francisco. During the middle of May, there were several other strikes in progress in the city—transit workers, iron workers and laundry workers. The linemen continued to stall and deferred making any decision about joining the walk-out.[112]

A settlement of the strike was reported to be "in sight" on May 13 and an "arrangement" was then being fine-tuned under which all the girls would return to work and arbitrate their differences later. Several members of the conciliation committee visited Pacific States president Henry T. Scott at his home and placed before him their plan. It consisted of letting the girls return to work and continue in the organization of their union, and all other differences would be arbitrated. Alice Lynch, president of the union, said that W.J. Phillips, city superintendent of the company, was making a house-to-house canvas of the union girls' homes, offering them $5 a day, three meals and a room inside the telephone building if they would come back to work and that he also promised to make supervising operators of them after the strike situation was settled.[113]

At the end of May 1907, Lynch was still optimistic and said, "We will show organized labor all over the country that men are not the only ones who can win a strike. And we will show the telephone corporation that girls are just as efficient strikers as they are employees." The wanted $30 a month for girls working their first three months; $35 a month for the next three months; and $60 a month after one year of service. They also wanted Pacific States to recognize their union. The strike had been on for nearly a month by then and every day telephone girls did picket duty around the telephone building. When a strikebreaker passed their picket line, she was asked to quit her job. If she refused to do so, she was liable to be called a "cat" or a "hen" or some other such epithet. Added Lynch, "If women had a voice in the government of the city, state and nation—well, things would be different. We would not be compelled to suffer the indignities the telephone company thrusts upon us."[114]

On May 28, Pacific States manager Phillips asserted that the company was gradually filling the ranks of the striking operators; Lynch maintained the company was making no such gains and that the union members were standing firm. Three picketers, Marion Maynard, Anna Aspelin and Evelyn McBride, surrendered themselves on that date at the central police station. They were accused of throwing eggs and insults at Bertha Culp and Edith Morton, non-union operators (strikebreakers). Lynch secured bail for all three.[115]

A brief profile of Lynch was published on June 1, 1907; part of the article headline called her a woman suffragist. The reporter noted, "Miss Lynch has her own idea on the status of women and her philosophy stamps her as a real character." One of her favorite bits of advice was said to be: "Girls, buy less candy and more books." Mostly, though, the piece was a collection of bits and pieces of quotes by Lynch gathered from previous articles on the strike. The journalist concluded his profile by declaring, "The secret was out. She is a Woman Suffragist of the dyed-in-the-wool kind and no doubt since the strike began she has converted many of her associates to the cause. Just how long the strike will last is hard to figure, but little Miss Lynch will never give up the fight."[116]

Finally, very early in June, some of the Pacific States electrical workers went out on a sympathy strike for the operators. However, on June 4, electrical workers of the Electrical Workers Union No. 151 were notified by union president J.C. Kelly that the 200 members who went out in sympathy to aid the striking operators had to return to

San Francisco operator and strike leader Alice Lynch in 1907.

their work at once. Kelly received a letter from C.J. Corcoran, special agent for the phone company, advising him of the action of some of the members of Local 151 and calling his attention to an agreement existing between the company and the Pacific District Council, with which Local 151 was affiliated, and which provided for labor peace between the parties for some time to come. Until that agreement expired, wrote Corcoran, there could be no strike called by the men. Kelly agreed, and so instructed his men. A stormy and bitter meeting with the 200 men was held with many of them favoring open rebellion. To a man, all 200 were in favor of staying out on their sympathy strike.[117]

Marion Maynard, one of the three striking operators accused of throwing eggs and insults, caused some excitement in Police Judge Weller's court on June 10 by fainting after a hung jury failed to agree on the charge against her of disturbing the peace. Maynard was carried into the judge's chambers, followed by about 20 strikers, and soon recovered. Scab operator Edith Norton accused Maynard of throwing eggs at her on May 23 at the telephone building. Her story was corroborated by three other witnesses. The jury stood eight for acquittal and two for conviction. The Maynard case was continued for a week, as were the cases of Evelyn McBride and Anna Aspelin. Nothing more was reported on these cases.[118]

On August 3, 1907, a brief press announcement stated that the San Francisco telephone operators, on strike against Pacific States Telephone would return to work under the same conditions as when they went out. The only concession made to the girls was that male operators would be discharged.[119]

That strike of about 500 telephone girls ended on August 2 when they held a five-hour long meeting and voted to go back to work. The girls then on strike would report to the general offices of Pacific States on Monday, August 5, and be assigned to all the old positions remaining vacant. The basis on which the strike was settled was listed in one account as an increase in wages granted voluntarily by the company shortly before the strike, amounting to from $8 to $20 a month. The working day would be eight hours with 30 minutes for a meal and two 15-minute recesses, one in the morning, one in the afternoon. The open shop would prevail. Operators would apply individually to manager Phillips for their positions but no one, because of affiliation with the union, would be discriminated against. The male chief operators would be withdrawn and women chief operators placed in direct charge of the girls, and "operators will be allowed to continue in the organization and maintenance of the union." Reportedly, the settlement came as a surprise because few people knew any talks were underway. Such talks had broken off shortly after the strike was called, some 14 weeks earlier. A meeting of the firm's electricians, who for the past eight weeks had been conducting a strike in sympathy with the operators, was scheduled for later that day. Rumor had it that those men would also vote to return to work. Both sides claimed victory. G.P. Robinson, general superintendent of Pacific States, said, "The operators who come back to work now will work under absolutely the same conditions as existed before the strike was called. The operators who remained faithful to the company and the recruits who joined our forces have been working under these conditions and we see no reason to make any changes." Union president Alice Lynch also claimed victory and stated,

> Our girls went out to gain their right as Americans to have a union and they got it. From the start we have never advocated a closed shop. Neither did we ask particularly for increased wages. Our right to organize was our first demand and without its being granted we never would have returned to work…. More than anything else besides our principal demand laid aside, we wanted the men operators the company had placed over us to go, and this we got also. Our eight-hour work day with the recesses which had been suspended are restored to us. The wages which the company had granted to us in a desperate effort to prevent the strike were allowed to stand. The only point we lost was the right to demand a closed shop.[120]

Lynch called a special meeting of her union for 1 p.m. August 5. An inference was drawn that harmonious relations had not been entirely established between the operators and the company. Lynch's announcement of the meeting said, "Important business relating to the affairs of the union will be transacted." Apparently many of the girls who had been on strike reported on August 3 at the offices of the phone company for their old positions. According to one account, "When they appeared, they were questioned relative to their connection with the union and practically put through the same catechizing to which they were subjected when the walkout was ordered. This reception was not agreeable to the girls and the union officers decided that the matter should be discussed at length in a meeting, which all union operators are urged to attend."[121]

Independent Telephone Company operators in Boise, Idaho, intended to walk out on May 13, 1907, should their demand for a salary increase be denied, but the discharge of one of their number led to an earlier walkout, on May 12. Independent Telephone declared it would not accede to the demands of the operators and vowed it would have a new workforce in place in a few hours.[122] Within a day of the Boise women's walk-out, the company brought some of its operators into Boise from outside exchanges and secured a few Boise girls to take the place of the strikers. But, said a reporter, "it is still short of persons to properly operate the system here."

A committee formed from the operators' union met incoming trains and tried to dissuade prospective operators from taking positions with the company and was doing the same work with the Boise girls. However, it was said that the company had proposed to take the operators back as individuals, at least some of them, but not as members of the union; that is, it declined to recognize the union and to pay only the former wages, an offer that the girls declined. Members of organized labor in Boise were aiding the strikers and the electrical workers employed by the firm were thought to be ready to walk out at any time. When the operators received their checks that month, they discovered that a cut had been made in their wages by the company, although nothing had previously been said to them about an imminent wage reduction.[123]

A committee from the Federated Trades and Labor Council of Boise and from the striking operators held a conference with manager Sinsel of the Independent Telephone Company on May 16 but no agreement was reached and each side seemed more determined. The biggest issue remained that of union recognition. The girls refused to go back to work until they achieved union recognition.[124]

On the evening of May 23, the operators reached an agreement with Sinsel whereby they would be taken back as a union with an increase in wages. The new scale of wages was that proposed by the company's management; "However, the agreement seems to represent a victory for the girls in that they were reinstalled as a union," said a journalist. Union recognition had been, reportedly, the only barrier to an agreement for the previous few days. The company's name was taken off the "unfair" list in Boise by the organized labor movement there and 12 of the girls went back to their switchboards on May 24.[125]

All the hello girls at the Butte, Montana, Rocky Mountain Bell Telephone Company went on a sympathy strike on June 25, 1907, in solidarity with the striking linemen of Idaho, Utah and Montana. The action was taken after a conference at which the girls decided the only way the linemen would win their strike was to totally tie up the company's business in the state. Business of the firm was reported to be "almost paralyzed." Local officials of the firm promised they would fill the places of operators and linemen with operators and linemen from other states, then said to be already on the way to Boise.[126]

On the night of August 5, at a meeting of the executive committee of the Montana Federation of Labor, it was decided to call out not only the girls employed by the Bell Telephone Company in cities where they were organized but also those in towns where they were not organized, in support of the linemen's strike. The phone service in Butte had been, reportedly, entirely suspended for a month by that time. The telephone girls' strike in Butte a month earlier and their successful effort to prevent their places being filled had strengthened the belief that the hello girls would win the strike for the linemen.

The phone girls' union had no organization in Montana outside of the larger cities. The girls there had been "orderly" but by moral suasion in Butte they had succeeded in keeping every girl out of the Bell Telephone Company. That request by the Montana Federation of Labor worked at least in one case because on August 6, 20 operators walked out in sympathy with the linemen, in compliance with the labor body's request.[127]

In Pocatello, Idaho, ten telephone girls spent ten days talking to management, asking for a wage increase. Getting nowhere, they went on strike on June 24, 1907. Phone company division superintendent Lanestrom claimed the girls had no occasion to strike and were to consider themselves discharged. Strikebreakers arrived on June 25 from Salt Lake City while the strikers were appealing to the public for sympathy and issued a statement saying they were only paid $20 to $30 a month and that amount of money was inadequate to live on. The girls wanted a raise of $10 a month. The operators formed themselves into committees and were petitioning phone subscribers to have their phones removed and, said a report, "are meeting with considerable success." The Trades and Labor Council of Pocatello was championing the case of the hello girls and sent a committee to see Lanestrom, who wouldn't meet with them. on June 27, a settlement was reached through a committee of citizens headed by Walter Cleare (an ex-mayor), a committee of striking operators and a committee from the Trades and Labor Council, meeting with Lanestrom. The agreement was that the girls would all go back to work the next day and work for one week at their old salary; after that week, they would receive the wage increase they demanded.[128]

When the Pocatello girls were back at work, the Bell Telephone firm suddenly announced they would not meet their demands but would make them a proposition to accept wages based on experience. With respect to the promises the company had made in order to get the women back to work, a reporter commented, "It has later developed, however, that the company made no such promises and that the citizens' committee misunderstood the agreement." Before returning to work, the operators had secured signatures to about 200 orders for the removal of phones. Unless the company granted an increase in pay within the time specified, they would be presented with the orders and the operators would be backed up by the citizens' committee and the Trades and Labor Council.[129]

Tucson, Arizona, telephone girls went on strike in August 1907 for a raise of $5 a month on top of their salary of $35 a month. J.H. Schneider, manager in Tucson for the Consolidated Telephone, Telegraph and Electric Company, told a reporter, "The telephone girls in this city have made no demand to me for an increase in their salary, and as I am manager of the local office it is only natural to suppose that if an increase was asked for, the demand would be made to me. So far as I know, there is absolutely no truth in the statement that the girls are going on a strike for higher wages or for any other cause. There have been no difficulty between the young ladies and the company whatever to my knowledge." The operators stated that they would strike as soon as Miss Henderson, the chief operator, returned to Tucson from Globe, Arizona. She did later that day and the girls went out on strike.[130]

Just a few days later, the strike was at an end. After a conference that lasted almost two full days, the hello girls were given a wage increase bringing their salary range from $30 a month to $40 a month. The ultimatum was that if they were not given the raise, they would all walk out and tie up phone service. The operators were said to be backed by a great number of Tucson telephone subscribers. Company officials were willing to give two long-serving ones, $40 a month but they objected to making that the general scale. They stated they would be willing to pay the newer girls $35 a month, an increase of $5.[131]

In December 1907, Andrew J. Gallagher, secretary of the San Francisco Labor Council, laid before an attorney the charges made to him by the members of the telephone girls' union that they had been persecuted by the Pacific States Telephone company even after leaving its employ. The young women stated that company agents had harassed them wherever they had secured employment. Gallaher had consulted a lawyer to learn if the accused persons and company could be prosecuted. No other details were given and nothing more was heard of this case.[132]

When Pacific States Telephone Company superintendent Reynolds arrived in Lewistown, Idaho, near the end of March 1908 with six strikebreakers from the Spokane office, the striking Lewistown operators let fly with jeers, insults, screams and hair-pulling, directed at the scabs. Those Lewistown operators had struck for the eight-hour day and, reportedly, the entire town was behind them. They and all their supporters met Reynolds and his scabs at the train depot where they extended to the newcomers what a reporter described as a "fierce welcome." However, the dispute was quickly settled with Pacific States conceding the eight-hour day to the girls, whereupon Reynolds and company returned to Spokane.[133]

Striking hello girls in Rockford, Illinois, clashed with the strikebreakers who took their places when the latter appeared at an exchange on December 19, 1908, and, noted a journalist, "a general free-for-all fight followed, in which half a dozen girls were slightly injured and which continued until the police were summoned. Umbrellas, fingernails, clenched fists and heavily booted tiny feet were the weapons and blood was streaming from the cheeks of several of the girls." The police finally arrived and quelled the melee.[134]

When the Maysville, Kentucky, exchange girls went on strike in September 1909 by reason of some objectionable rules of the company, the editor of a newspaper in that state wrote that they "have more to contend with than any other class of employee, and the *Climax* trusts they will get all concessions they ask, and then some."[135]

When You Ask Central for the Time, This Is the Clock She Consults
(At the left of the operator, in the circle of white, is its position at the switchboard.)

A 1916 photo showing New York City operators at work. At the bottom: the clock the operators consulted when a caller asked for the time.

In February 1910, San Francisco Mayor McCarthy's new police commissioner dismissed three telephone operators, all union members. Gertrude Foran (vice president of the telephone operators' union), and Mollie McMahon who was described as an "ardent" member of that same union. Amy Schiller was the third dismissed operator. They claimed that they were dismissed without warning. The new police commissioner was said to have started a reorganization campaign by firing the three women, the complete force of operators at the city's central police station. When Foran and McMahon visited the mayor to complain, he said the action was a surprise to him but that he would look into the matter. Three new operators were then in place. The fired hello girls had always been held in their positions under monthly appointment and the police commissioner who discharged them made an order just one week earlier that appointed them to their positions for the month of February. It was said that one of the new girls appointed by the commissioner, Margaret Welch, was a sister of California

AX PROVES BOOMERANG
UNION GIRLS SACRIFICED

Miss Mollie McMahon, one of the telephone operators dismissed by the police commissioners.

These San Francisco operators lost their jobs in 1910, perhaps due to municipal corruption or union activities.

State Senator Dick Welch, and that the appointment was a political debt being paid. Welch said he knew nothing about it but he did admit he had a sister named Margaret. It was also alleged by the dismissed women that Nellie Harvey, another new appointee, had been promised the position of police matron but she was given the position of operator when it was found impossible to comply with the original plan. Foran had been first vice-president of the union prior to the 1907 strike and took an active part in that strike but declined to seek re-election to her union post. McMahon also took a prominent role in the strike. Foran and McMahon threatened to take legal action but had decided to wait and see if the mayor was able to resolve the issue.[136]

When about 1200 hello girls, members of the newly formed Boston Telephone Operators' Union, threatened strike action in July 1912, they won their first big concession from their employers: the posting of an official notice in all Greater Boston telephone exchanges stating that beginning on July 15, the operators would be given an eight-hour day with no reduction in pay. The operators also secured these concessions: time and a half for all overtime, Sunday and holiday work; 30 minutes overtime allowance for work that exceeded five minutes after the regular hours; one round trip car fare per day for operators who worked split shifts; the elimination of compulsory split shifts for operators in the employ of the company for 18 months or longer; the question of wages was then being considered by the telephone company. Wages paid at the time ranged from $4 a week for beginners to $10 per week after 12 months service.[137]

The Boston Telephone Operators' Union was back in the news at the end of February 1913 when members of the Boston Telephone Operators' Union threatened to walk out. In one account, the membership total was put at 2200 in the metropolitan district. The employing firm was the New England Telephone Company. Back in the summer of 1912, the company had increased wages and readjusted the operators' working hours and their relief periods, and in January 1913 it initiated an insurance benefit plan for the employees.[138]

The threatened strike in Boston prompted the New England Telephone Company to bring into the city experienced operators to act as strikebreakers. At that time, early April, the demands of the operators were in the hands of the Massachusetts State Board of Arbitration and the operators were said to be ready to walk out if they found the board's report unsatisfactory. The fact that more than 1000 hello girls had been brought in from New York City, Philadelphia and various New England cities and housed in "the best hotels" ready for the emergency was communicated to the operators at one of their meetings and their vote for an immediate strike was averted only by the action of Boston Mayor Fitzgerald. The mayor rushed to the meeting hall and induced the operators to stick to their terms of the truce even though they believed the employer had violated its agreement to wait until the arbitration report was issued before taking any action. Manager D.S. Potter of the Chesapeake and Potomac Telephone Company (based in Washington, D.C.) stated on April 9 that he had been asked by the American Telephone and Telegraph Company to send operators to the Boston office "to keep the service open to and from Boston." He added, "We are not thoroughly familiar with the strike situation in Boston and we're not sending the girls as strikebreakers. We sent what operators we could spare without crippling the service here." It was explained to the reporter that the girls were not "sent" in the strict sense of the word but were asked to go and that they were all properly chaperoned. It was also declared that they were chosen from among the most experienced operators.

American Telephone and Telegraph, which was the long distance company, was asked why it should be asking for operators for protection against a possible local strike; it was stated that the connection between the long distance company and the local company in a city like Boston "is very intimate." In Washington, it was said, the long distance calls were handled in the main exchange. Hence, a strike in the exchanges of the local company might seriously affect the business of the long distance company; that is, they shared the same physical space. Twenty-five hello girls left for Boston on April 9 from Indianapolis to act as potential strikebreakers.[139]

What the operators were waiting for was the reply of New England Telephone President Spalding to their demand for higher wages. It was expected to be delivered by Spalding at 2 p.m. on April 9. The action of the company in bringing in New York City women already in the employ of American Telephone and Telegraph, coupled with the announcement that the whole Bell Telephone organization was behind its New England subsidiary in the local fight, was said to have "disappointed the girls." They had expected the company would make an effort to fill their places with new employees but they had not anticipated the coming of trained operators from other offices. Telephone operators were organized into unions in only a few cities in Massachusetts. Recently there had been a movement to organize the operators in New York City and the union members in Boston had hoped for much from the spread of unionism. That hope was dashed when a special train from New York City arrived in Boston on the afternoon of April 9 bringing 1000 women from the exchanges of New York

City, Brooklyn, Jersey City and Philadelphia. They were quartered at a prominent hotel in Boston's Back Bay area and were said to be ready to go to work immediately if needed. The Boston operators had the support of organized labor such as the Boston Central Labor Union. Practically every union in Boston connected with the American Federation of Labor was affiliated with the Central Labor Union.[140]

On April 10 it was announced there would be no strike of the Boston telephone girls. A committee representing the girls signed an agreement with the company at 5:25 a.m. on April 10, with the agreement going into effect on June 1. However, the U.S. federal government was to be asked to investigate the way in which the Bell company sent girls from all parts of the country to Boston. It was argued that the Bell company did not wait until it was seen that a strike was unavoidable before it began importing potential strikebreakers; that it was a tactic of intimidation. Most of the imported girls were young, many of them reportedly only 16 and 17. In some cases, the parents of the girls were not told where their daughters were being sent. In Boston they were housed in expensive hotels with their room and board paid for by Bell. All of them were paid a straight salary for the time they spent in Boston and were promised a bonus of $25 if they had to go to work. According to this account, the course of action taken by the Chicago Telephone Company (a Bell subsidiary) "was particularly flagrant." Some 300 girls were sent from Chicago to Boston on the evening of April 9. One hundred more were gathered together in Chicago early on the morning of April 10 ready to go to Boston, but in the end were not needed. Most of them were 16, 17 and 18 and all had suitcases with them.[141]

Another account of the averted Boston strike said that a compromise settlement was reached after 48 conferences were held by the two sides. A committee from the Boston Chamber of Commerce acted as an intermediary. Instead of the weekly wage increase of $1 which the union had demanded, the agreement provided for the establishment by the company of a plan of anniversary payouts. Those payments were to be $25 to each operator at the end of her second consecutive year of employment; $50 annually from the end of the third year to the end of the ninth year; and $100 at the end of the tenth year and each year thereafter. Other concessions were reported to be the "virtual abolition" of the split shift and a one-hour (instead of 45-minute) lunch period. That system of payouts was then being introduced in various cities by Bell on its own accord, apparently to try and keep employees; that is, no strike or threatened strike was necessary to win that concession.[142]

In another account of the Boston affair, it was reported, with respect to the agreement, that the company did not recognize the union and it did not "give up the split tricks or mention the eight-hour day, with rest periods of 15 minutes." Also, the Sunday, Saturday afternoon and holiday vacations given to operators would be dependent upon "consistency with the requirements of the service." At 3:15 p.m., the second section of a train arrived, bringing 130 girls to join the strikebreakers. These girls came from the "flood-stricken district," Toledo, Dayton, Columbus, Zanesville and Cincinnati, all in Ohio. Those girls were 30 hours on the road. That importation of strikebreakers had caused a certain level of political activity. Measures to protect wage earners against the interstate shipment of strikebreakers and against the forcing of an employee to work as a strikebreaker were reportedly to be introduced in the U.S. House of Representatives. Representative Frank Buchanan, of the committee on labor, said in an April 9 statement, "The fact that telephone girls in Washington have been shipped to Boston to break a strike in the plant of the corporation owning the telephones in both cities lends new emphasis to the need for legislation which will prevent an employer from forcing his employees to act as strikebreakers." He promised that legislation would be introduced before the close of the current session. It was also reported that the work of organizing a union among Washington operators had already begun under the direction of the Central Labor Union and the American Federation of Labor. Union officials were reluctant to talk about the state of the campaign. When asked their attitude toward the formation of a union among their employees, Chesapeake and Potomac Telephone Company officials declared, "We are not giving the matter any consideration."[143]

When some of those potential strikebreakers were imported to Boston, many were housed at the city's fashionable Copley-Plaza Hotel, where 350 rooms had been reserved for them. Those rooms had been renting for $8 to $10 a day. Besides the $25 bonus promised to them, and free room and board in the hotel, those girls had their laundry paid for and were entertained on free sightseeing trips and so forth, when not on duty. They were chaperoned by 12 female monitors and "protected from possible annoyance" by private detectives and 50 linemen. They had their own private dining room at the hotel, complete with an orchestra.[144]

Twenty-one Washington, D.C., hello girls who went to Boston as strikebreakers returned to their home city on April 13. Since the start of the excursion on April 8, inquiries at the offices of the Chesapeake and Potomac Telephone Company had been fruitless for reporters; no list of names could be obtained. One of those returning operators asked a journalist to imagine the manager walking up to you and saying, "'Miss Jones, you will please make arrangements to start for Boston at the expense of the company, at once. You will stop at the best hotel in the city. You may order anything you like.' How would you feel?" She added, "We were finely treated, and I am mighty glad I was chosen to go. From the time we left the telephone office in taxi cabs for the Union Station, we had everything we asked for.... It really does seem hard to return to work after such a good time."[145]

At an April 16 meeting of the Baltimore Federation of Labor, operators from that city who went to Boston as strikebreakers were bitterly criticized for their activities. The attack on the girls was led by Delegate Neal, who called them wolves in sheep's clothing.[146]

At the beginning of May 1913, the U.S. Department of Labor announced it would start a probe into the transportation of hello girls from Washington to Boston to be used as strikebreakers "just as soon as Congress appropriates the necessary money to carry on such an investigation." Secretary of Labor William Wilson declared that the Boston incident was then a closed one and that nothing would be done about it except that it would be studied in "every phase" so that laws could be drawn up to prevent a repetition of it. Said a reporter; "All of the precedents and laws on the matter will be gone into by the department to see what may be done to prevent the taking of young girls away from their homes without proper care and attention to act as strikebreakers."[147]

When the Cumberland Telephone Company in Madisonville, Kentucky, refused to grant their operators' demands for a salary increase, 12 of the 14 girls at the exchange in that city went out on strike on May 31, after which time the telephone service was reported as being "badly crippled." According to Maude Sullivan, chief operator, the salary request was $1 a day for operators, $1.25 a day for toll operators and $40 a month for the chief operator. Sullivan said the women were then being paid from $15 to $20 a month. Petitions were circulated on May 30 by two of the operators, assisted by citizens, and "practically every business house and phone user in the city signed them, asking that the company grant the increase in salary." Several hundred people were reported to have been in front of the telephone building when the girls walked out and gave them a hearty cheer, and also presented them with flowers.[148]

Union organizers were said to be at work in Chicago among the hello girls in June 1913 to organize them and to prevent another Boston from happening. Chicago operators had higher wages than department store girls, but still were poor objectively; they were also reported to be subject "to a great number of humiliating rules and regulations."[149]

On June 17, 1913, St. Louis operators employed by the Southwestern Telephone Company (a Bell company) went on strike. Company officials said that less than 50 percent of the girls quit work but union officials said the strike affected all of the city's Bell exchanges. Conflicting numbers were given out by the two sides. At union headquarters, it was said that all 23 operators at the Sidney exchange had walked out but Southwestern said that only seven operators there had gone on strike. Trouble between the two sides had been brewing for several weeks before it reached the crisis point.[150]

On June 18, about 100 strikebreaking girls arrived in St. Louis from Chicago and Kansas City. They were met at the Union Station by officials of Southwestern Telegraph and Telephone Company, who took them in automobiles to hotels. Fifty cops were on hand to preserve order; there was no sign of violence. On June 16, company officials said they would countenance no demands from strikers.[151]

According to one account, the majority of girls that Bell had sent to St. Louis were drawn from the Chicago Telephone Company. Altogether the Chicago branch of the Bell system had sent about 200 girls to St. Louis. They were put up at the best hotels and were said to receive double pay and short hours. On June 23, the striking girls in St. Louis received their first benefit payment. Each girl received $5, the amount paid each week to the 33 operators discharged by the company early in May for helping to organize the union. That relief action was taken by several unions in the area. For example, the Carpenters' District Council had already voted $500 to the strikers and pledged double that amount during the coming week.[152]

The St. Louis strike dragged on into July. According to Nebraska Telephone Company officials (who reportedly sent a large number of girls to St. Louis to act as strikebreakers there), fewer than a dozen girls had gone to that city. Those girls, telco officials said on July 18, had gone to St. Louis during their vacations and had not made the trips at the insistence of Nebraska Telephone. Fewer than 25 girls were away at a time during the summer on vacation and that was the maximum number, declared the company, that could possibly go as strikebreakers. It insisted that it was making no effort to recruit for St. Louis. Local operators in Omaha told a reporter that they were not being requested to go but were instead being asked whether they would not care to go for an added recompense over that which they were then receiving. Those queries by Nebraska Telephone officials were being made quietly, the operators said, but nevertheless they were being made. One operator, asked by a reporter what she knew about the situation, said, "I am afraid to tell."[153]

Rush hour at downtown exchanges.

Ogden, Utah, operators in 1916.

Lillian Miller was president of the Telephone Operators' Union of St. Louis and at the time of the strike she was a supervisor in the Sydney exchange of the system. On August 1, 1913, she had just been released from a St. Louis police station where she had been charged, said a news story, "with throwing something more solid and tangible than arguments at a taxi cab load of strikebreakers." She was described as five feet tall and in her middle 20s. Asked why they were on strike, Miller said; "Because the Bell company discharged 32 tried and faithful girls for participation in the organization of a union and 25 men for the same reason." Miller said there were then no other grievances. She added that the company had introduced a new scale of wages and had said it would grant the eight-hour day:

> We have not asked for recognition of the union but have asked for the re-employment of union girls who, after long and good service, were discharged and have been branded in the telephone company's statements as incompetent.... We are free Americans and insist upon our right to organize a union. The company, which sent agents to Jefferson City to oppose the passage of the woman's nine-hour labor law, insists that we must not organize. That is the whole trouble.

When the girls began to organize, the traffic chiefs called them one at a time and questioned them about the union. Thirty-two of those who favored it were notified that their services were no longer needed and they have been branded as incompetent, Miller explained. Every one of those women had been in the service of the company for at least three years and some had up to ten years of service. Miller was one of those discharged. She had nine years of service and had been a supervisor at the Sydney exchange for seven of those years; throughout those years she had never had a complaint of any kind lodged against her. Yet on May 9 she was discharged because she favored a union. The majority of the women who were fired had been receiving the maximum operator pay of $40 a month. That was reached by successive raises of $2.50 a month in the 65 months after a girl began her employment at $20 a month. Supervisors were paid $50 a month and were promoted from the ranks of the operators who were receiving the maximum pay for an operator.[154]

Mr. Hiss was the general manager of the Southwestern Telephone Company in St. Louis. According to Miller, the company had a system of demerits which, Hiss said, was abolished April 1 but which was in force in the Sydney exchange up to May 9 at least. There were 85 reasons for charging a girl with a demerit, and supervisors were charged with reporting laxity to the chief operator. For giving the wrong number to a subscriber, a girl was charged with four demerits; for "looking around," three demerits; for talking to the adjacent operator, three; for chewing gum, two; for cutting

St. Louis Telephone Girl Tells Story of Grievances

Leader In Strike Gives Reasons For The Trouble

Miss Lillian Miller, prominent in the trouble between the telephone operators and the Bell company in St.

Lillian Miller, president of the Telephone Operators' Union in St. Louis in 1913, was involved in a strike that year.

off a subscriber, five. Reportedly, the telco was then under the added expense of $5000 a day in railroad and taxi fares and for hotel room and board for the strikebreakers imported from other cities. Said a reporter,

> Boston's manager ... did not claim the right to interfere with the liberty of the operators and when they were organized conferred with them. As a result, Boston girls work eight hours, six days in the week, are paid time and a half for Sunday work; are paid every week at a maximum of $12 for operators and $15 for supervisors; have every third

Saturday off during the winter, and every other Saturday off during the summer, and split-time operators are paid $1 a week extra, with carfare.

Miller said,

In St. Louis the girls are on duty ten hours, have half an hour for lunch and two rest periods of 15 minutes each, morning and afternoon. They work six days a week with no extra for Sunday work. They are paid twice a month at the rate of $40 a month for operators and $50 a month for supervisors. They have no Saturdays off. Split-time operators get carfare but no extra pay.

Miller complained that this was not the first time the company had interfered with operators' liberty. A year or so earlier, some of the girls thought that, as the operators sat for long hours with a telephone headset strapped to their heads, their health might suffer and proposed to organize walking clubs. The girls were to go on little tours in the area around St. Louis on their days off. Miller went to a meeting in north St. Louis to arrange for those walks and a few days later was told, with the other participants, that the company forbade the organization of walking clubs. According to Miller, there were 750 members in the union, about 600 of whom were Bell employees and 150 Kinloch employees. Some 400 of them were on strike. She did not know if the other 200 would walk out or not: "The company is offering them every inducement to stay." And, she added, "Nearly all our girls live at home and we have offers of homes for all the girls who do not."[155]

An August 6 report declared that the strike of St. Louis operators and maintenance men against the Southwestern Telegraph and Telephone Company, which had been announced on August 5 as "settled," practically was renewed on the afternoon of August 6. An "indignation" meeting of the operators, called to protest the terms of settlement on which the girls had no vote, resulted in the announcement that none of the striking operators would return to work until the company first had made amends for the treatment of six of the first eight girls who sought reinstatement on August 5. The eight were delegated by the strikers to test the sincerity of the company's promise to take them back without discrimination. Two of the girls reported that when they went to the south exchange where they worked before the strike, they were told that all places were taken and that they had to apply at the main office. Two others went directly to the main office and, they said, were told to report again the next day. Two others said they were told they must enter the company's training school at $5 a week, although before the strike they were receiving $30 a month as experienced operators.[156]

A piece published in December 1913 discussed all the strikes that took place in the past six months in St. Louis and said that every strike ended in defeat: "In June last the telephone girls revolted…. Their defeat was almost instantaneous, and in the struggle, not a few girls had their heads battered by the yellow dogs—the police."[157]

Lexington, Kentucky, was threatened with an operators strike in May 1914. A committee of operators had presented a "communication" to President George S. Shanklin of the Fayette Home Telephone Company in which the girls' grievances were set forth: They had no Sundays off; they worked nine hours a day seven days a week and were only "allowed" a day off when they were unable to work due to sickness. The petition asked for a larger workforce of operators to handle the work load:

> Please remember that we are human and, unlike the instruments we serve, cannot go too rapid a pace without incurring the danger of a nervous breakdown. We ask that the company employ more operators to relieve the great strain due to an insufficient number of operators. We desire to call your attention to the unjust partiality of discrimination shown by those in charge to certain of the operators."[158]

Operators at both Scranton, Pennsylvania, exchanges had reportedly signified their willingness, in May 1914, to join a union that would remedy the split shift and other objectionable working conditions. According to an article, "The advances made by Boston organized telephone girls are being pointed to as an illustration of the power of unity."[159]

In Chicago in July 1915, Agnes Nestor, president of the Women's Trade Union League, said her organization hoped to break in among the employees of Bell Telephone and organize a union. Said Nestor,

> In the advertising spread so liberally in Chicago newspapers by the phone trust Chicago Telephone Co., the company has never explained why it operates a secret system for keeping all unions down. Not only in Chicago but all over the country, the Bell phone company is an enemy of organized labor. In Rochester, New York, a few days ago, the Rochester Home Telephone Co., a Bell phone branch, discharged ten young women operators for taking part in the organization of a union.[160]

At the end of October 1915, it was reported that the Herrin, Illinois, telephone girls had secured an agreement with the local telephone company after organizing a union affiliated with the International Brotherhood of Electrical Workers. Under that agreement, the union was recognized, wages were increased ten percent, an eight-hour work day was secured and a provision was made for settling disputes in an "amicable" manner.[161]

Four hello girls in Jackson, Missouri, went out on strike on March 27, 1916. Their dispute with exchange manager Charles W. Boutin was over wages and hours. Two places were quickly filled by strikebreakers from Cape Girardeau; one of the four relented and returned to her station. When a reporter contacted Boutin, the manager said; "It doesn't amount to anything. It isn't a strike. Two of them just quit. Don't say anything about it, because if this is kept quiet we'll get all this trouble settled quickly."[162]

A different account of the strike stated that at the close of the second day of the walkout, the three hello girls still out announced they had given up trying to reach a settlement with the company and were going to look for other jobs. After they declared they would not return, the phone company office was reportedly deluged with applications from women wanting those jobs. One striker was a local call operator while the other two were on the long distance boards. The one who returned to her post was Meta Meir, who had five years of service. Jennie Horn (13 years) was the only operator who did not join the strike. The other three were Frances Milde (eight years), Bertha Hartle (five years) and local call operator Pearl Beattie (three years). Those first two reported that they had been receiving $22.50 a month and had asked for an increase to $30. Others wanted a raise to $27. One of the women also said that on some days, they were required to work 18 hours, and then work six hours on the following day.[163]

Toledo, Ohio, operators formed a union in October 1916 and promised to immediately take up the question of the low wages and the split shifts that lengthened their day by several hours. That new union was to be affiliated with the International Brotherhood of Electrical Workers, the union that did the organizing work among the hello girls of Toledo.[164]

When those Toledo women organized, their employer, the Home Telephone Company, discharged four of them for organizing a union. The other operators all struck on November 18, 1916, as did the outside electrical workers. After a four-month strike, the employer acknowledged the right of the operators to join a union. Home Telephone agreed to reinstate all the strikers without discrimination and acknowledged the right of the operators to present grievances that would be adjusted by representatives of both parties. After work was resumed by the hello girls, the employees would present demands for wage increases to the company. Every union in Toledo had been behind the girls and every union contributed to a strike benefit fund. Many of the unions carried weekly assessments on every member to pay the girls an amount equal to their former wage. Reportedly, Home Telephone lost thousands of its subscribers. Federal Judge Killits issued an injunction "against violence" at the request of "prominent citizens" who were active in the Citizens' Alliance. That court was asked to act because the company was a subsidiary of an interstate corporation. The unionists denounced Killits for his usurpation of duties that belonged to officials charged with the enforcement of criminal law and showed that his honor was more interested in breaking the strike, as he insisted that "service to the public must not be interrupted." The four discharged operators were reinstated and the 90 strikers returned to work on February 28, 1917.[165]

Striking telephone operators in Hoquiam and Aberdeen, Washington, returned to work on the morning of July 6, 1917, following mediation. The operators were to get an increase in pay and the company agreed not to discriminate against union members. Experienced telephone girls who had been taken to Hoquiam and Aberdeen from Tacoma to fill the places of the strikers were sent home.[166]

Things on the West Coast remained uneasy but nothing much happened until October 1917 when it was announced that operators in all three Tacoma exchanges would go on strike on October 19 if their demands were not met. Wages then averaged $1.75 a day for eight hours with straight time paid for any overtime; the hello girls were asking for $2.75 a day with time and a half for overtime. The Pacific Telephone and Telegraph Company had persistently refused to recognize the new union at Tacoma although it raised wages (increases of from five to 25 cents a day) about a month earlier when the girls first started asking for more money.[167]

In nearby Seattle, telephone girls announced they would strike on October 20 unless the company gave them an eight-hour day and higher wages. Other members of the Electrical Workers' Union, of which the operators constituted a branch, would also be involved if the strike took place. Demands by the operators were that only union workers, when available, were to be employed; an eight-hour day was to be worked within 12 consecutive hours; no operator was to receive less than $1.50 a day; a minimum of $2.75 a day was to be paid after nine months on the job; at least 15 cents extra was to be paid for night work after 6 p.m.; night operators wages were to be 50 cents more than day workers; operators were to work every other Sunday with a day off during the week to compensate; double time was to be paid for Sunday work as well as for seven specified holidays; there was to be a 15-minute break each morning and afternoon "without being compelled to make up this 30 minutes"; two weeks' vacation with one weeks' pay after working 12 months; two weeks' vacation with full pay after working two years. Union president Rhoda Kerr said the minimum efficiency in the Seattle exchange was ten calls a minute and that some girls handled 16 calls a minute.[168]

At almost the same time, it was announced from San Francisco that a walkout of 3400 Pacific Telephone Company operators in Los Angeles and various other West Coast cities had been called for midnight on October 19. The announcement was made by John Morganthaler, an official of the International Brotherhood of Electrical Workers. The flat refusal of the company to recognize the operators' union was given by Morganthaler as the reason for the strike order.[169]

On October 20, 1917, Hazel Holmes, president of the Telephone Operators' Union Local A39 in Tacoma, announced that the strike there had been put off for at least a week at the request of the U.S. government. On October 1, the company had granted a wage increase of $1 a week to all classes of operators. The order to postpone the strike was delivered on the morning of October 20 at 2 a.m. from San Francisco. The postponement was the result of a conference between electrical workers and government authorities in San Francisco (no telephone girls were involved). The postponement was to last until after the second Liberty Loan (war effort) campaign was ended. Thus, the new tentative strike date was set for midnight on October 27, 12 hours after the Liberty Loan drive ended. Intervener in the affair was Mortimer Fleishhacker of the California State Council of Defense, at the request of federal authorities, and the appeal made to the unionists was that of "patriotism."[170]

At midnight on October 31, all the union operators and linemen in Washington and Oregon went on strike. In Tacoma that number was nearly 300 hello girls and linemen with more than 90 percent of all employees of the phone system walking out. Union officials declared there would be no settlement unless the phone company granted recognition of the operators' union. Messages from officials of the international union at San Francisco asking for a third postponement were received by Tacoma strike officials at 3:30 a.m. November 1 and were disregarded because of the lateness of their arrival. That 3:30 a.m. message said that the government had guaranteed that the phone company would recognize the girls' union in Aberdeen, Seattle and Portland. No mention was made of Tacoma.

Deputy sheriffs guarded the main phone exchange in Tacoma on November 1. The entrance to the building was locked and a guard stood inside the door. Printed notices were posted on the building warning against picketing and declaring that "appropriate action will be taken against any person who so acts." About a dozen girls and three linemen refused to join the strike.[171]

On November 23, the U.S. Labor Department announced the settlement of the operators' strike in California, Washington and Oregon. That settlement on the Pacific Coast still had to be ratified by the local union. Reportedly, the girls won recognition of their union and a 12.5 percent wage increase for operators receiving less than $50 a month and the right to negotiate through their organization for any further demands (that is, collective bargaining).[172]

5000 PHONE GIRLS STRIKE

TACOMA UNIONS OUT; SUBSTITUTE WORKERS HIRED

Hello Girls Directing Biggest Switchboard Strike

THE PHONE COMPANY'S MISTAKE!

Unidentified leaders in the Tacoma, Washington, operators' strike in 1917.

Then it was reported that after a strike of 26 days, the hello girls in Tacoma would return to work at 10 p.m. on November 26. Linemen had also accepted the deal but announced they would not go back to work until they saw that the girls were fairly treated. Although the operators were not granted a closed shop, they explained that was not insisted upon because of President Woodrow Wilson's request that closed shops be waived during the labor shortage caused by the war. All of the non-union strikebreakers hired by Pacific Telephone during the strike on offers of "permanent positions" were to be released by the company as fast as the union girls returned to their switchboards.[173]

One day later, on November 27, declaring that Tacoma officials of the Pacific Telephone Company had flatly repudiated the strike settlement signed by heads of the phone system and U.S. Secretary of Labor William Wilson at San Francisco, the Tacoma operators renewed their strike on November 27. A group of 27 operators appeared at the central exchange at 8:30 a.m. to resume work, in light of the settlement. However, armed guards of the company halted them. Company executive W.S. Moore came to the door and told the girls that they could enter the building two at a time and sign applications for work. The women said they understood they were to get their old positions back. "Most of our switchboards are full and we have space for only a few girls. But if you want to sign applications, I will notify you when there is work," said Moore. According to the settlement, all employees who had gone on strike were to be restored to their former positions without any discrimination and with no break in their service record with the company. That agreement had been signed by heads of the Pacific Telephone system at San Francisco and by Secretary Wilson, among others. Tacoma system manager John Schlarb announced on November 27 that he had no intention of removing any non-union girl from the switchboards in favor of a union girl. Operators and linemen who returned to work after signing an application blank would thus become new employees and would forfeit their entire service record.[174]

Secretary Wilson, the mediator in the dispute, was reported to be "ill" in Portland and unable to deal with this latest twist. Felix Frankfurter, secretary of President Woodrow Wilson's mediation commission, was then trying to bring the two sides together. Tacoma's phone system was not the only one that refused to take back its operators. Spokane union officials were told that the company would take back those they had vacancies for while the others would have to wait until vacancies occurred.[175]

In a November 29 editorial, the editor stated that the Pacific Telephone and Telegraph Company had

> proved itself faithless. Tacoma girls voted to return to work in accordance with the mediation agreement. They voted to end the strike. But when they returned to the telephone headquarters, the manager informed them they could not get their old jobs back, but would be considered as new applicants. They would have to take their turn for a vacancy.… This is a plain breach of faith.… The government of the United States has virtually been made a laughing stock in this affair.… Is the United States government going to stand for that?[176]

Tacoma operators were told to go back to work on December 4. The strike came to an abrupt end after Henry M. White of Seattle (appointed by William Wilson to mediate) advised the Tacoma strikers to report back to work at once. White had received word from Pacific Telephone headquarters in San Francisco that the company was ready to live up to the letter and spirit of the agreement. A list of all strikers at Tacoma, 145 hello girls and 52 linemen, was prepared and filed with Schlarb. No reason was given in this account for the reversal by the phone company.[177]

A report on the aftermath of the Tacoma strike, published on January 10, 1918, claimed that Pacific Telephone was making a determined effort to break up the new union of hello girls. That charge was made by officials of both the operators' union and the linemen's union. According to the girls and president James Stewart of the linemen, there had been discrimination against union girls who had returned to work since the strike. Non-union girls had been retained throughout the system and shown "extreme favoritism." Several girls had reportedly quit over what they described as unbearable conditions. At the same time, experienced union operators had been demoted and new operators (strikebreakers) with little or no experience had been elevated to positions above them. Said Stewart, "It has violated its agreement with the government, because it promised to put the girls all back in their former positions. It is a fact that scarcely a single union telephone operator has been given her former work and former hours." Pacific Telephone had advertised for recruits for its switchboards and was breaking in new girls every day. Before they could get employment, the new girls were forced to sign an agreement not to join the union. Not one of them had joined the union. According to one account, "A large number of the non-union girls who worked during the strike are now holding down the most important switchboard positions, and many of them have been made supervisors over girls who have worked in the telephone system for years."

Helen Bruce, one of the union operators who resigned because of poor treatment, said,

> The company is making life miserable for every union girl on the board. The union girls are forced to obey every slightest rule of the company, no matter how unimportant and no matter how much the rule was slighted before the strike. Non-union girls at the same time break the same rules continually without rebuke. When a union girl violates any rule she is publicly reprimanded by one of the non-union girls in such a nasty manner that the girls can hardly stand it.

Before the strike, Bruce had been a supervisor in the long distance department. When she returned to work after the strike, she was given an operator position at a lower salary and the supervisor placed over her had no experience at all. The girls claimed that whenever subscribers complained about poor service, Pacific Telephone told them that it could not provide adequate service now because the switchboards were unionized.[178]

A strike of 29 operators took place in Henryetta, Oklahoma, on November 18, 1917. The women organized the Telephone Operators' Union a week earlier and demanded a pay increase of 33.3 percent. Upon the refusal of the local manager to meet their demands, they walked out at 9 a.m. on Sunday morning. Using what non-union girls they could get and importing six operators from Muskogee, Oklahoma, the service resumed but the telephone building was picketed by 20 male strike sympathizers.[179]

Nearly 20,000 union operators and other workers employed by the New England Telephone and Telegraph Company and affiliated firms announced from Boston on April 12, 1919, that they would go on strike on April 15 unless a settlement was reached. At a strike vote held on April 11, 2000 operators representing unions from all parts of New England were present.[180]

Harry Henderson, business agent of the Telephone Operators' Union of Louisville, Kentucky, announced on April 16 that a vote was being taken throughout the country by telephone employees to force government recognition of their unions, with a nationwide strike as the alternative. He also declared that the New England operators strike was regarded as a test of strength for the union. American Telephone and Telegraph officials in New York said they were aware of a movement underway in practically all states to unionize the phone workers. They also said the organizers had the greatest success in New England (where a majority of operators were on strike), California and Montana. Elsewhere it was said that only a small minority of the operators had joined the unions.[181]

According to an April 15 report, telephone service in New England (except Connecticut) had been almost completely tied up by the strike of several thousand operators of New England Telephone and Telegraph and

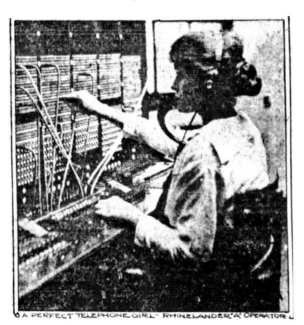

the Providence Telephone Company. The operators wanted a wage increase and the opportunity to bargain directly with the companies' officials. They said that since the operation of the wires had been taken over by the U.S. Post Office, they had been unable to get proper consideration of their demands. Postmaster General Burleson told reporters that every step was being taken to end the problem, and that the operators had walked out "without cause."

A 1920 photo depicting "a perfect telephone girl."

Boston phone service was completely tied up with all cities suffering a lesser disruption. A joint cablegram to President Woodrow Wilson, signed by Governors Coolidge of Massachusetts, Bartlett of New Hampshire and Beeckman of Rhode Island, stated, "New England urges your immediate action to relieve from great loss by telephone strike." Holding the New England strike to be without justification, the Post Office instructed the Boston phone company manager to replace the strikers or to take any other steps necessary to maintain the phone service. (Due to World War I, for a one-year period following July 31, 1918, the federal government took over the telephone system, under the Wire Control Board.)[182]

On April 17, the Wire Control Board declared it would act on New England Telephone strikers' demands on or before May 10. Postmaster Burleson said he had decided to act on behalf of the telephone operators by placing a statement of their demands before New England Telephone Company general manager Driver.[183]

On April 24 it was announced that the 20,000 striking operators and electrical workers of the two New England phone companies had returned to work under an agreement reached by representatives of the three sides involved (employees, employers, and J.C. Koonas, the country's first assistant postmaster. Hostility from all sectors of society, "especially the important ones," over the lack of phone service were said to be just too great to ignore.[184]

A few days later, a published piece singled out several women for the prominent role they played in "winning" the Boston strike. One was 28-year-old Julia S. O'Connor, an operator for about ten years. According to reporter Leary, when O'Connor started work in that industry, operators

> were not as well paid as now and the working conditions were not so good, especially in smaller towns. The girls had for years talked organization, but had got nowhere, partly from the inherent difficulty in organization, but mainly because of the opposition of company officials. There is nothing to indicate that the New England Telephone and Telegraph Company ever officially prohibited unions among the girls, but lesser officials did, and the result was the same.

That is, remarked Leary, until O'Connor, May Matthews, Anna Molly and a few others took it upon themselves in 1912 to form the Telephone Operators' Union of Boston. They made slow headway. During that same period, O'Connor was so active in the affairs of the Women's Trade Union League (in Boston) that she became its president, an office she held for several terms. A few years later, a big push was made among operators to unionize. Previously the union had been affiliated with the International Brotherhood of Electrical Workers and through them to the American Federation of

A 1919 photo showing a large group of striking Boston operators, milling about in the street after a union meeting.

Labor. By that time, 23 local unions existed in New England, all organized by O'Connor, and 97 in the nation with a total membership of 30,000. Then some friction developed with the Electrical Workers which ended in the agreement of both parties to set up a telephone department within the Brotherhood, to let the women do as they pleased, with wide limitations. As part of that settlement, the Brotherhood gave the women $25,000 to start their treasury. O'Connor made demands on the phone company but was told that they could not be done, that the wires were in the control of the government and the girls could not strike against Uncle Sam. Nonetheless, O'Connor led a strike. She reportedly got 100 percent of the operators to go out on that strike, and it was said they achieved most of their goals. Said O'Connor, "This strike, which was forced upon us and was not at all of our seeking, proves plainly that women can be organized as thoroughly as men, and it should prove to the satisfaction of everybody that by organization the exploitation of women in industry can be prevented. When they learn the lesson of coordination, exploitation will cease."[185]

Two companies of state militia were ordered to Linton, Indiana, on the night of April 28, 1919, to quell a riot resulting from a strike of operators. A mob of 400 was reported to have broken the door and windows of the exchange building and drove the eight women strikebreakers inside to the roof. Those girls were later rescued and taken to a place of safety.[186]

On the night of April 29, militia on duty at the Linton telephone strike fired into a crowd of men and women gathered at the exchange building. One man was shot, "though not seriously." One militiaman was hit on the head by a stone. Militiamen fired a total of ten rounds. Adjutant General Smith, in charge of the militia, "has ordered the men to fire low if shooting is necessary." The Department of Justice wired the U.S. Marshal's office at Indianapolis that the situation was growing more threatening as other union men were joining in. The Marshal's office dispatched 50 deputies to the scene. That strike had spread to other people with clerks and miners involved, and business houses, theaters and other places of amusement in Linton closed.[187]

Another Indiana town became involved when it was reported that 100 operators employed by the Citizens' Independent Telephone Company in Terre Haute went on strike on May 23, 1919. Those telephone girls had recently formed a union and were demanding recognition of their union by the company; a wage increase of about $2 a week; an eight-hour day; and time and a half for overtime. The current wage scale ranged from $8 to $15 a week.[188]

Rumors circulated in June 1919 that an attempt would be made to organize operators in New York City and New York State, with Julia O'Connor leading the campaign. A day after that rumor surfaced, American

Boston telephone operator Julia O'Connor was one of the organizers of a union in 1912 and a leader in the 1919 strike.

Telephone and Telegraph Company in New York City announced it
intended to develop a national organization of its employees similar to the
employees association maintained by the Western Union Telegraph Company. May Matthews, general organizer of the telephone operators department of the International Brotherhood of Electrical Workers, was in New
York City then, with O'Connor, to organize the hello girls. Matthews said

> We understand that the telephone company plans this association, which will include
> its 160,000 workers, in the hope that it will stop any possibility of our successfully
> unionizing the girls…. Of course they want to discourage a union among the
> workers…. But the New York girls' desire to unionize still remains.

The employer in New York City was the New York Telephone Company, a subsidiary of American Telephone and Telegraph. Formation of
company "associations" (company unions) were a common tactic used by
employers in the hope that such a tactic would prevent a true union being
formed by its employees, or at least forestalling that event. According to
one of the operators interested in the proposed union, a secret order had
gone out from the phone company a week earlier asking the girls on central
switchboards to listen in on the wires and report any conversations among
fellow operators concerning a union or a strike.[189]

A strike against Pacific Telephone and Telegraph Company started in
Washington state on the morning of June 29, 1919, with a walkout of the
Seattle operators followed by a strike of the linemen. The company
attempted to give service with non-union operators but the attempt was
said to have been a failure. California operators and linemen had gone out
several days before and Oregon and Nevada telephone employees went out
the Washington. Operators demanded a minimum of $2 a day for beginners
and $4 a day for experienced operators and the right to collective bargain-
ing. Negotiations with Pacific Telephone had been ongoing for months
and the order to strike did not come until the company indicated a deter-
mination not to comply with an order from Postmaster General Burleson
to grant the workers the right of bargaining collectively on wages and conditions. The only violence during the strike consisted of attacks on some
of the girls by civilian guards employed by the phone company. In Seattle,
two of the striking girls were struck several times in the face by those
guards. In Reno, Nevada, on July 9, Mayor Stewart took over the local
exchange of the Pacific Telephone Company, acting under the city charter's
police powers. The striking operators there were invited to return to work
with the city guaranteeing them the wages demanded when they went on
strike with the other Pacific Telephone employees. Stewart had sought to
have the strike mediated by himself and the mayors of San Francisco and

Sacramento but the offer was not accepted by Burleson. Several California cities had recently been threatening to take over the telephone service in their cities as a means of enforcing a settlement and guaranteeing service to business interests. An editorial comment was added, with respect to Burleson: "He will not agree to conciliation, to arbitration, to mediation, or even treat the employees of the telephone companies with common decency. He is about the dirtiest autocrat on the American continent. Striking telephone girls have been treated with violence and insult by his hired thugs."[190]

A strike of some 50 operators at the Cortlandt exchange in New York City, reported to have taken place in February 1910, was denied by the New York Telephone Company. However, it did admit that some 25 girls approached management with a view to discussing grievances, especially about wages. Under a new wage scale implemented by the company, beginners were granted a $3 a week raise while more experienced operators were given only $1 a week. One 13-year veteran explained that she and others in her position were then getting $21 a week while novices got $15. They resented the disproportionate nature of the increases. Those women who had briefly walked out returned to their posts, at the request of management. There had still been no union organized among the New York City hello girls and no efforts were then underway. There had been no organizing efforts there since Julia O'Connor's brief and unsuccessful foray the previous summer.[191]

A strike by Boston's telephone operators went into effect at 7 a.m. on June 26, 1923. Union president O'Connor said that between 5500 and 6000 answered the first strike call. A spilt in the ranks of strikers had reportedly developed with a rival union under the leadership of Annie Molloy having refused to join the O'Connor faction in the walkout. O'Connor's group had about 85 percent of the operators. When Molloy's faction would not join the strike, they were expelled from the International Union of Telephone Girls.[192]

That Boston strike was for increased wages and to get a seven-hour day. There was a special meeting of local unions in centers throughout the area served by the New England Telephone and Telegraph Company on July 19, some three and a half weeks after the action began. The purpose of those meetings was to discuss calling off the strike. It was a vote in favor of ending the dispute, and the strike ended.[193]

7

Goodbye to the Hello Girl

The hello girls had barely ousted the hello boys from the arena and then hardly had a chance to warm their seats up before a movement was launched that had as its aim the idea that the hello girl must go. That is, automation was going to sweep them out and allow users to dial directly. It did happen, of course, but nowhere near as quickly as the telcos would have liked. The idea of solving an operator shortage by no longer blaming the false image of the operators rushing off to get married en masse and instituting reasonable pay and working conditions was never contemplated; why bother when automation would soon solve all such problems?

A brief story published in November 1891 noted that a Kansas City, Missouri, man had invented a telephone attachment whereby anyone, by punching a certain number of buttons in a certain way a certain number of times, could make his own connections and, commented a newspaper editor. "the decree has gone forth that the telephone girl must go."[1]

During the summer of 1892, a new invention was announced that, it was claimed, would make the telephone girl a "back number" and provide every telephone subscriber his own "hello girl." The Strowger automatic telephone exchange was the invention that promised to make all connections automatically.[2]

Several people were said to have witnessed a demonstration of the device in La Porte, Indiana. Reportedly the Strowger automatic telephone exchange had been in use in that city for several months and was being studied and tested. It was, said this account, "soon to throw thousands of young ladies off the American labor market, reduce the price of telephones" and so forth.[3]

According to a June 1895 announcement from Syracuse, New York, a new system for telephony (allowing automatic connections) had been devised by Alexander T. Brown of that city. A reporter stated emphatically,

196

"The much abused 'hello girls' will not be necessary at all to make local connections."[4]

Chicago was reportedly set to try a new system of telephony in July 1899. The Illinois Telephone and Telegraph Company had acquired the rights to this new system for 30 years. The new service "will do away with telephone girls." Beside each subscriber's phone was a board containing press buttons. If the subscriber wanted number 682, he had only to press 6, 8 and 2 and the connection was automatically made at the central office. Another advantage touted for the new system was that of "absolute secrecy" as there would be no hello girls around to hear the conversation.[5]

An announcement out of New York City in March 1901 stated, "A new invention threatens to do away almost entirely with the telephone girl and to make every subscriber his own 'central.'" Under the new system, there would be no more "hellos" with central office operators; subscribers would be equipped with miniature switchboards and plugs. Each subscriber could call directly anyone he wished to converse with. That is, for local calls only; long distance calls would still require an operator. This piece did note, "[D]uring the 20 years that telephone lines have been in operation, various efforts have been made to invent some apparatus that would relieve the public of the annoyance of long waits to make connections in the central office."[6]

Emerging around 1901, the National Automatic Telephone Company touted the lack of hello girls with its automatic system and the enhanced privacy. A small in-house system could be set up in, say, a factory (in effect, an intercom system) or a public system with "hundreds of subscribers," although, of course, a subscriber could only call direct to those subscribers also on the system. This company finally went out of business around 1910.[7]

The Illinois Telephone and Telegraph Company announced in August 1901 that it had obtained a $5 million loan. Reportedly the money was to be used to complete the firm's telephone system in Chicago and, said the report; "The company will use an automatic telephone, doing away with the employment of telephone girls."[8]

When a Minneapolis newspaper commented on the Illinois Telephone plan to install an automatic system, the account declared that such a system had never been tried in Minneapolis but it had been used in several smaller Minnesota cities with the communities of Albert Lea and Rochester having automatic telephones. Some years earlier, it was said, the system was tried in Boston but was not a success. Said a Minneapolis telephone executive,

Men like to talk back. With an automatic phone they get a number or they do not get it. If they don't get it they have no recourse…. Of the two sexes, a man is usually more impatient over a telephone than a woman. He loses his temper more quickly, and he seems to forget that he is talking to a girl at the other end of the wire. We don't have much trouble that way, but occasionally the girls complain, and then we take steps to put a stop to the nuisance.

A few years earlier in Minneapolis, an attempt was made to use the graphophone (an early phonograph for recording and reproducing sounds) in connection with the work. When a call came for a number already in use, the girl pressed a button and the graphophone played the message "The line is busy … the line is busy…" That continued until the subscriber hung up, "but it was not satisfactory and never came into general use. Men don't like to talk to a machine."[9]

In November 1901, a news story announced an invention that was about to "knock out all the telephone girls. Each person does his own switching and no one can hear what he says to another." If the desired number was busy, "a buzzer prevents him from saying a word or understanding what is said." Reportedly, the system had been tried in New Bedford and "works like a charm." There was just one person at central—a troubleshooter. It was also claimed the new invention had already reduced the cost of phone service by 50 percent.[10]

After a New York City newspaper presented an article on the "passing" of the telephone girl—a passing made possible by the automatic telephone exchange—a Scranton, Pennsylvania, newspaper reprinted the piece and then added some material at the end about how Scranton played an important part in the automatic telephone:

> The "hello girl," presiding genius of the telephone ever since its installation, must seek fresh employment before long. For there has arrived, and is now in practical, successful operation, a girl-less, central-less telephone system, with which, with a few twists of a curious dial, anyone can get the number he wants, directly, in a few seconds.

And, as an added benefit, no one was ready to "listen in." In January 1902, Fall River, Massachusetts, was reported to have the most complete, largest and most practically operated of all the automatic telephone systems of America. It was closely followed by the systems of New Bedford, Massachusetts, and Augusta, Georgia; those cities each had more than 500 subscribers on those automatic wires. Fall River had 700. Geneva New York, Albuquerque New Mexico, Albert Lea Minnesota, Auburn New York, Madison Wisconsin, Princeton New Jersey, Ithaca New York, and Skagway Alaska, were all said to have automatic telephone systems. Chicago was then building a new automatic system that would take an estimated two years to complete. It was expected to start with 15,000 subscribers and perhaps increase it to 50,000. All of those automatic systems were owned and controlled in the U.S. and the world over by the Automatic Electric Telephone System, capitalized at $2 million. The company installing the Chicago plant was the Illinois Telegraph and Telephone Company, capitalized at $5 million. Much of the latter's ownership was held by the first named company. The phone was installed without cost to subscribers and there was an automatic meter connected to each phone to register all the calls. A charge of so-much per call was made until $85 was reached. Everything over that figure was "free." The Bell Telephone Company in Chicago then charged $175 a year for a business phone, without regard to the number of calls.[11]

A Salt Lake City, Utah, newspaper announced in November 1902 that the Utah Home Telephone Company was contemplating the use of an automatic system for that city. The cost of running such a system was much less than one that used hello girls. Three "expert" technicians in the central office were sufficient to keep switchboards with 3000 telephones in working order while, with the present manual system, 40 operators were needed to handle that many subscribers. Those 40 operators would draw about $1200 a month in salary while the three electricians would draw $600 in total, or less. The automatic switchboard, however, cost about 20 percent more than the kind then in use by the Bell Company. That new system being contemplated, the Strowger system, was then in use in Fall River and New Bedford, Massachusetts. Before such a system could be implemented, the mayor of Salt Lake had to sign a law granting the franchise to the new company. Rates for this new contemplated service were to be $4 a month for business phones and $2.50 a month for a residential phone. There were to be no party lines.

The Bell service had 31 different rates for its services. Price for a business phone, individual line and unlimited service was $90 a year. The same service for a residence was $60 a year. On a party line, unlimited service for a business house was $5 a month and for a residence it was $3. The charge for limited service for a business phone was $2.50 a month for 50 calls and 2.5 cents for all calls over that number. The cheapest cost for residential service was a party line with limited service, which cost $1 a month for 30 calls and 2.5 cents after that limit was passed. That last rate (if the call limit was not exceeded) was cheaper than anything offered by the new contemplated automatic service.[12]

With respect to the automatic phone systems, a very brief editorial comment appeared in a July 1904 California newspaper: "An invention to do away with the hello girl in telephone is announced. The public will have none of it. The chief attraction of the telephone is the hello girl, and the company that tries to run without her should be promptly boy-cotted."[13]

A September 12, 1905, dispatch from Allentown, Pennsylvania, stated that the management of the Consolidated Telephone Company decided to spend $20,000 in installing automatic plants in Allentown and Hazelton and in doing so would deprive more than 100 telephone girls of their jobs as soon as the new plants were ready, supposedly by December 1. The 60 girls who worked in the Allentown exchange were so angry about it that many left work immediately and, as a result, phone service in the city was greatly impaired. Company executives said they were sorry about the girls but they calculated on running each "girl-less exchange" at a savings of $20,000 a year. If the experiment was successful, the "girl-less system" was to be installed in the entire Consolidated system, which included 12 other large cities in Pennsylvania east of the Susquehanna River. More than 400 girls were employed in those exchanges.[14]

That Allentown news release reportedly got all the telephone girls in New York City talking about the idea and becoming worried. Said William Greer of the New York Telephone Exchange, "We have of course heard of these automatic telephone systems but we have never investigated them. We consider that New York has the best system but I am unprepared to pass judgment or give any information upon this automatic arrangement."[15] A few weeks later, another article about the automatic phone systems appeared in a Nebraska newspaper with the subhead; "New device insures absolute secrecy." Omaha was reported to be behind the times in terms of automatic telephone service, compared to the examples of Lincoln, Hastings and Sioux City, all within a radius of 100 miles of Omaha and all supposedly equipped with automatic phone service. According to this story,

> [T]he last years of the nineteenth century witnessed wonders in the way of hard labor being supplanted by machinery and with the best results, so far as certainly, uniformity and rapidity of operation are concerned. Perhaps this is more noticeable in the automatic switchboard than in any other mechanical device. Today this telephone apparatus is thoroughly standardized and is one of the greatest triumphs in the field of automatics.

This reporter contended that the manual phone system contained many annoyances and delays due largely to carelessness and poor articulation either by the operator or by the customer: "Every thinking man will admit that these imperfections cannot be remedied in manual practice and that they can only be eliminated by the introduction of an automatic device which places the calling and connecting processes entirely in the hands of a machine." It was said to have been more than 12 years since the first automatic exchange was placed in commission and that the total of all automatic phone services then in use had more than 100,000 subscribers. Other cities besides Lincoln, Hastings and Sioux City that had automatic systems included Chicago (IL), Grand Rapids (MI), Columbus (OH), Portland (ME), Portland (OR), Auburn (NY), Lewiston (ME), Fall River (MA), New Bedford (MA), Los Angeles (CA), San Diego (CA), Hopkinsville (KY), Cleburne (TX), Columbus (GA), South Bend (IN), Aberdeen (SD), Miamisburg (OH), Auburn (ME), Medford (WI), Dayton (OH), St. Marys (OH), Woodstock (NY), Westerly (RI), Manchester (IA), Princeton (NJ), Albuquerque (NM) Van Wert (OH), Battle Creek (MI), Clayton (MI), Pentwater (MI), Toronto Junction (CA), Wilmington (DE), Riverside (CA), Traverse City (MI), Wausau (WI), El Paso (TX), Havana, Cuba, Marianao, Cuba, and Berlin, Germany. The U.S. government had reportedly installed an automatic system in four of its arsenals, at the naval station in New Orleans and at the Sandy Hook proving grounds at Fort Hancock, New Jersey.[16]

A March 1906 article on automatic systems began by enthusing, "The tireless, talkless, waitless, girl-less central is no longer a myth but an accomplished fact." It was estimated there were then over five million phones in America and, allowing one operator for every 150 instruments, along with relief operators, that meant a grand total of over 45,000 operators in the nation. Allowing for five calls per day for each instrument led the reporter to conclude that those telephone girls responded to over 25 million calls a day. The journalist declared; "A careful comparison of the two will show that, irrespective of the advanced mechanical side of the principles involved, yet the personal element, with its attendant fallibility, is a part of the system which, when eliminated, cannot be replaced by the most perfect mechanism. The feeling of assurance given by the friendly voice of central will be missing and instead there will arise a sense of incompleteness which will be difficult to overcome."[17]

As of March 1909, what was described as a "syndicate of capitalists" in Portland, Oregon, had reportedly taken over the automatic telephone companies of Portland, Tacoma, Bellingham, Walla Walla and other cities in the area. It was headed by a prominent lawyer named Samuel Hill and included other lawyers, bankers and merchants. They had then taken over the Home Telephone Company of Puget Sound, among many others. According to a story, the deal meant that the syndicate would control the business of the girl-less companies in Seattle, Tacoma, Walla Walla, Spokane, San Francisco and Los Angeles and the long distance lines between those cities and points in Nevada, Colorado and Arizona. All of

the Home Telephone companies on the West Coast had been purchased with the new firm being a rival to the Pacific States Telephone and Telegraph Company.[18]

A news story published in March 1918 declared that Washington, D.C., would have an automatic telephone system within the coming 18 months. T.P. Sylvan, assistant to the president of the Chesapeake and Potomac Telephone Company, predicted that when the full system was in effect nine out of every ten telephone girls then employed would lose their jobs.[19]

Until this point, the stories about automatic systems taking over, and so forth, had all failed to materialize. All the firms that sprang up to deliver automatic systems had failed, some quicker than others. When the 1920s started, there was no effective automatic telephone system in use. But then it all started to change. New York Telephone Company announced in April 1920 that it would install an automatic system and that the first phase would be ready for use in early 1921. It did not talk about the end of operators but stated they would be needed for years to come, and always needed on toll and long distance services. In New York City, the company had 12,000 operators, with 9500 recruited during the previous 12 months, and they then needed 1500 more.[20]

New York Telephone was somewhat delayed but in March 1922 it was reported to be installing automatic machinery and was expected to have its first automatic exchange in operation in the summer of that year. It was estimated it would take ten years to fully convert the system. New York City then had 989,000 phones in use and every one of them had to be replaced. For the following ten years, the system could be a hybrid with some subscribers dialing the numbers themselves with others giving their desired numbers to the operators, as usual. Hello girls were still needed with no dismissals contemplated then or into the future as the turnover among the telephone girls was so great that turnover would cover any eventualities.[21]

New York Telephone subscribers connected to the Pennsylvania exchange dialed their own numbers on October 15, 1922, for the first time and things went off without a problem. A total of 9000 telephones and 1700 truck lines had been converted. Said a reporter, "Although the new machinery, which makes the subscriber act as his own telephone operator, was adopted largely because of the labor problem, the telephone company

Opposite, top and bottom: **Some 1905 photos of automatic telephone equipment. Note the absence of hello girls from the operating room.**

YOUR
TELEPHONE—
IF YOU ARE
ON AN AUTOMATIC
"CENTRAL"

The DIAL of The
AUTOMATIC 'PHONE

The New York Telephone Company displayed its automatic equipment in 1920. It wasn't until 1922 that the first subscribers made automatic local calls.

has not reduced the number of girls employed." In fact, the company was still advertising for operators and thought the number of operators employed on the phones would be steadily increased during the coming ten years.[22]

As of September 1923, the New York Telephone Company had seven exchanges on the automatic system. Each conversion had gone smoothly and the firm then had some 42,000 phones converted to automatic, but much work remained to be done. Other major world cities such as London and Paris also began the conversion to automatic phone systems. The era of the hello girl, at least for local calling, was coming to an end. That end began in the period of 1922 and 1923 but would take many years before it was completed. As was the case of New York Telephone Company, the major impetus for an automatic system was the huge turnover of telephone operators. Low pay and poor working conditions caused that turnover and the telcos, rather than deal with those issues, had chosen to put their faith in a technological fix. As early as 1891, the automatic system was touted but all efforts were abject failures until 1922–1923 when a functioning and efficient system began to be adopted and installed.[23]

Chapter Notes

Chapter 1

1. "The telephone." *The Arizona Citizen* (Tucson), December 7, 1887.
2. "All about the telephone." *Evening Star* (Washington), January 29, 1881.
3. "Question of labor." *Omaha Daily Bee*, October 15, 1882.
4. "Through the telephone." *Evening Star* (Washington), November 18, 1882.
5. "The telephone Babel." *Omaha Daily Bee*, March 8, 1883.
6. "Evidently an untruth." *Sun* (NY), November 18, 1883.
7. "From shop and mill." *St Paul Globe*, May 31, 1885.
8. No title. *St. Johns Herald* (St. Johns, Arizona), February 18, 1892.
9. "The telephone. Hello there." *San Francisco Call*, February 7, 1892.
10. "The telephone girl." *Hickman Courier* (KY), March 2, 1894.
11. "The telephone girl." *Evening Times* (Washington), July 8, 1898.
12. "Soft answer to hello." *New York Tribune*, October 2, 1898.
13. "Telephone girls talk too much." *Valentine Democrat* (Nebraska), June 21, 1900.
14. "Equal to hello girls." *Times Dispatch* (Richmond, VA), March 25, 1906.
15. "Hello girl." *Hopkinsville Kentuckian*, February 27, 1908.
16. "Hello girls used to be boys who cussed cranks 'n' everything." *Washington Times*, May 8, 1921.
17. "Hello girl." *Carbondale Free Press* (Illinois), July 2, 1930.
18. Mildred Adams. "And now thank you saves time for us." *New York Times*, June 19, 1927.

Chapter 2

1. "Proposed change in the telephone service." *Evening Star* (Washington), April 25, 1884.
2. "Telltale telephones." *Evening Star* (Washington), January 3, 1885.
3. "From shop and mill." *St. Paul Globe*, May 31, 1885.
4. "Hello, there, central." *Omaha Daily Bee*, August 1, 1886.
5. "At the hello center." *St. Paul Globe*, February 26, 1888.
6. Eva Gay. "That you, central?" *St. Paul Globe*, August 12, 1888.
7. "Long-range gossip." *Pittsburg Dispatch*, December 8, 1889.
8. "Patient, useful, practical." *Omaha Daily Bee*, August 3, 1890.
9. No title. *St. Johns Herald* (St. Johns, Arizona), February 18, 1892.
10. "The telephone. Hello! There." *San Francisco Call*, February 7, 1892.
11. No title. *Pittsburg Dispatch*, October 19, 1892.
12. Marie Evelyn. "For other ears." *San Francisco Call*, November 26, 1892.
13. "Telephonic trials." *St. Paul Globe*, July 9, 1893.
14. "With the hello girls." *Salt Lake Herald*, July 29, 1894.
15. "Beauty wins." *Sacramento Record-Union*, April 27, 1895.
16. "An important change." *Kansas City Daily Journal* (MO), May 2, 1895.

17. "Telegraph innovations." *San Francisco Call*, January 15, 1896.

18. Mamie Loretta Nallin. "The telephone girl." *Scranton Tribune* (PA), May 14, 1896.

19. "New Switchboard in." *Norfolk Virginian*, December 18, 1896.

20. "The girls at the phone." *Sun* (NY), February 7, 1897.

21. *Ibid.*

22. "Amusements." *Evening Star* (Washington), November 11, 1897.

23. "Farces with music." *New York Tribune*, December 26, 1897.

24. "She rings the bell." *Richmond Dispatch* (VA), December 18, 1898; Ad. *Washington Times*, December 25, 1898.

25. "Boycott play." *Spokane Press*, December 8, 1902.

26. Eva Mitchell Cook. "The treadmill of the telephone." *Los Angeles Herald*, January 23, 1898.

27. "No working woman is happier than a telephone girl." *Chicago Eagle*, June 11, 1898.

28. "Soft answer to hello." *New York Tribune*, October 2, 1898.

29. "There are purchasable spies in many households." *San Francisco Call*, January 1, 1899.

30. Cromwell Childe. "Hello! The telephone girl." *New York Times*, June 11, 1899.

31. "Anita Byrne was overworked and demented." *San Francisco Call*, July 14, 1899.

32. "Hello girl writes about her troubles." *San Francisco Call*, July 16, 1899.

33. Marian West. "My experience as a telephone operator." *San Francisco Call*, August 20, 1899.

34. "Haunted to death by phantom 'hello' bells." *San Francisco Call*, September 14, 1899.

35. "Death of the telephone Nettie Friebel." *San Francisco Call*, September 15, 1899.

36. "Long arms, big girls." *Monroe City Democrat* (MO), January 25, 1900.

37. "Have you noticed the change in the telephone girl's voice?" *St. Louis Republican*, May 20, 1900.

38. No title. *Kentucky Irish American* (Louisville), June 9, 1900.

39. "The field of electricity." *Omaha Daily Bee*, June 15, 1900.

40. "For the better half." *El Paso Herald*, July 21, 1900.

41. "Woman workers—telephone girl." *Omaha Daily Bee*, August 12, 1900.

Chapter 3

1. "Busy work of the telephone girls." *Honolulu Republican*, February 10, 1901.

2. "The telephone girl." *Arizona Republican* (Phoenix), February 11, 1901.

3. "East Liverpool telephone girl." *Stark County Democrat* (Canton, Ohio), March 123, 1901.

4. "Providing a rest room for business women." *St. Louis Republic*, April 7, 1901.

5. "No more morning hellos." *Brooklyn Eagle*, June 16, 1901.

6. "Chicago hello girls are singing the praises of President Sabin." *San Francisco Call*, June 27, 1901.

7. "Hello girls get a raise." *Start County Democrat* (Canton, Ohio), July 19, 1901.

8. "The telephone girl." *Philipsburg Mail* (Montana), August 9, 1901.

9. "Fair eavesdroppers." *Nebraska Advertiser* (Omaha, August 23, 1901.

10. "Hello girls to elocute." Daily Ardmoreite (Ardmore, OK), December 31, 1901.

11. "A good telephone girl." *Virginia Gazette* (Williamsburg, VA), January 11, 1902.

12. "School for hello girls is New York's very latest." *Evening World* (NY), January 16, 1902.

13. "Into new quarters." St. Paul Globe, April 4, 1902.

14. "Long hours for hello girls." *Evening Star* (Washington), September 29, 1902.

15. "Census shows that 5,319,912 women are bread winners." *St. Louis Republic*, September 7, 1902.

16. "Bell Telephone girls may slide down a new spiral fire escape." *St. Louis Republic*, November 13, 1902.

17. "Telephone girls wanted." *San Francisco Call*, December 16, 1902.

18. "Troubles that beset the telephone girl." *Washington Times*, December 14, 1902.

19. "Hello central." *Minneapolis Journal*, March 26, 1903.

20. "Bell Telephone Company established school of instruction for hello girls." *St. Louis Republic*, May 31, 1903.

21. "A summer day with the hello girl." *Sun* (NY), August 2, 1903.

22. "Telephone girl's training." *Evening Star* (Washington), October 3, 1903.

23. "A Paris Waldorf-Astoria for telephone girls." *Minneapolis Journal*, October 10, 1903.

24. "Training hello girls." *Wichita Eagle*, December 8, 1903.

25. "The new north Washington telephone exchange." *Washington Times*, December 27, 1903.

26. "Hello girl gets $15,000 for shock." *Salt Lake Tribune*, April 6, 1904.

27. "Here is the telephone central's story." *Salt Lake Herald*, February 19, 1905.

28. "Hello girls hard to get." *Omaha Daily Bee*, March 28, 1905.

29. "Hello girls of Gotham no longer alarm clocks for sleepy-heads." *San Francisco Call*, August 18, 1905.

30. "Hello girls' alarm clocks." *Omaha Daily Bee*, August 26, 1905.

31. "Life of the hello girl." *Evening Star* (Washington), October 22, 1905.

32. "The story of two want ads." *Spokane Press*, November 20, 1905.

33. "Millions use the telephone." *Los Angeles Herald*, May 21, 1906.

34. "Hello girls vocation both pleasant and remunerative." *Los Angeles Herald*, September 2, 1906.

35. "The telephone girl her strenuous days." *Arizona Republican* (Phoenix), September 10, 1906.

36. "May train hello girls' voices to attain proper modulation." *Washington Times*, October 28, 1906.

37. "The hello girls are kept busy." *Rogue River Courier* (Grants Pass, OR), December 14, 1906.

38. "Clergyman takes up hello girls cause." *San Francisco Call*, February 26, 1907.

39. "Clergyman discusses telephone religion." *San Francisco Call*, March 4, 1907.

40. "When in doubt just ask the information telephone girl." *Evening Star* (Washington), March 17, 1907.

41. "Telephone co. worst employer in Spokane." *Spokane Press*, April 19, 1907.

42. "Telephone operators succumb to epidemic." *Los Angeles Herald*, July 22, 1907.

43. "School of special instruction for employees multiply in big cities." *Omaha Daily Bee*, September 29, 1907.

44. "Hello girls now have libraries." *Los Angeles Herald*, October 13, 1907.

45. "With the hello girl at main." *Evening Star* (Washington), November 17, 1907.

46. "Terrors for hello girls." *Bourbon News* (Paris, KY), December 20, 1907.

47. Priscilla Prim. "American women who work." *Tacoma Times*, February 18, 1909.

48. "Increased use of telephones." *Gainesville Daily Sun* (FL), April 3, 1909.

49. Julia Creswell. "The hello girls of Spokane." *Spokane Press*, November 2, 1909.

50. "Hello girls overworked." *Anadarko Daily Democrat* (OK), November 29, 1909.

51. "Telephone girls are now trilling their r's." *Times Dispatch* (Richmond, VA), December 28, 1909.

52. Marion Lowe. "School for courtesy is established in Seattle." *Seattle Star*, January 7, 1910.

53. "If hello girl gets angry blame Commissioner Neill." *Washington Herald*, February 28, 1910.

54. "All about the hello girls." *Sun* (NY), February 28, 1910.

55. "Short girl? You can't say hello." *San Francisco Call*, February 28, 1910.

56. "Tel. girls must be over 5 feet." *Paducah Evening Sun* (KY), February 28, 1910.

57. "Telephone girls rarely marry." *Morning Examiner* (Ogden, Utah), April 10, 1910.

58. Laura S. Smith. "Great care is exerted for telephone girls' comfort." *Salt Lake Herald*, May 15, 1910.

59. "Telephone sweetness." *Los Angeles Herald*, June 19, 1910.

60. "New York's orgy of telephones." *Ogden Standard*, July 16, 1910.

61. "Hello girls work hard." *New York Times*, September 23, 1910.

62. "Girls from country desirable operators." *Arizona Republican* (Phoenix), October 16, 1910.

63. "The girl and the dividends." *Tacoma Times*, January 5, 1911.

64. "The Women, new Belasco play, to open at National." *Washington Times*, April 16, 1911.

65. "It's all on the switchboard." *Goodwin's Weekly* (Salt Lake), March 9, 1912.

66. "Actress wins praise of hello girls." *San Francisco Call*, October 17, 1912.

67. Mary Marshall. "Your daughter's vocation." *New York Tribune*, December 17, 1911.

68. *Ibid.*

69. "Matron will care for hello girls." *Bisbee Daily Review*, March 5, 1912.

70. "The girl at the switchboard." *University Missourian* (Columbia), March 14, 1912.

71. "Telephone girls here may powder." *Washington Times*, September 9, 1912.

72. "Telephone service subject of report." *El Paso Herald*, October 5, 1912.

73. "Hello girls are happy; their pay has been raised." *Evening World* (NY), October 21, 1912.

74. "Bonus for telephone girls." *Sun* (NY), January 27, 1913.

75. "Increased wages for all hello girls." Washington Herald, April 30, 1913.

76. "Shorter hours for telephone girls." *Labor World* (Duluth, MN), May 10, 1913.

77. "Increase in salary of telephone girls comes at Cleveland." *Omaha Daily Bee*, June 17, 1913.

78. "The world uses 12,318,000 telephones." *San Francisco Call*, December 16, 1913.

79. "Working girls need minimum of $12.11." *San Juan Islander* (Friday Harbor, WA), January 30, 1914.

80. "Fix $9 wage for telephone girls." *Seattle Star*, June 27, 1914.

81. "Minimum wage for phone girls is fixed at $9." *Seattle Star*, July 10, 1914.

82. "The most beautiful telephone girl in the United States." *Seattle Star*, January 14, 1915.

83. "Higher pay to telephone girl is asked by Frank Walsh." *Day Book* (Chicago), February 15, 1915.

84. "Government inquiry shows hello girls underpaid in 7 cities." *Evening World* (NY), July 22, 1915.

85. "Plea made for telephone girls." *Ogden Standard*, July 24, 1915.

86. "There are more than 8,000,000 women workers in the U.S." *Bemidji Daily Pioneer* (MN), April 10, 1916.

87. "Girl answers many calls." *Evening Herald* (Klamath Falls, OR), September 14, 1916.

88. "Uncle Sam raids hello girls' ranks." *Washington Times*, June 27, 1917.

89. Echo June Zahl. "Echo Zahl works as hello girl." *Seattle Star*, July 2, 1917.

90. Echo June Zahl. "Hello girl's pay at start is $1.10 a day." *Seattle Star*, July 3, 1917.

91. "Hello girls stop telling time." *Watchman and Southron* (Sumter, SC), July 9, 1919.

92. "City phone efficiency drops 60% in 3 years." *New York Tribune*, August 25, 1919.

93. "Busy Manhattan calls in vain for 700 hello girls." *New York Tribune*, December 3, 1919.

94. "Bad phone service laid to low wages." *New York Times*, December 18, 1919.

95. "Poor telephone service is due to cheap labor." *Labor World* (Duluth, MN), January 17, 1920.

96. "Capital hello girls best paid operators in telephone service." *Washington Times*, November 29, 1920.

97. "Hello girls used to be boys who cussed cranks 'n' everything." *Washington Times*, May 8, 1921.

Chapter 4

1. "Telephone girls deprived of gum." *National Tribune* (Washington), May 3, 1888.

2. Marie Evelyn. "For other ears." *San Francisco Call*, November 26, 1892.

3. "Miss Means wins her case." *Los Angeles Herald*, December 6, 1893.

4. "Telephone girls protest." *Evening World* (NY), February 6, 1894.

5. "Among the telephone girls." *Chicago Eagle*, August 4, 1900.

6. "Girls must not talk." *New York Times*, October 7, 1900.

7. "Girls must toe the mark." *Salt Lake Herald*, November 13, 1901.

8. "Regulate telephone girls." *Omaha Daily Bee*, January 12, 1902.

9. "To abolish hello." *San Francisco Call*, April 14, 1902.

10. "Cost a manager $12,500 to hurt hello girl." *Washington Times*, March 5, 1903.

11. "Teaches hello girl." *St. Paul Globe*, March 21, 1903.

12. "Hello, prunes and prisms." *Brownsville Herald* (TX), April 2, 1903.

13. "Discharged girl gets new job." *Evening World* (NY), April 27, 1904.

14. "Dance and darn that company." *Sun* (NY), May 16, 1904.

15. "Hello girls trip it, trip it." *Sun* (NY), May 31, 1904.

16. "50 hello girls flirted too much." *Evening World* (NY), August 31, 1904.

17. "Hist, new d'ye hear?" *Seattle Star*, December 18, 1905.

18. "Hello girls picnic too sporting, 'tis said." *San Francisco Call*, May 29, 1907.

19. "Hello girls must throw away rats." *Seattle Star*, December 24, 1909.

20. "Telephone girls say spies follow them after work." *Evening World* (NY), April 7, 1911.

21. "Breaking the hello girl dead line." *Evening World* (NY), April 11, 1911.

22. "Strict rules for telephone girls." *Washington Times*, July 24, 1912.

23. "Capital hello girls not held in check." *Washington Times*, July 26, 1912.

24. "Instructive talks to telephone girls." *Bisbee Daily Review*, October 12, 1915.

25. No title. *San Francisco Call*, October 3, 1892.

26. "Blue and black." *San Francisco Call*, December 5, 1893.

27. No title. *Sacramento Record-Union*, December 7, 1893.

28. "The hello girls." *Salt Lake Herald*, December 9, 1893.

29. "Hello girls mad." *Fort Worth Gazette*, April 5, 1894.

30. "Telephone girls in black." *Evening World* (NY), May 1, 1894.

31. No title. *Wichita Daily Eagle*, September 8, 1895.

32. "Low necked dresses not for hello girls." *Spokane Press*, June 25, 1903.

33. "Boss taboos girls' finery." *San Francisco Call*, July 18, 1903.

34. "St. Louis hello girls can wear peek-a-boos." *Wenatchee Daily World* (WA), June 18, 1906.

35. "Life for telephone girl loses its charm." *Rogue River Courier* (Grants Pass, OR), May 18, 1916.

36. "Business men need dress censor nowadays to keep girls modest." *Evening Public Ledger* (Philadelphia), September 15, 1916.

Chapter 5

1. "Evidently an untruth." *Sun* (NY), November 18, 1883.

2. "Hello, girls, were you shocked." *Stark County Democrat* (Canton, Ohio), November 24, 1887.

3. "The girls all right." *Pittsburg Dispatch*, January 25, 1889.

4. Marie Evelyn. "For other ears." *San Francisco Call*, November 26, 1892.

5. "Telephone ears." *San Francisco Call*, May 17, 1893.

6. "More telephone ear." *Sun* (NY), November 11, 1894.

7. "The telephone ear." *Stark County Democrat* (Canton, Ohio), December 14, 1900.

8. "Hello girls, be sure you're healthy and then go ahead." *San Francisco Call*, March 22, 1901.

9. "Like their work." *Nebraska Advertiser* (Nemaha City), June 28, 1901.

10. "Diphtheria breaks out among hello girls." *Seattle Star*, November 10, 1905.

11. "Corns on ears of hello girls." *Hopkinsville Kentuckian*, November 23, 1905.

12. "Many maladies of phone girls." *Los Angeles Herald*, July 1, 1906.

13. "Out of sight gallantry." *Tacoma Times*, March 6, 1909.

14. "Telephone girls' eyes." *Princeton Union* (MN), November 13, 1913.

15. "Flash lights hurt phone girls' eyes." *Labor World* (Duluth, MN), November 15, 1913.

16. "One thing and another." *St. Paul Daily Globe*, June 28, 1891.

17. "Women swear the most." *Evening Statesman* (Walla Walla, WA), February 4, 1905.

18. "Swearing at hello girl may be costly to doctor." *Washington Times*, September 2, 1907; "Local news." *Plymouth Tribune* (Indiana), January 30, 1908.

19. "Rights of telephone girls." *Salt Lake Herald*, February 9, 1908.

20. "You can't swear over phone any more—in Texas." *Evening World* (NY), February 15, 1909.

21. "Gramophone comes to aid of hello girls." *San Francisco Call*, May 15, 1910.

22. "Swore at hello girl." *Medford Mail Tribune* (OR), April 12, 1912.

23. "$60 fine for swearing at telephone girl." *San Francisco Call*, December 17, 1913.

24. "All about the telephone." *Evening Star* (Washington), January 29, 1881.

25. "He annoyed the central." *St. Paul Daily Globe*, February 8, 1888.

26. "Talks for her living." *Evening World* (NY), June 10, 1890.

27. "Hello! You central." *St. Paul Daily Globe*, July 13, 1890.

28. "Marks the masher." *Wichita Daily Eagle*, April 31, 1895.

29. "Telephone girl's voice." *The Bourbon News* (Paris, KY), February 22, 1898.

30. "Cupid has a merry time among Oakland's telephone operators." *San Francisco Call*, July 24, 1900.

31. "Teaching her to talk well." *St. Louis Republic*, August 24, 1902.

32. "Hello girls ring up Hymen's office often." *Washington Times*, September 29, 1902.

33. "Millionaire Tower and the hello girl who will become his bride Wednesday." *Evening World* (NY), January 5, 1903.

34. "Will society receive her?" *St. Paul Globe*, March 10, 1903.

35. "Sweet voice wins hello girl a millionaire for a husband." *St. Louis Republic*, May 3, 1903.

36. "Jack hugger runs big risk." *San Francisco Call*, December 20, 1903.

37. Nixola Greeley-Smith. "The telephone girl and matrimony." *Evening World* (NY), April 7, 1904.

38. "The telephone girl has the best chance of matrimony." *Times Dispatch* (Richmond, VA), April 24, 1904.

39. "Five hello girls resign to marry." *Washington Times*, September 19, 1904.

40. "Cupid busy among the hello girls." *Sun* (NY), January 8, 1905.

41. "Hello girls tell how to marry rich." *Evening World* (NY), November 23, 1905.

42. "Hello girls practice punching bags in telephone gymnasium." *Paducah Evening Sun* (KY), June 13, 1906.

43. "Telephone girls wanted." *Daily Capital Journal* (Salem, OR), January 29, 1908.

44. "50 pretty Spokane hello girls wed in three months." *Spokane Press*, August 25, 1909.

45. "Hello girls; girls hello." *Tacoma Times*, March 9, 1911.

46. "Hello girls are Cupid's harvest." *San Francisco Call*, November 15, 1912.

47. "Hello girls quit places to marry." *University Missourian* (Columbia, MO), November 18, 1912.

48. "Cupid wrecking phone service." *Times Dispatch* (Richmond, VA), January 14, 1913.

Chapter 6

1. "The girls strike." *Sacramento Daily Record-Union*, February 11, 1887.

2. "Of general interest." *Wichita Daily Eagle*, April 25, 1893.

3. "Telephone girls out on a strike." *Washington Post*, November 29, 1899.

4. "Striking telephone girls." *St. Louis Republican*, July 15, 1900.

5. "Telephone girls." *St. Louis Republican*, July 16, 1900.

6. "The telephone strike." *Houston Daily Post*, July 17, 1900; "Telephone strike settled." *Houston Daily Post*, July 18, 1900.

7. "Hello! Hello! Alas!" *Independent* (Honolulu), October 5, 1900.

8. "Be sure and register." *Honolulu Republican* (Honolulu), October 5, 1900.

9. "The strike rung off." *Hawaiian Star* (Honolulu), October 5, 1900.

10. "They want Cassidy." *Evening Bulletin* (Honolulu), October 5, 1900.

11. No title. *Hawaiian Star* (Honolulu), October 5, 1900.

12. "Men operators also strike for more pay." *Honolulu Republican*, October 7, 1900.

13. "John Cassidy is out and Corcoran is in." *Hawaiian Gazette* (Honolulu), October 9, 1900.

14. "Telephone strike." *El Paso Daily Herald*, November 3, 1900.

15. "Telephone strike still on." *Houston Daily Post*, November 9, 1900.

16. "The telephone strike." *Houston Daily Post*, November 9, 1900.

17. "Telephone strike." *Houston Daily Post*, November 11, 1900.

18. *Ibid.*

19. "Subscribers on strike." *Houston Daily Post*, November 13, 1900.

20. "San Antonio strike." *El Paso Herald*, November 13, 1900.

21. "Strike extends to Temple." *St. Louis Republican*, November 16, 1900.

22. "Telephone girls." *El Paso Herald*, November 27, 1900.

23. "San Antonio budget." *El Paso Herald*, December 6, 1900.

24. "Not organized in St. Louis. St. Louis Republican*, December 18, 1900.

25. "Talk of central union." *New York Tribune*, January 16, 1901.

26. "Hello girls would strike." *Akron Daily Democrat* (Ohio), August 22, 1901.

27. "Hello girls secured reinstatement of linemen." *Akron Daily Democrat* (Ohio), November 2, 1901.

28. "Hello girls on strike." *St. Paul Globe*, March 5, 1902.

29. "Hello girls on strike." *St. Paul Globe,* March 26, 1902.

30. "Hello girls satisfied." *Washington Times,* April 15, 1902; "Strike declared off." *Evening Star* (Washington), April 15, 1902.

31. "Hello girls on a strike." *Akron Daily Democrat* (Ohio), June 21, 1902.

32. "Telephone girls strike." *Omaha Daily Bee,* June 22, 1902.

33. "To erect a state fishway." *Omaha Daily Bee,* June 28, 1902.

34. "Linemen on sympathy strike." *Omaha Daily Bee,* June 29, 1902.

35. "Laboring men assist girls." *Omaha Daily Bee,* June 30, 1902.

36. "Turns down asphalt bill." *Omaha Daily Bee,* July 1, 1902.

37. "Telephone girls win out." *Omaha Daily Bee,* July 10, 1902.

38. No title. *Commoner* (Lincoln, Nebraska), July 18, 1902.

39. "Hello girls strike settled." *Ocala Banner* (FL), December 19, 1902.

40. "Hello girls." *Stark County Democrat* (Canton, Ohio), August 29, 1902.

41. "Hello girls strike." *Seattle Star,* November 27, 1902.

42. "Comment on current events." *Labor World* (Duluth, MN), January 24, 1903.

43. "Hello girls form union." *Spokane Press,* April 8, 1903.

44. "To take places of union hello girls." *Spokane Press,* April 16, 1903.

45. "Hello girls go to Butte." *Salt Lake Herald,* April 16, 1903.

46. "Hello girls strike." *Daily Journal* (Salem, OR), April 17, 1903.

47. "Don't like local phone girls." *Deseret Evening News* (Salt Lake), April 17, 1903.

48. "Butte phone girls battle with company." *Spokane Press,* April 18, 1903.

49. "Butte strike is called off." *Salt Lake Herald,* April 20, 1903.

50. "Return from Butte." *Salt Lake Herald,* April 22, 1903.

51. "Hello girls strike." *Hopkinsville Kentuckian,* April 21, 1903.

52. "Hello girls." *Paducah Sun* (KY), April 23, 1903.

53. "Telephone strike ended." *Hopkinsville Kentuckian,* May 1, 1903.

54. "Hello girls given increase in wages." *Spokane Press,* April 21, 1903.

55. "Admit hello girl delegates to council." *Spokane Press,* May 20, 1903.

56. "New girls employed." *Minneapolis Journal,* May 27, 1903.

57. "Fear no strike of St. Paul hello girls." *St. Paul Globe,* May 28, 1903.

58. "Call out wire men." *Minneapolis Journal,* May 28, 1903.

59. "Hello girls are still out." *St. Paul Globe,* May 29, 1903.

60. "Privileges for the hello girl." *St. Paul Globe,* May 30, 1903.

61. "Hello girls seem to be out." *St. Paul Globe,* May 30, 1903.

62. "Looks like defeat." *Minneapolis Journal,* June 3, 1903.

63. "Hello girls at Spokane." *Spokane Press,* June 30, 1903.

64. "Telephone girls join Western Conference." *Spokane Press,* July 1, 1903.

65. "The telephone operators' strike." *Spokane Press,* July 1, 1903.

66. "Girls confident of winning strike." *Spokane Press,* July 2, 1903.

67. "Threaten boycott." *Evening Statesman* (Walla Walla), July 3, 1903.

68. "To place telephones upon the unfair list." *Spokane Press,* July 3, 1903.

69. "Telephone company is refused police cannot show any need of specials." *Spokane Press,* July 4, 1903

70. "How others view it." *Spokane Press,* July 6, 1903.

71. "Trades Council boycotts phones." *Spokane Press,* July 8, 1903.

72. "Young ladies secure 1500 phone removals." *Spokane Press,* July 11, 1903.

73. "Busy hello girls." *Daily Journal* (Salem, OR), July 21, 1903.

74. "Telephone girls on company's blacklist." *Spokane Press,* July 24, 1903.

75. "Telephone girls not discouraged." *Spokane Press,* September 11, 1903.

76. "Hello girls enlist with striking linemen." *Guthrie Daily Leader* (OK), June 30, 1903; "Turmoil." *Wichita Daily Eagle,* July 1, 1903.

77. "Telephone operators at Fresno quit work." *San Francisco Call,* July 4, 1903.

78. "Striking telephone girls." *Evening Bulletin* (Maysville, KY), July 25, 1903.

79. "Hello girls on a strike." St. Louis Republic, October 14, 1903.

80. "Telephone girls out on strike." *Palestine Daily Herald* (TX), November 23, 1903.

81. "A just strike." *Palestine Daily Herald* (TX), November 24, 1903.

82. "Telephone girls strike." St. Louis Republic, February 2, 1904.

83. "Portland hello girls on strike." *Spokane Press*, October 12, 1904.

84. "Hello girls on strike." *San Francisco Call*, October 13, 1904.

85. "After hello girls." *Salt Lake Tribune*, October 16, 1904.

86. "Play for her sake." *Seattle Star*, October 20, 1904.

87. "Hello girls organize." *Salt Lake Herald*, March 25, 1905.

88. "Colfax hello girls strike." *Seattle Star*, June 15, 1905.

89. "Hello girls angry." *Colfax Gazette* (WA), December 8, 1905.

90. "No telephone strike." *Colfax Gazette* (WA), December 22, 1905.

91. "Out on a strike." *Mt. Sterling Advocate* (KY), July 5, 1905.

92. "Hello girls quit." *Deseret Evening News* (Salt Lake), September 6, 1905.

93. "Telephone girls on strike." *Wenatchee Daily World* (WA), February 24, 1906.

94. "Ashland Telephone girls go on strike." *Labor World* (Duluth, MN), March 10, 1906.

95. "Telephone girls strike." *Red Cloud Chief* (Red Cloud, Nebraska), June 22, 1906.

96. O. M. Boyle. "News of the labor world." *San Francisco Call*, June 27, 1906.

97. "Hello girls strike over alley entrance." *Minneapolis Journal*, August 23, 1906.

98. "Telephone girls walk out and quit." *Times Dispatch* (Richmond, VA), September 4, 1906.

99. "Hello girls refuse to return to work." *Daily Arizona Silver Belt* (Globe, AZ), February 16, 1907.

100. "Hello girls win strike." *Spokane Press*, February 16, 1907; "Bell telephone girls." *Montana News* (Lewistown), February 21, 1907.

101. "Strike settled." *Montana News* (Lewistown), February 28, 1907.

102. "Mayor makes a bad break." *Montana News* (Lewistown), February 28, 1907.

103. "Telephone tie-up general." *Montana News* (Lewistown), March 14, 1907.

104. *Ibid.*

105. "Manifesto of striking telephone girls." *Montana News* (Lewistown), March 14, 1907.

106. "Hello girls organize union and will insist on higher wage rate." *San Francisco Call*, March 31, 1907.

107. "Chief operators in pants must go, say the hello girls." *San Francisco Call*, April 1, 1907.

108. "Hello girls believe that a strike will be averted by compromise." *San Francisco Call*, April 3, 1907.

109. "Frisco hello girls strike." *Daily Arizona Silver Belt* (Globe, AZ), May 4, 1907.

110. "San Francisco harassed by strikes." *Albuquerque Evening Citizen*, May 4, 1907.

111. "Labor Council seeking peace." *Daily Arizona Silver Belt* (Globe, AZ), May 8, 1907.

112. "Peace Council meets secretly." *Daily Arizona Silver Belt* (Globe, AZ), May 9, 1907.

113. "Strike of telephone girls seems likely to be settled today." *San Francisco Call*, May 13, 1907.

114. "Striking girls holler cat and hen." *Spokane Press*, May 28, 1907.

115. "Girls deny company is filling up ranks." *San Francisco Call*, May 29, 1907.

116. "Leader of striking hello girls is a woman suffragist." *Seattle Star*, June 1, 1907.

117. "Telephone linemen ordered back to work." *San Francisco Call*, June 5, 1907.

118. "Striking telephone girl faints in court." *San Francisco Call*, June 11, 1907.

119. "Hello girls return to work at Frisco." *Seattle Star*, August 3, 1907.

120. "Telephone girls to go back to work Monday." *San Francisco Call*, August 3, 1907.

121. "Harmony in telephone situation incomplete." *San Francisco Call*, August 4, 1907.

122. "Hello girls strike." *Salt Lake Tribune*, May 13, 1907.

123. "Telephone girls of Boise remain out." *Salt Lake Tribune*, May 14, 1907.

124. "War on telephone company likely." *Salt Lake Tribune*, May 17, 1907.

125. "Hello girls win at Boise." *Deseret Evening News* (Salt Lake), May 24, 1907.

126. "Butte hello girls have gone on strike." *Albuquerque Evening Citizen*, June 26, 1907.

127. "Montana hello girls will all join strikers." *Albuquerque Citizen*, August 5, 1907; "Montana hello girls in sympathetic strike." *Salt Lake Tribune*, August 6, 1907.

128. "Girls win strike at Pocatello." *Deseret Evening News* (Salt Lake), June 29, 1907.

129. "Hello girls strike is not at an end." *Salt Lake Tribune*, July 1, 1907.

130. "Hello girls strike." *Daily Arizona Silver Belt* (Globe, AZ), August 18, 1907.

131. "Hello girls win strike in Tucson." *Daily Arizona Silver Belt* (Globe, AZ), August 20, 1907.

132. "Union telephone girls charge persecution." *San Francisco Call*, December 20, 1907.

133. "Hello girls sail in savage and win their strike." *Spokane Press*, March 30, 1908.

134. "Girls in riot." *Times Dispatch* (Richmond, VA), December 20, 1908.

135. "Girls on strike." *Richmond Climax* (Richmond, KY), September 15, 1909.

136. "Trouble over the dismissal of three women." *San Francisco Call*, February 5, 1910.

137. "Telephone girls win concessions." *Washington Times*, July 14, 1912.

138. "Hello girls may strike." *Sun* (NY), March 29, 1913.

139. "Hub phone girls ready for strike." *Washington Times*, April 9, 1913.

140. "1,000 hello girls to break Boston strike." *New York Tribune*, April 9, 1913.

141. "U.S. probes shipping of local girls to Boston to intimidate girls here." *Day Book* (Chicago), April 10, 1913.

142. "Telephone girls' strike avoided by concessions." *Evening World* (NY), April 10, 1913.

143. "Hello girls not to strike." *Washington Herald*, April 11, 1913.

144. "Hello girls from N.Y. stay at swell hotels phone people spend." *Tacoma Times*, April 14, 1913.

145. "Treated fine, phone girls say." *Washington Herald*, April 14, 1913.

146. "Hello girls or wolves." *Washington Herald*, April 18, 1913.

147. "Investigation is probable." *Washington Herald*, May 3, 1913.

148. "The hello girls go out at Madisonville." *Hartford Herald* (KY), June 4, 1913.

149. "Union organizers working among local phone girls—big strike threatened." *Day Book* (Chicago), June 17, 1913.

150. "Hello girls on strike." *Ogden Standard*, June 17, 1913.

151. "Chicago slaves." *Day Book* (Chicago), June 21, 1913.

152. "Chicago Telephone Co. helps St. Louis fight girls." *Day Book* (Chicago), June 23, 1913.

153. "Telephone girls go to St. Louis to help break strike." *Omaha Daily Bee*, July 18, 1913.

154. "St. Louis telephone girl tells story of grievances." *Honolulu Star-Bulletin*, August 2, 1913.

155. *Ibid.*

156. "Hello girls on strike." *Ogden Standard*, August 6, 1913.

157. J. Gabriel Soltis. "St. Louis A.F.L. crushed." *Voice of the People* (New Orleans), December 18, 1913.

158. "Hello girls ask more pay." *Mountain Advocate* (Barbourville, KY), May 22, 1914.

159. "More hello girls to organize union." *Labor World* (Duluth, MN), May 23, 1914.

160. "Says organization will come to hello girls in Chi.—would be big power." *Day Book* (Chicago), July 8, 1915.

161. "Girls depend on themselves." *Labor Advocate* (Cincinnati), October 30, 1915.

162. Hello girls at Jackson strike for more dough." *Weekly Tribune and the Cape County Herald* (Cape Girardeau, MO), March 31, 1916.

163. "Hello girls now look for new jobs." *Weekly Tribune and the Cape County Herald* (Cape Girardeau, MO), March 31, 1916.

164. "Hello girls unionized." *Labor World* (Duluth, MN), October 28, 1916.

165. "Telephone girls win." *Labor Advocate* (Duluth, MN), March 10, 1917.

166. "Phone girls win; go back to work." *Tacoma Times*, July 6, 1917.

167. "Phone girls vote strike." *Tacoma Times*, October 11, 1917.

168. "Hello girls make demands." *Labor Journal* (Everett, WA), October 19, 1917.

169. "Hello girls may heed strike call." *Bisbee Daily Review*, October 20, 1917.

170. "Postpone telephone strike for week on government request." *Tacoma Times*, October 20, 1917.

171. "5000 phone girls strike." *Tacoma Times*, November 1, 1917.

172. "Strikes ended and averted by U.S. mediators." *Washington Herald*, November 24, 1917.

173. "Girls will go back to work at 10 o'clock." *Tacoma Times*, November 26, 1917.

174. "Phone strike is on again today." *Tacoma Times*, November 27, 1917.

175. "Still no end to strike in sight." *Tacoma Times*, November 28, 1917.

176. "Telephone girls tricked." *Tacoma Times*, November 29, 1917.

177. "Telephone girls go back to work." *Tacoma Times*, December 4, 1917.

178. "Charge phone co. has broken faith." *Tacoma Times*, January 10, 1918.

179. "Telephone girls strike." *Tulsa Daily World*, November 19, 1917.

180. "20,000 hello girls to go on strike." *Washington Herald*, April 13, 1919.

181. "Phone strike may spread to entire country." *New York Tribune*, April 17, 1919.

182. "New England phone service is almost completely tied up." *Burlington Weekly Free Press* (VT), April 17, 1919.

183. "Burleson refers phone strike to Wire Board." *Washington Herald*, April 18, 1919.

184. "New England phone strike is adjusted." *Labor World* (Duluth, MN), April 26, 1919.

185. John J. Leary Jr. "How the girls won the Boston strike." *New York Tribune*, April 27, 1919.

186. "Hello girls strike; troops called out." *Sun* (NY), April 29, 1919.

187. "Militia fires upon strikers." *Washington Herald*, April 30, 1919.

188. "Terre Haute telephone girls strike." *New York Times*, May 24, 1919.

189. "Telephone co. plans union of all employees." *New York Tribune*, June 17, 1919.

190. "Phone strike." *Labor Journal* (Everett, WA), July 11, 1919.

191. "Telephone official denies operators are out on strike." *New York Tribune*, February 19, 1920.

192. "Boston phone strike operators in split." *Hammond Lake County Times* (IN), June 26, 1923.

193. "Telephone strike all over—will be called off." *Portsmouth Herald* (NH), July 19, 1923.

Chapter 7

1. No title. *Anaconda Standard* (Montana), November 5, 1891.

2. "Will retire the hello girl." *Rock Island Daily Argus* (Illinois), July 27, 1892.

3. "New telephonic device." *Rock Island Daily Argus* (Illinois), November 9, 1892.

4. "Against hello girls." *St. Paul Daily Globe*, June 5, 1895.

5. "Chicago drops telephone girls." *Wichita Daily Eagle*, July 7, 1899.

6. "Does away with telephone girls." *St. Louis Republic*, March 2, 1901.

7. "The National Automatic Telephone." *Wichita Daily Eagle*, March 7, 1901.

8. "The telephone girl." *Philipsburg Mail* (Montana), August 9, 1901.

9. "Like to talk to central." *Minneapolis Journal*, August 20, 1901.

10. "Hello girl is doomed." *Daily Journal* (Salem, OR), November 13, 1901.

11. "Scranton men in big scheme." *Scranton* (PA), January 6, 1902.

12. "Would banish the hello girl." *Salt Lake Herald*, November 26, 1902.

13. No title. *Imperial Press* (Imperial, CA), July 9, 1904.

14. "Hello girls discharged." *Evening Star* (Washington), September 13, 1905.

15. "What! Phones without the hello girls?" *Evening World* (NY), September 13, 1905.

16. "Wonders worked by the automatic telephone—no more hello girls." *Omaha Daily Bee*, October 1, 1905.

17. "The passing of the telephone girl: a retrospect." *New York Times*, March 4, 1906.

18. "Syndicate takes girlless phone." *Evening Statesman* (Walla Walla, WA), March 23, 1909.

19. "9 out of every 10 phone girls may soon lose jobs." *Washington Times*, March 14, 1918.

20. "What the automatic telephone will mean to subscribers." *Sun* (NY), April 18, 1920.

21. "Automatic phones soon to work here." *New York Times*, March 12, 1922.

22. "Dial phone system meets Sunday test." *New York Times*, October 16, 1922.

23. "Dial phones soon in common use here." *New York Times*, September 2, 1923.

Bibliography

"Actress wins praise of hello girls." *San Francisco Call*, October 17, 1912.

Ad. *Washington Times*, December 25, 1898.

Adams, Mildred. "And now thank you saves time for us." *New York Times*, June 19, 1927.

"Admit hello girl delegates to council." *Spokane Press*, May 20, 1903.

"After hello girls." *Salt Lake Tribune*, October 16, 1904.

"Against hello girls." *St. Paul Globe*, June 5, 1895.

"All about the hello girls." *Sun* (NY), February 28, 1910.

"All about the telephone." *Evening Star* (Washington), January 29, 1881.

"Among the telephone girls." *Chicago Eagle*, August 4, 1900.

"Amusements." *Evening Star* (Washington), November 11, 1897.

Anaconda Standard (Montana), no title, November 5, 1891.

"Anita Byrne was overworked and demented." *San Francisco Call*, July 14, 1899.

"Ashland telephone girls go on strike." *Labor World* (Duluth, MN), March 10, 1906.

"At the hello center." *St. Paul Globe*, February 26, 1888.

"Automatic phones soon to work here." *New York Times*, March 12, 1922.

"Bad phone service laid to low wages." *New York Times*, December 18, 1919.

"Be sure and register." *Honolulu Republican*, October 5, 1900.

"Beauty wins." *Sacramento Record-Union*, April 27, 1895.

"Bell telephone company established school of instruction for hello girls." *St. Louis Republic*, May 31, 1903.

"Bell telephone girls may slide down a new spiral fire escape." *St. Louis Republic*, November 13 1902.

"Bell telephone girls." *Montana News* (Lewistown, Montana), February 21, 1907.

"Blue and black." *San Francisco Call*, December 5, 1893.

"Bonus for telephone girls." *Sun* (NY), January 27, 1913.

"Boss taboos girls' finery." *San Francisco Call*, July 8, 1903.

"Boston hello girls to go on strike tomorrow." *Washington Times*, April 6, 1913.

"Boston phone strike operators in split." *Hammond Lake County Times* (Hammond IN), June 26, 1923.

"Boycott play." *Spokane Press*, December 8, 1902.

Boyle, O. M. "News of the labor world." *San Francisco Call*, June 27, 1906.

"Breaking the hello girl dead line." *Evening World* (NY), April 11, 1911.

"Burleson refers phone strike to wire board." *Washington Herald*, April 18, 1919.

"Business men need dress censor nowadays to keep girls modest." *Evening Public Ledger* (Philadelphia), September 15, 1916.

"Busy hello girls." *Daily Journal* (Salem, OR), July 21, 1903.

"Busy Manhattan calls in vain for 700 hello girls." *New York Tribune*, December 3, 1919.

"Busy work of the telephone girls." *Honolulu Republican*, February 10, 1901.

"Butte hello girls have gone on strike." *Albuquerque Evening Citizen*, June 26, 1907.

"Butte phone girls battle with company." *Spokane Press*, April 18, 1903.

"Butte strike is called off." *Salt Lake Herald*, April 20, 1903.

"Call out wire men." *Minneapolis Journal*, May 28, 1903.

"Capital hello girls best paid operators in telephone service." *Washington Times*, November 29, 1920.

"Capital hello girls not held in check." *Washington Times*, July 26, 1912.

"Census shows that 5,319,912 women are bread winners." *St. Louis Republic*, September 7, 1902.

"Charge phone co. has broken faith." *Tacoma Times*, January 10, 1918.

"Chicago drops telephone girls." *Wichita Daily Eagle*, July 7, 1899.

"Chicago hello girls are singing the praises of president Sabin." *San Francisco Call*, June 27, 1901.

"Chicago slaves." *Day Book* (Chicago), June 21, 1913.

"Chicago telephone co. helps St. Louis fight girls." *Day Book* (Chicago), June 23, 1913.

"Chief operators in pants must go, say the hello girls." *San Francisco Call*, April 1, 1907.

Childe, Cromwell. "Hello! The telephone girl." *New York Times*, June 11, 1899.

"City phone efficiency drops 60% in 3 years." *New York Tribune*, August 25, 1919.

"Clergyman discusses telephone religion." *San Francisco Call*, March 4, 1907.

"Clergyman takes up hello girls cause." *San Francisco Call*, February 26, 1907.

"Colfax hello girls strike." *Seattle Star*, June 15, 1905.

"Comment on current events." *Labor World* (Duluth, MN), January 24, 1903.

Commoner (Lincoln, NE), no title, July 18, 1902.

Cook, Eva Mitchell. "The treadmill of the telephone." *Los Angeles Herald*, January 23, 1898.

"Corns on ears of hello girls." *Hopkinsville Kentuckian*, November 23, 1905.

"Cost a manger $12,500 to hurt hello girl." *Washington Times*, March 5, 1903.

Creswell, Julia. "The hello girls of Spokane." *Spokane Press*, November 2, 1909.

"Cupid busy among the hello girls." *Sun* (NY), January 8, 1905.

"Cupid has a merry time among Oakland's telephone operators." *San Francisco Call*, July 24, 1900.

"Cupid wrecking phone service." *Times Dispatch* (Richmond, VA), January 14, 1913.

"Dance and darn that company." *Sun* (NY), May 16, 1904.

"Death of the telephone Nettie Friebel." *San Francisco Call*, September 1899.

"Dial phone system meets Sunday test." *New York Times*, October 16, 1922.

"Dial phones soon in common use here." *New York Times*, September 2, 1923.

"Diphtheria breaks out among hello girls." *Seattle Star*, November 10, 1905.

"Discharged girl gets new job." *Evening World* (NY), April 27, 1904.

"Does away with telephone girls." *Omaha Daily Bee*, August 18, 1901.

"Does away with telephone girls." *St. Louis Republic*, March 2 1901.

"Don't like local phone girls." *Deseret Evening News* (Salt Lake), April 17, 1903.

"East Liverpool telephone girl." *Stark County Democrat* (Canton, OH), March 12, 1901.

"Echo Zahl works as hello girl." *Seattle Star*, July 2, 1917.

"Equal to hello girls." *Times Dispatch* (Richmond, VA), March 25, 1906.

Evelyn, Marie. "For other ears." *San Francisco Call*, November 26, 1892.

"Evidently an untruth." *Sun* (NY), November 18, 1883.

"Fair eavesdroppers." *Nebraska Advertiser* (Omaha), August 23, 1901.

"Farces with music." *New York Tribune*, December 26, 1897.

"Fear no strike of St. Paul hello girls." *St. Paul Globe*, May 28, 1903.

"The field of electricity." *Omaha Daily Bee*, June 15, 1900.

"50 hello girls flirted too much." *Evening World* (NY), August 31, 1904.

"50 pretty Spokane hello girls wed in three months." *Spokane Press*, August 25, 1909.

"Five hello girls resign to marry." *Washington Times*, September 19, 1904.

"5000 phone girls strike." *Tacoma Times*, November 1, 1917.

"Fix $9 wage for telephone girls." *Seattle Star*, June 27, 1914.

"Flash lights hurt phone girls' eyes." *Labor World* (Duluth, MN), November 15, 1913.

"For the better half." *El Paso Herald*, July 21, 1900.

"Frisco hello girls strike." *Daily Arizona Silver Belt* (Globe, AZ), May 4, 1907.

"From shop and mill." *St. Paul Globe*, May 31, 1885.

Gay, Eva. "That you, central?" *St. Paul Globe*, August 12, 1888.

"The girl and the dividends." *Tacoma Times*, January 5, 1911.

"Girl answers many calls." *Evening Herald* (Klamath Falls, OR), September 14, 1916.

"The girl at the switchboard." *University Missourian* (Columbia, MO), March 14, 1912.

"The girls all right." *Pittsburg Dispatch*, January 25, 1889.

"The girls at the 'phone." *Sun* (NY), February 7, 1897.

"Girls confident of winning strike." *Spokane Press*, July 2, 1903.

"Girls deny company is filling up ranks." *San Francisco Call*, May 29, 1907.

"Girls depend on themselves." *Labor Advocate* (Cincinnati), October 30, 1915.

"Girls from country desirable operators." *Arizona Republican* (Phoenix), October 16, 1910.

"Girls in riot." *Times Dispatch* (Richmond, VA), December 20, 1908.

"Girls must not talk." *New York Times*, October 7, 1900.

"Girls must toe the mark." *Salt Lake Herald*, November 13, 1901.

"Girls on strike." *Richmond Climax* (KY), September 15, 1909.

"The girls strike." *Sacramento Daily Record-Union*, February 11, 1887.

"Girls will go back to work at 10 o'clock." *Tacoma Times*, November 26, 1917.

"Girls win strike at Pocatello." *Deseret Evening News* (Salt Lake), June 29, 1907.

"A good telephone girl." *Virginia Gazette* (Williamsburg, VA), January 11, 1902.

"Government inquiry shows hello girls underpaid in 7 cities." *Evening World* (NY), July 22, 1915.

"Gramophone comes to aid of hello girls." *San Francisco Call*, May 15, 1910.

Greeley-Smith, Nixola. "The telephone girl and matrimony." *Evening World* (NY), April 2, 1904.

"Harmony in telephone situation incomplete." *San Francisco Call*, August 4, 1907.

"Haunted to death by phantom 'hello' bells." *San Francisco Call*, September 14, 1899.

"Have you noticed the change in the telephone girl's voice." *St. Louis Republican*, May 20, 1900.

Hawaiian Star (Honolulu), no title, October 5, 1900.

"He annoyed the central." *St. Paul Globe*, February 8, 1888.

"Hello central." *Minneapolis Journal*, March 26, 1903.

"Hello girl." *Hopkinsville Kentuckian*, February 27, 1908.

"Hello girl." *Carbondale Free Press* (IL), July 2, 1930.

"Hello girl gets $15,000 for shock." *Salt Lake Tribune*, April 6, 1904.

"Hello girl is doomed." *Daily Journal* (Salem, OR), November 13, 1901.

"Hello girl writes about her troubles." *San Francisco Call*, July 16, 1899.

"The hello girls." *Salt Lake Herald*, December 9, 1893.

"Hello girls." *Stark County Democrat* (Canton, NE), August 29, 1902.

"Hello girls." *Paducah Sun* (KY), April 23, 1903.

"Hello girls' alarm clocks." *Omaha Daily Bee*, August 26, 1905.

"Hello girls angry." *Colfax Gazette* (WA), December 8, 1905.

"Hello girls are Cupid's harvest." *San Francisco Call*, November 15, 1912.

"Hello girls are happy; their pay has been raised." *Evening World* (NY), October 21, 1912.

"The hello girls are kept busy." *Rogue River Courier* (Grants Pass, OR), December 14, 1906.

"Hello girls are still out." *St. Paul Globe*, May 29, 1903.

"Hello girls ask more pay." *Mountain Advocate* (Barbourville, KY), May 22, 1914.

"Hello girls at Jackson strike for more dough." *Weekly Tribune and the Cape County Herald* (Cape Girardeau, MO), March 31, 1916.

"Hello girls at Spokane." *Spokane Press*, June 30, 1903.

"Hello girls, be sure you're healthy and then go ahead." *San Francisco Call*, March 22, 1901.

"Hello girls believe that a strike will be averted by compromise." *San Francisco Call*, April 3, 1907.

"Hello girls discharged." *Evening Star* (Washington), September 13, 1905.

"Hello girls enlist with striking linemen." *Guthrie Daily Leader* (OK), June 30, 1903.

"Hello girls form union." *Spokane Press*, April 8, 1903.

"Hello girls from N.Y. stay at swell hotels phone people spend." *Tacoma Times*, April 14, 1913.

"Hello girls get a raise." *Stark County Democrat* (Canton, OH), July 19, 1901.

"Hello girls; girls hello." *Tacoma Times*, March 9, 1911.

"Hello girls given increase in wages." *Spokane Press*, April 21, 1903.

"Hello girls go on strike." *San Francisco Call*, October 13, 1904.

"The hello girls go out at Madisonville." *Hartford Herald* (KY), June 4, 1913.

"Hello girls go to Butte." *Salt Lake Herald*, April 16, 1903.

"Hello girls hard to get." *Omaha Daily Bee*, March 28, 1905.

"Hello girls mad." *Fort Worth Gazette*, April 5, 1894.

"Hello girls make demands." *Labor Journal* (Everett, WA), October 19, 1917.

"Hello girls may heed strike call." *Bisbee Daily Review*, October 20, 1917.

"Hello girls may strike." *Sun* (NY), March 29, 1913.

"Hello girls must throw away rats." *Seattle Star*, December 24, 1909.

"Hello girls not to strike." *Washington Herald*, April 11, 1913.

"Hello girls now have libraries." *Los Angeles Herald*, October 13, 1907.

"Hello girls now look for new jobs." *Weekly Tribune and the Cape County Herald* (Cape Girardeau, MO), March 31, 1916.

"Hello girls of Gotham no longer alarm clocks for sleepyheads." *San Francisco Call*, August 18, 1905.

"Hello girls on a strike." *Akron Daily Democrat* (OH), June 21, 1902.

"Hello girls on strike." *Ogden Standard*, August 6, 1913.

"Hello girls on strike." *Ogden Standard*, June 17, 1913.

"Hello girls on a strike." *St. Louis Republic*, October 14, 1903.

"Hello girls on strike." *St. Paul Globe*, March 5, 1902.

"Hello girls on strike." *St. Paul Globe*, March 26, 1902.

"Hello girls or wolves." *Washington Herald*, April 18, 1913.

"Hello girls organize." *Salt Lake Herald*, March 25, 1905.

"Hello girls organize union and will insist on higher wage rate." *San Francisco Call*, March 31, 1907.

"Hello girls overworked." *Anadarko Daily Democrat* (OK), November 29, 1909.

"Hello girls picnic too sporting, 'tis said." *San Francisco Call*, May 29, 1907.

"Hello girls practice punching bags in telephone gymnasium." *Paducah Evening Sun* (KY), June 13, 1906.

"Hello girls quit." *Deseret Evening News* (Salt Lake), September 6, 1905.

"Hello girls quit places to marry." *University Missourian* (Columbia, MO), November 18, 1912.

"Hello girls refuse to return to work." *Daily Arizona Silver Belt* (Globe, AZ), February 16, 1907.

"Hello girls return to work at Frisco." *Seattle Star*, August 3, 1907.

"Hello girls ring up Hymen's office often." *Washington Times*, September 29, 1902.

"Hello girls sail in savage and win their strike." *Spokane Press*, March 30, 1908.

"Hello girls satisfied." *Washington Times*, April 15, 1902.

"Hello girls secured reinstatement of linesmen." *Akron Daily Democrat* (OH), November 2, 1901.

"Hello girls seem to be out." *St. Paul Globe*, May 30, 1903.

"Hello girls stop telling time." *Watchman and Southron* (Sumter SC), July 9, 1919.

"Hello girls strike." *Daily Arizona Silver Belt* (Globe, AZ), August 8, 1907.

"Hello girls strike." *Daily Journal* (Salem, OR), April 17, 1903.

"Hello girls strike." *Hopkinsville Kentuckian*, April 21, 1903.

"Hello girls strike." *Salt Lake Tribune*, May 13, 1907.

"Hello girls strike." *Seattle Star*, November 27, 1902.
"Hello girls strike is not at an end." *Salt Lake Tribune*, July 1, 1907.
"Hello girls strike over alley entrance." *Minneapolis Journal*, August 23, 1906.
"Hello girls strike settled." *Ocala Banner* (FL), December 19, 1902.
"Hello girls strike; troops called out." *Sun* (NY), April 29, 1919.
"Hello girls tell how to marry rich." *Evening World* (NY), November 23, 1905.
"Hello girls to elocute." *Daily Ardmoreite* (Ardmore, OK), December 31, 1901.
"Hello girls trip it, trip it." *Sun* (NY), May 31, 1904.
"Hello girls unionized." *Labor World* (Duluth, MN), October 28, 1916.
"Hello girls used to be boys who cussed cranks 'n' everything." *Washington Times*, May 8, 1921.
"Hello girls vocation both pleasant and remunerative." *Los Angeles Herald*, September 2, 1906.
"Hello girls win at Boise." *Deseret Evening News* (Salt Lake), May 24, 1907.
"Hello girls win strike." *Spokane Press*, February 16, 1907.
"Hello girls win strike in Tucson." *Daily Arizona Silver Belt* (Globe, AZ), August 20, 1907.
"Hello girls work hard." *New York Times*, September 23, 1910.
"Hello girls would strike." *Akron Daily Democrat* (OH), August 22, 1901.
"Hello prunes and prisms." *Brownsville Herald* (TX), April 2, 1903.
"Hello there, central." *Omaha Daily Bee*, August 1, 1886.
"Hello! You central." *St. Paul Globe*, July 13, 1890.
"Hello! Hello! Alas!" *Independent* (Honolulu), October 5, 1900.
"Hello, girls, were you shocked." *Stark County Democrat* (Canton, Ohio), November 24, 1887.
"Here is the telephone central's story." *Salt Lake Herald*, February 19, 1905.
"Higher pay to telephone girls is asked by Frank Walsh." *Day Book* (Chicago), February 15, 1915.
"Hist, now d'ye hear?" *Seattle Star*, December 18, 1905.
"How others view it." *Spokane Press*, July 6 1903.
"Hub phone girls ready for strike." *Washington Times*, April 9, 1913.
"If hello girl gets angry blame Commissioner Neill." *Washington Herald*, February 28, 1910.
Imperial Press (Imperial, CA), no title, July 9, 1904.
"An important change." *Kansas City Daily Journal* (MO), May 2, 1895.
"Increase in salary of telephone girls comes at Cleveland," *Omaha Daily Bee*, June 17, 1913.
"Increased use of telephones." *Gainesville Daily Sun* (FL), April 3, 1909.
"Increased wages for all hello girls." *Washington Herald*, April 30, 1913.
"Instructive talks to telephone girls." *Bisbee Daily Review*, October 12, 1915.
"Into new quarters." *St. Paul Globe*, April 4, 1902.
"Investigation is probable." *Washington Herald*, May 3, 1913.
"It's all on the switchboard." *Goodwin's Weekly* (Salt Lake), March 9, 1912.
"Jack Hugger runs big risk." *San Francisco Call*, December 20, 1903.
"John Cassidy is out and Corcoran is in." *Hawaiian Gazette* (Honolulu), October 9, 1900.
"A just strike." *Palestine Daily Herald* (TX), November 24, 1903.
Kentucky Irish American (Louisville), no title, June 9, 1900.
"Labor council seeking peace." *Daily Arizona Silver Belt* (Globe, AZ), May 8, 1907.
"Laboring men assist girls." *Omaha Daily Bee*, June 30, 1902.
"Leader of striking hello girls is a woman suffragist." *Seattle Star*, June 1, 1907.
Leary, John J. Jr. "How the girls won the Boston strike." *New York Tribune*, April 27, 1919.
"Life for telephone girl loses its charm." *Rogue River Courier* (Grants Pass, OR), May 18, 1916.
"Life of the hello girl." *Evening Star* (Washington), October 22, 1905.
"Like their work." *Nebraska Advertiser* (Nemaha City), June 28, 1901.
"Like to talk to central." *Minneapolis Journal*, August 20, 1901.
"Linemen on sympathy strike." *Omaha Daily Bee*, June 29, 1902.
"Long arms, big girls." *Monroe City Democrat* (MO), January 25, 1900.
"Long hours for hello girls." *Evening Star* (Washington), September 29, 1902.
"Long-range gossip." *Pittsburg Dispatch*, December 8, 1889.

"Looks life defeat." *Minneapolis Journal*, June 3, 1903.

"Low necked dresses not for hello girls." *Spokane Press*, June 25, 1903.

Lowe, Marion. "School for courtesy is established in Seattle." *Seattle Star*, January 7, 1910.

"Manifesto of striking telephone girls." *Montana News* (Lewistown, Montana), March 14, 1907.

"Many maladies of phone girls." *Los Angeles Herald*, July 1, 1906.

"Marks the masher." *Wichita Daily Eagle*, April 3, 1895.

Marshall, Mary. "Your daughter's vocation." *New York Tribune*, December 17, 1911.

"Matron will care for hello girls." *Bisbee Daily Review*, March 5, 1912.

"May train hello girls' voices to attain proper modulation." *Washington Times*, October 28, 1906.

"Mayor makes a bad break." *Montana News* (Lewistown, Montana), February 28, 1907.

"Men operators also strike for more pay." *Honolulu Republican*, October 7, 1900.

"Militia fires upon strikers." *Washington Herald*, April 30, 1919.

"Millionaire Tower and the hello girl who will become his bride Wednesday." *Evening World* (NY), January 5, 1903.

"Millions use the telephone." *Los Angeles Herald*, May 21, 1906.

"Minimum wage for phone girls is fixed at $9." *Seattle Star*, July 10, 1914.

"Miss Means wins her case." *Los Angeles Herald*, December 6, 1893.

"Montana hello girls in sympathetic strike." *Salt Lake Tribune*, August 6, 1907.

"Montana hello girls will all join strikers." *Albuquerque Citizen*, August 5, 1907.

"More hello girls to organize union." *Labor World* (Duluth, MN), May 23, 1914.

"More telephone ear." *Sun* (NY), November 11, 1894.

"The most beautiful telephone girl in the United States." *Seattle Star*, January 14, 1915.

Nallin, Mamie Loretta. "The telephone girl." *Scranton Tribune* (PA), May 14, 1896.

"The National Automatic Telephone." *Wichita Daily Eagle*, March 7 1901.

"New England phone service is almost completely tied up." *Burlington Weekly Free Press* (VT), Apr 17, 1919.

"New England phone strike is adjusted." *Labor World* (Duluth, MN), April 26, 1919.

"New girls employed." *Minneapolis Journal*, May 27, 1903.

"The new north Washington telephone exchange." *Washington Times*, December 27, 1903.

"New switchboard in." *Norfolk Virginian*, December 18, 1896.

"New telephone device." Rock Island Daily Argus (IL), November 9, 1892.

"New York's orgy of telephones." *Ogden Standard*, July 16, 1910.

"9 out of every 10 phone girls may soon lose jobs." *Washington Times*, March 14, 1918.

"No more morning hellos." *Brooklyn Eagle*, June 16, 1901.

"No telephone strike." *Colfax Gazette* (WA), December 22, 1905.

"No working woman is happier than a telephone girl." *Chicago Eagle*, June 11, 1898.

"Not organized in St. Louis." *St. Louis Republican*, December 18, 1900.

"Of general interest." *Wichita Daily Eagle*, April 25, 1893.

"One thing and another." *St. Paul Globe*, June 28, 1891.

"1,000 hello girls to break Boston strike." *New York Tribune*, April 9, 1913.

"Out of sight gallantry." *Tacoma Times*, March 6, 1909.

"Out on a strike." *Mt. Sterling Advocate* (KY), July 5, 1905.

"A Paris Waldorf-Astoria for telephone girls." *Minneapolis Journal*, October 10, 1903.

"The passing of the telephone girl: a retrospect." *New York Times*, March 4, 1906.

"Patient, useful, practical." *Omaha Daily Bee*, August 3, 1890.

"Peace council meets secretly." *Daily Arizona Silver Belt* (Globe, AZ), May 9, 1907.

"Phone girls vote strike." *Tacoma Times*, October 11, 1917.

"Phone girls win; go back to work." *Tacoma Times*, July 6, 1917.

"Phone strike." *Labor Journal* (Everett, WA), July 11, 1919.

"Phone strike is on again today." *Tacoma Times*, November 27, 1917.

"Phone strike may spread to entire country." *New York Tribune*, April 17, 1919.

Pittsburg Dispatch, no title, October 19, 1892.

"Play for her sake." *Seattle Star*, October 20, 1904.

"Plea made for telephone girls." *Ogden Standard*, July 24, 1915.

"Poor telephone service is due to cheap labor." *Labor World* (Duluth, MN), January 17, 1920.

"Portland hello girls on strike." *Spokane Press*, October 12, 1904.

"Postpone telephone strike for week on government request." *Tacoma Times*, October 20, 1917.

Prim, Priscilla. "American women who work." *Tacoma Times*, February 18, 1909.

"Privileges for the hello girl." *St. Paul Globe*, May 30, 1903.

"Proposed change in the telephone service." *Evening Star* (Washington), April 25, 1884.

"Providing a restroom for business women." *St. Louis Republic*, April 7, 1901.

"Question of labor." *Omaha Daily Bee*, October 15, 1882.

"Regulate telephone girls." *Omaha Daily Bee*, January 12, 1902.

"Return from Butte." *Salt Lake Herald*, April 22, 1903.

"Rights of telephone girls." *Salt Lake Herald*, February 9, 1908.

Sacramento Record-Union, no title, December 7, 1893.

St. Johns Herald (St. Johns, AZ), no title, February 18, 1892.

"St. Louis hello girls can wear peek-a-boos." *Wenatchee Daily World* (WA), June 18, 1906.

"St. Louis telephone girl tells story of grievances." *Honolulu Star-Bulletin*, August 2, 1913.

"San Antonio budget." *El Paso Herald*, December 6, 1900.

"San Antonio strike." *El Paso Herald*, November 13, 1900.

San Francisco Call, no title, October 3, 1892.

"San Francisco harassed by strikes." *Albuquerque Evening Citizen*, May 4, 1907.

"Says organization will come to hello girls in Chicago—would be big power." *Day Book* (Chicago), Jul 8, 1915.

"School for hello girls is New York's very latest." *Evening World* (NY), January 16, 1902.

"School of special instruction for employees multiply in big cities." *Omaha Daily Bee*, September 29, 1907.

"Scranton men in big scheme." *Scranton Tribune* (PA), January 6, 1902.

"She rings the bell." *Richmond Dispatch* (VA), December 18, 1898.

"Short girl? You can't say hello." *San Francisco Call*, February 28, 1910.

"Shorter hours for telephone girls." *Labor World* (Duluth, MN), May 10, 1913.

"$60 fine for swearing at telephone girl." *San Francisco Call*, December 17, 1913.

Smith, Laura A. "Great care is exerted for telephone girls' comfort." *Salt Lake Herald*, May 15, 1910.

"Soft answer to hello." *New York Tribune*, October 2, 1898.

Soltis, J. Gabriel. "St, Louis A.F.L. crushed." *Voice of the People* (New Orleans), December 18, 1913.

"Still no end to strike in sight." *Tacoma Times*, November 28, 1917.

"The story of two want ads." *Spokane Press*, November 20, 1905.

"Strict rules for telephone girls." *Washington Times*, July 24, 1912.

"Strike declared off." *Evening Star* (Washington), April 15, 1902.

"Strike extends to Temple." *St. Louis Republican*, November 16 1900.

"Strike of telephone girls seems likely to be settled today." *San Francisco Call*, May 13, 1907.

"The strike rung off." *Hawaiian Star* (Honolulu), October 5, 1900.

"Strike settled." *Montana News* (Lewistown, Montana), February 28, 1907.

"Strikes ended and averted by U.S. mediators." *Washington Herald*, November 24, 1917.

"Striking girls holler cat and hen." *Spokane Press*, May 28, 1907.

"Striking telephone girl faints in court." *San Francisco Call*, June 11, 1907.

"Striking telephone girls." *Evening Bulletin* (Maysville, KY), July 25, 1903.

"Striking telephone girls." *St. Louis Republican*, July 15, 1900.

"Subscribers on strike." *Houston Daily Post*, November 13, 1900.

"A summer day with the hello girl." *Sun* (NY), August 2, 1903.

"Swearing at hello girl may be costly to doctor." *Washington Times*, September 2, 1907.

"Sweet voice wins hello girl a millionaire for a husband." *St. Louis Republic*, May 3, 1903.

"Swore at hello girl." *Medford Mail Tribune* (OR), April 12, 1912.

"Syndicate takes girl-less phone." *Evening Statesman* (Walla Walla, WA), March 23, 1909.

"Talk of central union." *New York Tribune*, January 16, 1901.

"Talks for her living." *Evening World* (NY), June 10, 1890.

"Teaches hello girl." *St. Paul Globe*, March 21, 1903.

"Teaching her to talk well." *St. Louis Republic*, August 24, 1902.

"Tel. girls must be over 5 feet." *Paducah Evening Sun* (KY), February 28, 1910.

"Telegraph innovations." *San Francisco Call*, January 15, 1896.

"The Telephone." *Arizona Citizen* (Tucson), December 7, 1877.

"The telephone Babel." *Omaha Daily Bee*, March 8, 1883.

"Telephone co. plans union of all employees." *New York Tribune*, June 17, 1919.

"Telephone co. worst employer in Spokane." *Spokane Press*, April 19, 1907.

"Telephone company is refused police cannot show any need of specials." *Spokane Press*, July 4, 1903.

"The telephone ear." *Stark County Democrat* (Canton, OH), December 14, 1900.

"Telephone ears." *San Francisco Call*, May 17, 1893.

"The telephone girl." *Arizona Republican* (Phoenix), February 11, 1901.

"The telephone girl." *Evening Times* (Washington), July 8, 1898.

"The telephone girl." *Hickman Courier* (KY), March 2, 1894.

"The telephone girl." *Philipsburg Mail* (Montana), August 9, 1901.

"The telephone girl has the best chance of matrimony." *Times Dispatch* (Richmond, VA), April 24, 1904.

"The telephone girl her strenuous days." *Arizona Republican* (Phoenix), September 10, 1906.

"Telephone girls." *St. Louis Republican*, July 16, 1900.

"Telephone girls." *El Paso Herald*, November 27, 1900.

"Telephone girls are now thrilling their r's." *Times Dispatch* (Richmond, VA), December 28, 1909.

"Telephone girls deprived of gum." *National Tribune* (Washington), May 3, 1888.

"Telephone girls go back to work." *Tacoma Times*, December 4, 1917.

"Telephone girls go to St. Louis to help break strike." *Omaha Daily Bee*, July 18, 1913.

"Telephone girls here may powder." *Washington Times*, September 9, 1912.

"Telephone girls in black." *Evening World* (NY), May 1, 1894.

"Telephone girls join Western Conference." *Spokane Press*, July 1, 1903.

"Telephone girls not discouraged." *Spokane Press*, September 11, 1903.

"Telephone girls of Boise remain out." *Salt Lake Tribune*, May 14, 1907.

"Telephone girls on company blacklist." *Spokane Press*, July 24, 1903.

"Telephone girls on strike." *Wenatchee Daily World* (WA), February 24, 1906.

"Telephone girls out on strike." *Palestine Daily Herald* (TX), November 23, 1903.

"Telephone girls out on a strike." *Washington Post*, November 29, 1899.

"Telephone girls protest." *Evening World* (NY), February 6, 1894.

"Telephone girls rarely marry." *Morning Examiner* (Ogden), April 10, 1910.

"Telephone girls say spies follow them after work." *Evening World* (NY), April 7, 1911.

"Telephone girls strike." *Omaha Daily Bee*, June 22, 1902.

"Telephone girls strike." *Red Cloud Chief* (Red Cloud, NE), June 22, 1906.

"Telephone girls strike." *St. Louis Republic*, February 2, 1904.

"Telephone girls strike." *Tulsa Daily World*, November 19, 1917.

"Telephone girls talk too much." *Valentine Democrat* (NE), June 21, 1900.

"Telephone girls to go back to work Monday." *San Francisco Call*, August 3, 1907.

"Telephone girl's training." *Evening Star* (Washington), October 3, 1903.

"Telephone girls tricked." *Tacoma Times*, November 29, 1917.

"Telephone girl's voice." *Bourbon News* (Paris, KY), February 22, 1898.

"Telephone girls walk out and quit." *Times Dispatch* (Richmond, VA), September 4, 1906.

"Telephone girls wanted." *Daily Capital Journal* (Salem, OR), January 29, 1908.

"Telephone girls wanted." *San Francisco Call*, December 16, 1902.

"Telephone girls win concessions." *Washington Times*, July 14, 1912.
"Telephone girls win." *Labor Advocate* (Duluth, MN), March 10, 1917.
"Telephone girls win out." *Omaha Daily Bee*, July 10, 1902.
"Telephone girls' eyes." *Princeton Union* (MN), November 13, 1913.
"Telephone girls' strike avoided by concessions." *Evening World* (NY), April 10, 1913.
"The telephone, Hello! There." *San Francisco Call*, February 7, 1892.
"Telephone linemen ordered back to work." *San Francisco Call*, June 5, 1907.
"Telephone official denies operators are out on strike." *New York Tribune*, February 19, 1920.
"Telephone operators at Fresno quit work." *San Francisco Call*, July 4, 1903.
"The telephone operators' strike." *Spokane Press*, July 1, 1903.
"Telephone operators succumb to epidemic." *Los Angeles Herald*, July 22, 1907.
"Telephone service subject of report." *El Paso Herald*, October 5, 1912.
"Telephone strike." *El Paso Daily Herald*, November 3, 1900.
"The telephone strike." *Houston Daily Post*, July 17, 1900.
"The telephone strike." *Houston Daily Post*, November 9, 1900.
"Telephone strike." *Houston Daily Post*, November 11, 1900.
"Telephone strike all over—will be called off." *Portsmouth Herald* (NH), July 19, 1923.
"Telephone strike ended." *Hopkinsville Kentuckian*, May 1, 1903.
"Telephone strike still on." *Houston Daily Post*, November 9, 1900.
"Telephone sweetness." *Los Angeles Herald*, June 19, 1910.
"Telephone tie-up general." *Montana News* (Lewistown, Montana), March 14, 1907.
"Telephone trials." *St. Paul Globe*, July 9, 1893.
"Telltale telephones." *Evening Star* (Washington), January 3, 1885.
"Terre Haute telephone girls strike." *New York Times*, May 24, 1919.
"Terrors for hello girls." *Bourbon News* (Paris, KY), December 20, 1907.
"There are more than 8,000,000 women workers in the U.S." *Bemidji Daily Pioneer*, April 10, 1916.
"There are purchasable spies in many households." *San Francisco Call*, January 1, 1899.
"They want Cassidy." *Evening Bulletin* (Honolulu), October 5, 1900.
"Threaten boycott." *Evening Statesman* (Walla Walla, WA), July 3, 1903.
"Through the telephone." *Evening Star* (Washington), October 15, 1882.
"To abolish hello." *San Francisco Call*, April 14, 1902.
"To erect a state fishway." *Omaha Daily Bee*, June 28, 1902.
"To place telephones upon the unfair list." *Spokane Press*, July 3, 1903.
"To take places of union hello girls." *Spokane Press*, April 16, 1903.
"Trades council boycotts phones." *Spokane Press*, July 8, 1903.
"Training hello girls." *Wichita Daily Eagle*, December 8, 1903.
"Treated fine, phone girls say." *Washington Herald*, April 14, 1913.
"Trouble over the dismissal of three women." *San Francisco Call*, February 5 1910.
"Troubles that beset the telephone girl." *Washington Times*, December 14, 1902.
"Turmoil." *Wichita Daily Eagle*, July 1, 1903.
"Turns down asphalt bill." *Omaha Daily Bee*, July 1, 1902.
"20,000 hello girls to go on strike." *Washington Herald*, April 13, 1919.
"Uncle Sam raids hello girls' ranks." *Washington Times*, June 27, 1917.
"Union organizers working among local phone girls—big strike threatened." *Day Book* (Chicago), June 17, 1913.
"Union telephone girls charge persecution." *San Francisco Call*, December 20, 1907.
"U.S. probe shipping of local girls to Boston to intimidate girls here." *Day Book* (Chicago), April 10, 1913.
"War on telephone company likely." *Salt Lake Tribune*, May 17, 1907.
West, Marian. "My experience as a telephone operator." *San Francisco Call*, August 20, 1899.
"What! Phones without hello girls?" *Evening World* (NY), September 13, 1905.
"What the automatic telephone will mean to subscribers." *Sun* (NY), April 18, 1920.

"When in doubt just ask the information telephone girl." *Evening Star* (Washington), March 17, 1907.

Wichita Daily Eagle, no title, September 8, 1895.

"Will retire the hello girl." *Rock Island Daily Argus* (IL), July 27, 1892.

"Will society receive her?" *St. Paul Globe*, March 10, 1903.

"With the hello girl at main." *Evening Star* (Washington), November 17, 1907.

"With the hello girls." *Salt Lake Herald*, July 29, 1894.

"Woman workers—telephone girl." *Omaha Daily Bee*, August 12, 1900.

"The women, new Belasco play, to open at National." *Washington Times*, April 16, 1911.

"Women swear the most." *Evening Statesman* (Walla Walla, WA), February 4, 1905.

"Wonders worked by the automatic telephone—no more hello girls." *Omaha Daily Bee*, October 1, 1905.

"Working girls need minimum of $12.11." *San Juan Islander* (Friday Harbor, WA), January 30, 1914.

"The world uses 12,318,000 telephones." *San Francisco Call*, December 16, 1913.

"Would banish the hello girl." *Salt Lake Herald*, November 26, 1902.

"You can't swear over phone any more—in Texas." *Evening World* (NY), February 15, 1909.

"Young ladies secure 1500 phone removals." *Spokane Press*, July 11, 1903.

Zahl, Echo June. "Hello girl's pay at start is $1.10 a day." *Seattle Star*, July 3, 1917.

Index